METALLIC COATING
OF PLASTICS

VOLUME I

METALLIC COATING OF PLASTICS

by

WILLIAM GOLDIE

VOLUME I

ELECTROCHEMICAL PUBLICATIONS LIMITED

1968

ELECTROCHEMICAL PUBLICATIONS LIMITED
18 Colburn Avenue, Hatch End, Middlesex, England

PRINTED IN GREAT BRITAIN

To my wife
Elizabeth
and our children
Lorraine and Alison

PREFACE

ALTHOUGH the electroplating of plastics is by no means new, it is only within comparatively recent times that any significant progress has been made. To the best of the writer's knowledge, there is no book in existence which covers these technological advances in their entirety. This book was therefore written in an attempt to cover such advances.

The writer also recognises that other techniques exist for depositing metals on to plastics, either as an initial thin conducting film or as a thick deposit. Consequently, an effort has been made to accommodate them into the text, highlighting the essentials of these processes. Although very little use is being made of some of these processes at present, it is quite conceivable that they may assume some importance in the not too distant future.

In writing this book, an attempt has been made to appeal to the designer as well as to the electrochemist and plastics technologist. Consequently, in addition to the chapters which suggest why metallised plastics should be used and detailed discussions given on their design, many unusual and diverse applications have been cited throughout to enable the designer to appreciate the magnitude and wealth of possible uses he has at his disposal. Furthermore, individual polymers are discussed in some detail and their properties tabulated to assist the designer to choose the most suitable material for his particular application.

Although some effort has been made throughout the text to standardise units, it has not been possible in a number of cases since a direct conversion resulted in too many difficulties. For example, graphs would need to be changed as well as formulae, operating conditions and results; to do this would be presumptious of the writer inasmuch that some danger existed in misquoting the works of the investigators involved and thereby presenting a false reflection of their work.

One point however which should be mentioned is the reluctance of some investigators to be precise in their presentation of formulae. A typical example in this category is that of compounds which exist in the hydrated state. In the many instances where molar concentrations are not stated, it would have been an asset to have the water of crystallisation figures available.

Without knowledge of such figures, the composition of certain solutions could be misconstrued, leading to possible erroneous results in their application.

About references. In order to facilitate checking and to maintain uniformity, all sources, with a few exceptions, are referred to by the abbreviations and contractions suggested and recommended in the World List of Scientific Periodicals, 4th Edition, published by Butterworth of London. The exceptions are references to those journals of very recent origin which have not yet been classified and to those which flourished prior to 1900 but were not published thereafter.

At the end of most chapters a bibliography accompanies the references cited in the text. This includes papers and books that are of specialised or general interest relating to the chapter in question but which were not used as specific references. Appearing in the bibliography are sources of information which also appear among the references; in the writer's opinion they are sufficiently comprehensive to enable the reader to obtain a great deal of background knowledge relating to the text of the particular chapter concerned.

For convenience, the book is published in two volumes. In the first, following a few introductory chapters, the accent is primarily directed towards the techniques of depositing the metal. The second volume discusses the individual polymers and cites methods for their preconditioning. In the concluding chapters, electroplating processes and equipment are highlighted and discussed in some detail.

ACKNOWLEDGMENTS

During the preparation of this book various authorities were asked to read and comment on the manuscript. The writer wishes to thank these gentlemen for their painstaking attention to detail, their helpful suggestions and, not least, their encouragement.

VOLUME ONE:

Preconditioning: Mr. K. R. Gadsby of Kirkby Processes and Equipment, Thatcham, Berks.

Sensitisers and Activators: Mr. G. D. R. Jarrett of M. L. Alkan, Ruislip, Middx.

Adhesion: Mr. A. Rantell of the Borough Polytechnic, London.

Electroless Deposition: Dr. E. B. Saubestre of Enthone, Newhaven, Conn., U.S.A.

Aerosol Deposition: Mr. D. J. Levy of Lockhead Missiles, Palo Alto, Calif., U.S.A.

Physical Vapour Deposition
{ Mr. H. F. W. Shepherd of Ultra Electronics, London.
Mr. A. Rantell of the Borough Polytechnic, London.
Mr. B. Francis of Bee Chemical, London.

Chemical Vapour Deposition: Mr. L. W. Owen of the Atomic Weapons Research Establishment, Aldermaston, Berks.

Metal Spraying: Mr. V. C. Handy of Metallisation, Dudley, Worcs.

CONTENTS

CONTENTS

CONTENTS

PART I

INTRODUCTION

CHAPTER 1

HISTORICAL BACKGROUND

Plastics have been recognised from time immemorial and although electroplating is a comparative newcomer to engineering, metal finishing, as such, is undoubtedly thousands of years old. The earliest applications of metal coatings were on metals but, with the coming of the Industrial Age, it was only a question of time before the search would begin for methods of applying metals to non-metallic materials and only a matter of time before such methods were discovered.

Archæological examples exist of metallised wood and terra cotta, made by Egyptians using methods unknown. However, beyond mechanically sheathing such objects, no practical method was available for metallising non-metallic materials.

The first example of a metallised non-metal probably dates back to 1835 when von Liebig first produced metallic silver by the reducing action of an aldehyde and, in the course of the experiment, successfully metallised the inside of the test tube in which the reaction took place. This was followed by metallised samples exhibited by H. Jacobi in 1838 in which the non-adherent coatings could be separated from the base for use as a negative mould. In 1840 Robert Murray applied graphite to non-metallic surfaces to make them conductive and later reproduced engraved copper plates by this " galvano-plastic " method.

Alexander Jones obtained a patent in 1841 for sensitising to render conductive the surfaces of lace, wood, leather, porcelain, glass and other materials by the application of copper. In the same year, Alexander Parkes was granted a patent for metallising animals, insects, flowers and fruit by the application of a silver nitrate solution. Silver nitrate formed a part of many other processes which varied simply in their method of application. For example, a patent obtained by Noualheir and Provost in 1857 described the metallisation of a soft surface such as a human corpse by placing the body in a suitable position and spreading pulverised silver nitrate over it with a brush then electroplating it in a copper sulphate bath, producing a copper plated mummy. The following years saw numerous patents for the electrolytic deposition of metal on all types of non-metallic materials.

Meanwhile the mirror industry was now in existence and the literature, both patent and technical, began to escalate. However, the majority of this was frivolous to say the least and instead of advancing the science of electroplating and allied topics, probably did more damage by drawing attention to itself with the result that the science was reduced to the status of an art carried out by back street operators. As such, little progress was made until the late 1940's when newer plastics arrived on the scene and coincided with the demands of the electronics industry for the production of various metal-dielectric combinations for a wide variety of applications which could not be produced satisfactorily by other means. Before proceeding with a description of these developments, it is probably helpful to retrace our steps and describe the individual progress of the electroplating and plastics industries to make the picture more complete.

Electroplating Industry

Metal finishing, as previously mentioned, has been known since early times. The alchemist Zozimus for example described the reduction of copper from its solutions using iron while Parascelsus was aware of the fact that copper and iron could be coated with silver by simple immersion in a silver solution.

Prior to the discovery by Luigi Galvani of the galvanic couple, there was no such thing as the reduction of metals from solutions by electricity. In 1799 Alexander Volta constructed his famous Volta pile which Nicholson and Carlisle used in 1800 to decompose water electrolytically thereby forming oxygen and hydrogen.

Cruickshank (1803) investigated the behaviour of solutions of copper sulphate, silver nitrate, and similar compounds, towards an electric current. He found that the metals were completely reduced from their solutions, suggesting to him a method by which metals could be quantitatively analysed, a technique which was to be perfected by Sands among others many years later.

In 1805 Brugnatelli succeeded in gilding two silver coins by connecting them with copper wire to the negative pole of the Volta pile and immersing them in a solution of gold in potassium cyanide while a piece of metal was suspended in the solution from the positive pole. He also observed that if the positive plate was an oxidisable metal it dissolved.

In 1827 Ohm put forward his well known law which was appropriately called after him to be followed in 1833 by Faraday's Laws of Electrolysis.

Professor Jacobi, whom we have already encountered earlier in the chapter, announced to the Academy of Sciences at St. Petersburg (Leningrad) in 1838 that galvanic electricity could be used as a means of metal forming and for reproducing objects in metal. He produced an exact mould of metals and artistic objects in wax and then rendered the wax impression electrically conductive by means of a graphite coating. This was suspended in an electrolytic bath containing a suitable metal salt and connected to the negative pole, the corresponding metal of the salt in solution was connected to the positive pole. On passing a current through the bath, the conductive wax became coated with metal. The metal forming the anode was dissolved in the bath as quickly as it was deposited on the cathode.

Although Brugnatelli was probably the first to demonstrate the technique, Jacobi is generally considered to be the father of electroplating since he was the first to utilise and make use of practically, the discoveries made up to that time.

Within the next few years rapid progress was made in the field. Scheele's observations on the solubility of the cyanide combinations of silver and gold in potassium cyanide led Wright (1840), an associate of the Elkingtons who were foremost in the field of electroplating (and, incidentally, the employers of Alexander Parkes), to employ such solutions to obtain thick deposits of gold which up to that time had not been achieved.

In a similar fashion the Elkingtons themselves obtained thick deposits of silver and are credited with the discovery of silver plating as it is known today.

The same year witnessed the discovery of a chloride bath for depositing platinum and the deposition of zinc. It has been suggested in the case of the latter metal that this took place prior to 1827 since Dr. John Revere exhibited samples of zinc coated articles at the Lyceum of Natural History, New York, in 1829. The reference to electrochemical terms in Revere's work indicates that the coating was accomplished by electroplating. The other notable event to take place in 1840 was the deposition of nickel from the nitrate. However, it was not until two years later that Professor Boettger discovered that nickel would deposit in a dense and lustrous form from the double salt, nickel ammonium sulphate.

The year preceding Boettger's discovery, Smee published an account of his findings which included references to the deposition of antimony, palladium, iron, lead, copper and zinc, and referred to the subject as electro-metallurgy.

In 1843 De Ruolz succeeded in depositing alloys such as brass from solutions of the mixed salts. Morewood and Rogers took out the first patent for the electrodeposition of tin. A power source other than the voltaic cell was first employed by Poole in this same year when he took out a patent for a thermo-electric pile. The following year the deposition of metals from solutions using a permanent current of electricity was practiced in Birmingham, England.

The only other item of interest to take place towards the end of the first half of the nineteenth century was the first inkling of the use of brighteners in electrolytic solutions. In 1845, wax moulds which were phosphorised by means of a solution of phosphorus in carbon disulphide, were transferred to a copper sulphate solution to receive an electrodeposit, and resulted in a bright copper deposit being obtained. This is of considerable interest since many of the brighteners used in the past, and in the present, are sulphur containing organic compounds related in some ways to carbon disulphide. Furthermore, for many years this compound was

5

used as a brightening agent in silver plating baths prior to the introduction of sodium thiosulphate in 1931 and its subsequent replacement by other more sophisticated compounds.

Major events which occurred in the latter half of the nineteenth century include, among the patents, the first one on zinc plating (1852) and the first on the use of alkaline zinc electrolytes (1855). Papers on rhodium plating initially appeared in 1891 (Joly and Leidre, and E. F. Smith). However, like palladium, interest in this metal did not take place until about 1930 when their importance was realised. The first commercially successful process for electroplating nickel was initiated in 1860 (Adams).

The development of the dynamo and the construction of suitable motor generators as the source of low voltage required for plating in 1880, supplanted the ordinary cell and supplied industry with a further boost, since many limitations were imposed on electroplating as an industrial tool by the power sources orginally available.

During the first thirty years of the twentieth century, the technique of electroplating made steady progress. Watts disclosed details of the well-known nickel solution ascribed to his name. Sargent took out his patent on chromium plating in 1920 and in 1923 the first commercial plant was in operation at the Fletcher Electro Salvage Company.

A number of advances were made in the 1930's. Schlötter (1932) introduced the first of what may be regarded as the modern brighteners when he patented aromatic sulphonates as brighteners for nickel plating solutions. This triggered off a considerable amount of research in the field and the arrival of primary brighteners for use in conjunction with the Schlötter type of secondary brightener soon appeared. Wetting agents were incorporated into nickel solutions to prevent pitting of the deposits which was a characteristic inherited with brightener systems. Rectifiers were introduced during this decade.

In the 1940's and early 1950's attention appeared to be focussed on finding other basic electrolytes to replace those in common use at the time. For example, other electrolytes of copper investigated included the fluoroborate and pyrophosphate. The use of periodic reversed current was reported. Undoubtedly one of the most important disclosures was the report by Brenner and Riddell on electroless nickel in 1946 and this may be regarded as one of the important milestones in the metallising of nonconductors although this was not the prime concern of the authors at that time.

From the middle fifties up to the present time the industry has advanced at a colossal rate. Much more fundamental research is being carried out in conjunction with development work. New applications are appearing which demand a more scientific approach to the problems. Who, twenty years ago, would have envisaged depositing magnetic films with pre-selected magnetic properties? The sudden upsurge in the 1960's of gold plating and the introduction of innumerable tailor-made solutions was a direct result of demands made by the electronics industry. More has been discovered about gold plating in the last seven years than in the previous 120 years of its history. Exceptionally bright and level copper and nickel solutions have also been available commercially over the past three or four years and have contributed greatly, both scientifically and economically, to the furtherance of the technology.

Plastics Industry

The term plastics is something of a misnomer. It is vague, ambiguous and often misleading. In present day semantics it describes a wide variety of substances from which are made all manner of consumer goods. In their finished form these plastic products are often hard and rigid, displaying none of the properties normally associated with plastic materials.

These materials however have been endowed with the terminology since they have at some stage during their fabrication displayed certain plastic properties. Although we tend to regard plastics as synthetic materials which have appeared within recent years, it may be pointed out that nature herself produces plastics which have been used for thousands of years. Gums and resins for instance have been oozing from trees for generations. Some of these materials display the combination of properties which are associated with modern plastics. When heated the resins will soften and become plastic; they will change shape if subjected to pressure, yet these resins have sufficient of the firmness of a solid to retain their final shape when the pressure is no longer applied. Such resinous substances are therefore examples of natural plastics and are of animal or vegetable origin. Shellac and amber are two examples in these categories.

Glass, of mineral origin, is another example of a material which exhibits plastic behaviour. Glass can be softened by heating until it possesses the ability to flow and then moulded or blown into any desired shape and set in that shape by cooling.

However, it is with the synthetic plastics with which we are primarily interested in and the bounds within which these come may be aptly described by the following definition quoted in the Glossary of Terms published by the British Standards Institute. " Plastics—A wide group of solid composite materials which are largely organic, usually based on synthetic resins or upon modified polymers of natural origin and possessing appreciable mechanical strength. At a suitable stage in their manufacture most plastics can be cast, moulded or polymerised directly to shape. Some plastics are rubber-like while some chemically modified forms of rubber are considered to be plastics."

Semi Synthetic Plastics

The era of synthetic plastics begins in the nineteenth century. On this point most historians are agreed. On the other hand there is general disagreement as to who may be given the honour of having founded it. The author does not propose to enter into any discourse on this subject but will merely present the facts as recorded.

About 1832, Henri Bracconot, Professor of Natural Philosophy at the Lyceum, Nancy, studied the effect of concentrated nitric acid on cotton and wood fibres. The product, after washing in acetic acid, was a hard, water resistant film which Bracconot termed Xyloidine. A few years later in 1838, Théophile Jules Pelouze of the University of Paris suggested that the reaction between cotton and nitric acid could be used to make explosives, but this idea was not pursued. Then, in 1846, Christian Frederik Schönbein, a professor at the University of Basle, succeeded in isolating a substance from the product obtained by treating paper with a mixture of nitric and sulphuric acids. This transparent material which was capable of being shaped was cellulose nitrate. As such, Schönbein might well be considered indirectly to be the founder of the plastics industry.

The publication of Schönbein's findings prompted Pelouze to re-examine his work on cellulose. He examined the effect of nitric acid on many different kinds of cellulose and from one of his experiments he obtained a material which he called pyroxylin. In the following year, Waldo Maynard, a Boston chemist repeated some of Pelouze's work and found that pyroxylin was soluble in a mixture of ethyl alcohol and ether forming a solution to which was given the name collodion.

Up till now the work on cellulose nitrate had been unproductive. Information of scientific interest had emerged but no one had observed any significant factor to suggest that the discovery might lead to commercial exploitation.

When all interest in cellulose nitrate appeared to have lapsed, Alexander Parkes, with whom we have already become acquainted earlier in this chapter, became interested in the process. Parkes felt that cellulose nitrate was the material that the electrical industry, which was in its infancy, was looking for to replace natural materials, such as shellac and gutta percha. In addition to these materials being in short supply they were becoming technically inadequate to the demands of the industry for better and more reliable insulators.

Beginning in 1854, Parkes began investigating cellulose nitrate as a potential mouldable material. The two serious disadvantages associated with this material were its flammability and high shrinkage rate, the latter precluding it from making accurate mouldings. To counteract the shrinkage problem, Parkes examined a number of solvents, plasticisers and fillers. During the course of these experiments he found that cellulose nitrate could be dissolved in molten camphor. As it cooled, the mixture passed through a putty-like stage during which it could be moulded. It then set to a flexible horn-like material. Parkes exhibited this new material, which he termed "Parkesine," in the Great International Exhibition of 1862 in London. From this it may be seen why Parkes is a popular choice among critics as the originator of the plastics industry.

The introduction of cellulose acetate may be regarded as a logical development in cellulose chemistry. The need to eradicate the serious defects associated with cellulose nitrate, namely flammability and explosive tendencies, led to a search for an alternative. The field was somewhat limited since the number of esterifying agents available on an industrial scale was small. Progress was made by Schützenberger in the production of the acetate in 1869, Cross and Bevan who were responsible for promoting the first industrial process and G. W. Miles who produced secondary cellulose acetate in 1905.

For many years chemists have been familiar with the tarry masses that sometimes accompany organic reactions. These apparently useless by-products in the past were accepted philosophically as an unavoidable nuisance and promptly discarded. It was these by-products, particularly that obtained by the reaction between phenol and formaldehyde, which aroused the interest of a Belgian chemist, Leo Hendrik Baekeland in 1902.

The ability of formaldehyde to form resinous masses was by no means new. It had been observed as early as 1859 by the Russian chemist Butlerov who described formaldehyde polymers. In 1872 Adolf Bayer reported that the condensation of phenol and acetaldehyde in the presence of sulphuric acid produced a white, sticky substance and that a colourless resin was obtained by the reaction of pyrogallol and benzaldehyde. In 1883 Michael obtained similar products using an alkaline catalyst.

The commercial production of formaldehyde by the oxidation of methyl alcohol was introduced in 1890, resulting in a decrease in the price of formaldehyde and an increased interest in the reaction of formaldehyde with phenol. During this period a number of scientists including Kleeberg, Tollens and Abel studied the reaction but it was Baekeland who perceived that the failure of the others to produce a homogeneous material which could be moulded arose from the fact that neither the temperature of the reaction nor the proportion of the reactants had been controlled. The first patent to Baekeland was issued in 1907 and the success associated with this material is now history. Whereas celluloid was the first plastics material obtained by chemical modification of a natural material to be commercially exploited, the phenolics were the first truly synthetic material to be successfully marketed.

The success of phenol formaldehyde polymers stimulated research with other resins. Hans John prepared resins by reacting urea with form-aldehyde. This reaction was also studied by Pollak and by Ripper around 1920 in an attempt to make an organic glass. In 1923 the first urea-form-aldehyde moulding powder (Pollopas) appeared on the market.

Appearance of the Thermoplastics

In spite of the generalisations levelled against many chemists regarding their inability or oversight in investigating such resinous by-products as encountered above, it should be noted that a number of alert chemists did observe the unusual behaviour of such materials. Many reasons exist to explain why these observations were not pursued, or if they were, abandoned at an early stage. For example, a number of workers involved in these researches were academicians. Since at that time chemists were still influenced by the methods and results of classical organic chemistry, they regarded any substance which could not be crystallised, or which did not possess a sharply defined melting point, as a waste product and the experiment which produced it as a failure. Secondly, the time was premature since manipulative techniques and the necessary equipment were not then available. Another important absentee was the necessary driving force in the form of industrial demand. In other words, it was an inopportune time for such discoveries. It is therefore not surprising that a number of plastics are actually rediscoveries.

A further stimulus towards the appearance of plastics was in the replacement of natural materials which were in short supply. This had already been witnessed in the case of cellulose nitrate which was a substitute for ivory, and casein which replaced horn. This point was to be further evidenced at a later date when rubber, among other commodities in short supply, was replaced by polyvinyl chloride and polystyrene. Ironically enough, in some cases not only did the substitute suffice, but in a vast number of applications proved to be better than the original material it was replacing.

The Period 1900 to 1930

The years 1900 to 1930 brought forth a spate of scientific information regarding various polymers which were in the embryo stage. Rohm published his thesis on acrylate polymers in 1901 and eleven years later Ostromislenski patented the polymerisation of vinyl chloride. The year 1925 heralded the first (unsuccessful) attempt to produce styrene on an industrial scale in the U.S.A. Four years later industrial research was initiated in Germany. Successful copolymerisation of vinyl chloride and vinyl acetate took place in 1928.

Other notable events were occuring during this period which were divorced from the field of thermoplastics. Alkyd resins were discovered by Smith in 1901 and in 1921 Eichengrün designed the first modern injection moulding machine.

The Period 1930 to 1939

This period witnessed the initial industrial development of the major thermoplastics of today, polystyrene, polyvinyl chloride and polymethyl methacrylate. Attention may be drawn to the fact that these polymers had been known previously for some considerable time, in the case of the first two mentioned this was in the region of one hundred years. By comparison, polyamides and polyethylene both had a meteoric rise to fame having been synthesised and produced commercially within the space of a few years.

During this period butadiene-styrene rubber was introduced (1933), Henkel made melamine-formaldehyde resins (1935) and polyurethanes were first produced (1938).

Patents were granted to Ellis for unsaturated polyester resins (1935) and the first patent on epoxides appeared (1939).

Polytetrafluoroethylene was first observed (1938) and the first extruder designed for thermoplastics produced by Troester (1935).

The Period 1939 to 1945

It is often said that necessity is the mother of invention. This statement is probably a true reflection of the plastics industry during the war years. With the supply of rubber from Malaya cut off, polyvinyl chloride underwent a phenomenal rate of development in the U.K. to counteract the rubber shortage. The same may be said of polystyrene in the U.S.A. Polyethylene which had been manufactured on little more than a pilot plant scale in 1939 became involved in a crash programme for the production of radar which initially used all of the polymer manufactured since its outstanding performance at high frequencies made it an excellent insulator for radio frequency applications.

Polyethylene terephthalate (terylene fibre) was discovered by Whinfield and Dickson in 1941. Dow Corning produced silicones industrially in 1942, although silicone chemistry dates back to Friedel and Crafts (1863) and Kipping (1901). The pilot plant production of polytetrafluoroethylene was first inaugurated in 1943.

The Period 1945 to 1967

While there was a marked improvement in the quality of existing plastics and an increase in the range of goods made available following the cessation of warlike activities, the only important newcomer to arrive on the scene was high impact polystyrene.

By the middle 1950's theoretical polymer chemistry had advanced to such a high level that the empirical routes which had characterised the discoveries of the earlier synthetic plastics were being replaced by more systematic studies and an overall scientific approach to the problems. The chemist was approaching his ideal of synthesising tailor-made polymers with preselected properties for specific applications. For example, it had been recognised that the spatial arrangement of the atoms in the polymer molecule had a profound influence on the properties of the material and this theory was successfully translated into fact by Professor Giulio Natta of the Polytechnic Institute in Milan through the development of polypropylene. Here the chemist had actually introduced a known pattern of atoms to achieve the desired properties.

In 1959 polycarbonates (Bayer, General Electric) and polyacetals (Bayer, Du Pont) were introduced commercially. Polyphenylene oxide (General Electric) first appeared in 1964 and this was followed by 4-methyl-pentene-1 (I.C.I.) and polysulphone (Union Carbide) in 1965.

In order to pick up the main theme once again, it is necessary to retrace our steps and return to the immediate pre-war years. Up till this time, the only significant outlet for depositing metals on non-conductors was provided by the mirror and printing (electrotyping) industries. The former of course used glass as a substrate and, since the latter involved separation of the metal from the plastic at some stage during its manufacture, this precludes both of them from discussion. Outside of these two applications, all other outlets were extremely small and could not be considered as production on a commercially viable scale. About this time some activity in the field of electroplated plastics became apparent. In one factory situated in Maidenhead, England, production quantities of electroplated plastic motifs for the automobile industry were being turned out and in the United States large quantities of buttons, mementoes and novelties appeared, the production of which was limited to one or two sources at the most.

A possible shortage of zinc which threatened the United States towards the end of the 1939-1945 war resulted in some discussion about the suitability of electroplated plastics for interior hardwear fittings of automobiles, thereby releasing zinc for essential war purposes. As the war came to rather an abrupt end this did not materialise.

There are records of electroplated plastics being used on a more utilitarian level during this period, notably in the electroplating (lead) of plastics as shields for radio equipment in aircraft. Reports also indicate that some interested parties were experimenting with electroplated helical designs for use as induction coils.

The plastics which were being utilised during this period included the cellulosics (nitrate, acetate, butyrate), phenolics, ureas and methacrylates. The deposition of copper, nickel, chromium, tin, lead, cadmium, zinc, silver, gold, palladium and rhodium has been reported. Applications include escutcheon rings, crucifixes and religious medals (cellulose acetate), letter openers (cellulose nitrate) and buttons (polymethyl methacrylate). Among other applications where an unidentified base has been used are cigarette boxes, refrigerator door handles, costume jewellery, light switches and bottle caps.

As has already been mentioned, it is usually a combination and accumulation of events which finally turns the wheels of any technological process. In the late forties and early fifties the scene was set inasmuch that innumerable new polymers were available on the market with a wide variety of properties and the young, imaginative, effervescent electronics industry in an attempt to cater for, and solve, spaceage problems, was demanding better and more reliable metal dielectric combinations. However, there is normally one event which can be isolated as the one which finally triggers the reaction off. In this case it may be attributed to the advent of the two-sided printed wiring board where plated-through holes were being used as a means of interconnection, this allowing both sides of the board to be used with a subsequent saving in space.

As a result of this innovation, a considerable amount of activity was evident within the electronics industry to solve the various problems associated with the technique, such as developing production-worthy electroless solutions which up till that time had (with the exception of electroless nickel) only been laboratory curiosities. A few applications appeared requiring the use of the most recent and more sophisticated plastics. In the middle and late fifties the deposition of ferromagnetic materials on polyethylene terephthalate, for example, was a large departure from that of the electroplating of polymethyl methacrylate buttons for decorative use.

Until the early sixties most of these applications were purely functional, the necessary impetus required in the decorative field being absent. However, in 1963 the missing impetus was supplied by the arrival of ABS, a polymer which was found to be readily plated following chemical conditioning, with good adhesion characteristics.

Although this was not the first polymer to be plated in this manner (PTFE had been successfully plated following chemical conditioning, exhibiting excellent adhesion characteristics, three years previous) the principal difference was that electroplated ABS was commercially interesting, since the mechanical properties of the polymer were sufficiently good and economics favoured the process for commercial exploitation.

As already mentioned the arrival of bright, level copper and nickel solutions on the market about this time greatly contributed to the success of this process since they allowed the buffing stage to be dispensed with. Without them it is perhaps doubtful if the technology would have progressed so fast in such a short time and been on such a sound footing as it is at present. Nevertheless, even allowing for this it should not detract from the fact that the plating of ABS must be considered a major break-through in metal finishing technology.

Today, a considerable amount of research is being devoted to the subject, not only by the metal finishing industry, but by the plastics manufacturers themselves who see very valuable and profitable outlets for their materials. Already it has been disclosed that another two polymers, polypropylene and polysulphone have been successfully electroplated and launched on the commercial market. Others are expected to follow suit in the near future.

Within an amazingly short period, this field, which was virtually an inventors paradise and rather looked down upon by the scientist, has done a quick turnabout. Today there is little room for the inventor of yesteryear. He will have to seek pastures new. Replacing him is the scientist who will approach the problems in a more systematic and scientific manner. As a result, more headway will probably be made by the science in the next few years than in the first century of its inception.

BIBLIOGRAPHY

1 " Metallising Non Conductors," S. Wein, Metals & Plastics Publ., New Jersey (1945).
2 " A Complete Treatise on the Electrodeposition of Metals," G. Langbein, Baird, Philadelphia (1913).
3 " The Story of Nickel Plating," G. Dubpernell, *Plating*, **46,** 6, 599 (1959).
4 " Tin in Electroplating," R. M. MacIntosh, *Plating*, **46,** 6, 617 (1959).
5 " Precious Metals," E. A. Parker, *Plating*, **46,** 6, 621 (1959).
6 " Copper Plating During the Last Fifty Years," F. Passal, *Plating*, **46,** 6, 628 (1959).
7 " Zinc in the World of Electroplating," E. W. Horwick, *Plating*, **46,** 6, 639 (1959).
8 " The History of Nickel Plating Developments in the U.S.A.," R. J. McKay, *Plating*, **38,** 1, 41 (1951); **38,** 2, 147 (1951).
9 " The First Century of Plastics—Celluloid and its Sequel," M. Kaufman, Plast. Inst., London (1963).
10 " Landmarks of the Plastics Industry," (1862-1962), I.C.I., Welwyn Garden City (1962).
11 " The Story of B.I.P.," C. S. Dingley, British Industrial Plastics, Birmingham (1963).
12 " History of Bakelite Ltd.," T. J. Fielding, Bakelite Ltd., London (1948).
13 " Cellulose—the Chemical that Grows," W. Haynes, Doubleday, New York (1953).
14 " A Historical Survey of Plastics," J. H. Collins, *Trans. Plast. Inst.*, Lond., **24,** 100 (1956).
15 " The Story of Polythene," M. W. Perrin, *Research*, Lond., **6,** 111 (1953).
16 " Twenty-Five Years of Polyolefines," J. C. Swallow, *Chemy. Ind.*, 1367 (1959).

CHAPTER 2

ADVANTAGES OF DEPOSITING METALS ON PLASTICS

There are many advantages to be obtained from the metallising of plastics. In the past their use was purely decorative, but nowadays they fulfil a functional need as well. Various applications within the electronics industry, for instance, require the combination of properties derived from both the dielectric and the metal, which neither can supply alone.

Certain properties exhibited by metals but not possessed by plastics are sometimes desirable in products for special purposes; this gives rise to the need for the metallising of plastics. As a result these properties may be improved electrically, physically, optically, thermally, chemically or mechanically.

The following list illustrates how metallising not only upgrades the performance of plastics, but in some cases produces improvements which cannot be attained by any other known method. Other advantages of metal-dielectric combination are also cited.

1 By depositing a metal on the surface, the plastic becomes electrically conductive.

2 Metallising the surface of the plastic may be necessary for electro-magnetic and anti-static screening purposes.

3 The polymer can be protected from possible degradation and structural changes (e.g., cross linking) by electrical phenomena such as corona discharge.

4 Protection is obtained from harmful radiation sources. The metal film may reflect infra-red energy and absorb ultra-violet which has a degrading effect on a number of polymers. With optical polymers, visible light may still be transmitted using thin metallic films. Glare will also be eliminated. Furthermore, it is envisaged that when certain alloys are deposited this may vary the transmission spectra of various optical plastics (table 2.1)[1].

5 When the dissipation of heat is necessary, the metal may act as a heat sink. Thin metallic films are used for their heat reflecting powers. Thermal stability of the polymer is improved. The heat distortion point is also much higher (table 2.2)[2].

6   The metallic film acts as a flame retardent medium, reducing possible fire hazard. Electroplated cellulose nitrate is a good example of this.

7   Various polymers are dissolved or attacked by certain solvents, but a metallised coating will protect them from such an attack. Depending on the metal used, protection may be afforded from acids, bases and other chemicals. The ingress of moisture is avoided (table 2.3)[2]. Permeability to vapours and gases is also reduced.

8   An improvement is obtained in the mechanical properties (table 2.4)[2]. Tensile, flexural and impact strength, together with abrasion resistance, are higher. Elongation is the only property adversely affected.

9   There is an increase in dimensional stability.

10   An improvement in weatherability is achieved.

11   Materials may be joined together by soldering the metallised films.

12   The plastic may act simply as a mechanical support for thin metallic films, as in the case of magnetic tapes.

13   Since the metal is in intimate contact with the dielectric, this will effectively reduce the noise level experienced in certain electronic applications.

14   It may not be possible to apply metals to plastics satisfactorily by other means, as, for example, in the production of complex shapes like paraboloids.

15   Advantages are obtained over mechanical fabrication techniques in providing metal-plastic combinations in that they are cheaper, easier and quicker to manufacture and the result is more reliable (e.g., plated through holes in printed wiring boards).

16   An improvement is obtained in anti-vibration characteristics over other metal-plastic fabrications.

Comparison Between Electroplated Plastics and Metals

There are a number of advantages and disadvantages to be obtained by using electroplated plastics as opposed to the use of electroplated metals. The principal advantages are outlined below.

Advantages

1   Economics generally favours the utilisation of electroplated plastics, which is of the utmost importance in decorative applications. As time passes this differential is likely to increase. The cost is of course dependent on a number of factors, not the least of them being the basic costs of the metal and plastic, since these vary considerably (table 2.5). Two of the most important rivals in the fields of decorative plating for similar applications are zinc based die-castings and ABS polymers. Although the die-casting generally requires less thickness of plating

and the pre-treatment is less involved, the polishing operation can be eliminated in the plating process for ABS, giving rise to a considerable cost saving. Therefore the cost of the finished article is the criterion on which the economics must be based. This is illustrated in table 2.6 by a number of examples[3]. It may be deduced that if, for example, brass replaces zinc as the base metal, the price differential increases.

2 Corrosion resistance is considerably enhanced. Tests have shown that an enormous improvement is obtained when plastics are substituted for metals as the base material. A Cu-Ni-Au electroplate for example[4], will protect Mg for 24 hours, Al for 90 hours and plastics for several thousand hours when exposed to salt spray corrosion testing. As a result, electroplated plastics are ideally suited for marine equipment where resistance to a salt water environment is essential.

With no base metal present, particularly one so electro-negative as zinc, there is a distinct improvement in corrosion resistance, but it should be emphasised that it is not completely eliminated as some misinformed people would have us believe. Corrosion can still take place between the electroplated metals and this is more than likely with a Cu-Ni-Cr system. The nearest approach to an ideal state is when a noble metal such as gold is deposited directly on to a polymer thereby avoiding any form of bimetallic system.

3 A large saving in weight is obtained (table 2.7). This is of particular importance in military equipment and space research applications. The saving will obviously depend on the polymer employed and on its geometric configuration, together with the specific metal deposited and thickness required. Transport costs are also reduced since they are normally based on weight.

Disadvantages

1 Physical properties of plastics are inferior to metals at all temperatures.

2 The coefficients of thermal expansion are less compatible, which means that the thermal shock characteristics of plated plastics are much poorer than plated metals. As a result, the size of the plastic mouldings which can be satisfactorily plated at present is limited.

3 Scrap rate is higher. Recovery of scrap material is not as practicable with plastics as it is with metals.

4 Plastics are not very compatible with metal inserts.

Tables

The tables discussed in the text are shown on the following pages.

Table 2.1

Colours Transmitted by Various Metals

Metal	Colour	Metal	Colour
Silver	Blue-violet	Gold	Green
Chromium	Brown	Copper	Green
Aluminium	Blue	Selenium	Orange

Single metals or alloys may form the basis of a filter. Alloys are used where transmission of a specific colour is required and where the characteristic cannot be obtained with a single metal.

Table 2.2

Comparison of the Heat Distortion Temperatures of some Unplated and Plated Plastics

Polymer	Heat Distortion Temperature °C*		
	Unplated	Plated**	%Increase
Phenolic (unfilled)	127	254	100
Urea-formaldehyde	127	160	33·9
Melamine-formaldehyde	132	210	59·1
Polyvinyl chloride	77	107	39·0
Polystyrene	77	113	46·8
Polymethyl methacrylate	68	121	78·0
Cellulose acetate	71	96	35·2

*   Temperature values given are average of three test specimens (Source—Electrochemical Society).

** Samples electroplated with 0.0003 in. copper approximately and 0·0005 in. cadmium.

Table 2.3

Comparison of the Water Absorption Properties of some Unplated and Plated Plastics

Polymer	% Water Absorption, 24 hr. immersion*		
	Unplated	Plated**	% Decrease
Phenolic	0·21	0·04	80·9
Urea-formaldehyde	1·6	0·05	96·9
Melamine-formaldehyde	0·14	0·02	86·7
Polyvinyl chloride	0·42	0·11	73·9
Polystyrene	0·01	0·00	100·0
Polymethyl methacrylate	0·35	0·03	91·4
Cellulose acetate	3·1	0·09	97·1

*   Values given are average of three test specimens (Source—Electrochemical Society).

** Sample electroplated with 0·0003in. copper and 0·0005in. cadmium. It should be pointed out that the water absorption of the plated polymer will be influenced by the porosity of the deposit which, in turn, will be governed by the deposition conditions.

Table 2.4

Comparison of the Mechanical Properties of some Unplated and Plated Plastics

Polymer	Tensile Strength* lb/in²			Impact Strength* (Notched) Izod ft-lb/in notch			Flexural Strength* lb/in²		
	Unplated	Plated**	%Increase	Unplated	Plated**	%Increase	Unplated	Plated**	%Increase
Phenolic (moulding)	9,525	10,500	10·2	0·33	0·40	21·2	14,000	16,775	19·8
Urea-formaldehyde	7,500	8,775	17·0	0·28	0·33	21·4	12,000	13,500	12·5
Melamine-formaldehyde	6,500	7,250	11·5	0·24	0·31	29·2	9,500	10,750	13·1
Polyvinyl chloride	6,775	8,650	27·7						
Polystyrene	4,775	6,225	30·4	0·30	0·36	20·0	12,750	14,750	15·9
Polymethyl methacrylate	10,250	11,750	14·7	0·35	0·41	17·1	10,000	12,000	20·0
Cellulose acetate	5,775	6,725	16·4	2·40	2·95	22·9	6,500	7,765	17·9

* Values given are the average of three test specimens.
** Polymers plated with 0·0003 in. (7·6µ) copper and 0·0005 in. (12·7µ) cadmium.

Table 2.5

Cost of Basic Materials—Metals and Plastics

Metal	Cost per in³		Polymer	Cost per in³	
	pence	cents		pence	cents
Magnesium	1·7	2·0	Polyethylene	0·6	0·7
Aluminium	1·8	2·1	Polystyrene	0·5-1·0	0·6-1·2
Zinc	3·3	3·7	Polypropylene	1·0	1·2
Stainless Steel	11·3	13·3	ABS	1·3	1·53
Copper	16·4	19·3	Polyamide	3·3-4·3	3·9-5·1
Nickel	22·1	26·1	Polycarbonate	3·8	4·5
Silver	63·1	74·0	PTFE	30-51	35·3-60

Table 2.6

Comparison of Costs

		SMALL KNOB 0·625in. high, 0·188in. dia. Material vol: 0·095in³	LARGE KNOB 1·5in. high, 1in. dia. Material vol: 0·60in³	REFRIG. DOOR HANDLE 10in. long, 2in. wide, 1·625in. high Material vol: 3·5in³	FOOD BLENDER BASE 6in. high, 6in. dia., 0·095in. wall Material vol: 10in³
Unplated part cost, material plus moulding or die casting	d ABS ¢	1·40 1·65	2·63 3·09	13·10 15·41	30·79 36·22
	d ZINC ¢	1·45 1·71	4·00 4·70	26·56 31·25	62·48 73·5
Finishing and plating cost	d ABS ¢	1·53 1·80	3·16 3·72	16·25 19·59	66·05 77·7
	d ZINC ¢	1·83 2·15	3·60 4·23	19·38 22·80	60·78 71·5
Total cost	d ABS ¢	2·93 3·45	5·79 6·81	29·75 35·00	96·83 113·92
	d ZINC ¢	3·28 3.86	7·59 8·93	45·94 54·05	123·25 145·0

d=pence   ¢=cents

Cost includes all mark-up to buyer, including overhead and profit. Tooling costs are not included in the cost figures. Generally, they have an equal effect on both the zinc and ABS parts, and their inclusion would not significantly affect the relative economics.

ADVANTAGES OF DEPOSITING METALS ON PLASTICS

Table 2.7

Comparison of the Specific Gravities of some Common Metals and Plastics

Metal	Sp. Gravity	Polymer	Sp. Gravity
Magnesium	1·74	Polyurethane (foams)	0·03 upwards
Beryllium	1·83	Polypropylene	0·902—0·906
Aluminium	2·70	Polyethylene	0·93 —0·965
Titanium	4·5	Polystyrene	1·04 —1·065
Vanadium	6·0	ABS	1·01 —1·15
Chromium	7·1	Polyamide	1·09 —1·15
Zinc	7·1	Polyester	1·01 —1·46
Tin	7·29	Cellulose acetate butyrate	1·15 —1·22
Iron	7·87	Acrylics (Methyl methacrylate)	1·17 —1·20
Cobalt	8·6	Epoxies	1·11 —1·40
Cadmium	8·64	Polyvinyl chloride	1·15 —1·35
Nickel	8·9	Polycarbonate	1·2
Copper	8·93	Cellulose acetate	1·23 —1·34
Silver	10·5	Phenol-formaldehyde	1·25 —1·30
Lead	11·37	Diallyl phthalate	1·3 —1·4
Palladium	11·40	Polyacetal	1·41 —1·425
Gold	19·32	Melamine-formaldehyde	1·48
Platinum	21·50	Polyvinylidene fluoride	1·76 —1·77
		FEP	2·12 —2·17
		PCTFE	2·1 —2·2
		PTFE	2·13 —2·22

REFERENCES

1 Wein S., " Vacuum Methods," PB111335, OTS, U.S. Dept. Commerce (1953).
2 Narcus H., " Metallising of Plastics," Reinhold, New York (1960).
3 Chandler W. N., *Modern Plastics*, **43**, 4, 91 (1965).
4 MacNeill C. E., Chiurazzi G. T., *Mat. Des. Engng*, **11**, 22 (1962).

CHAPTER 3

METHODS OF PRECONDITIONING THE POLYMER

The polymer may be preconditioned by various means to obtain a surface which is readily bondable. Chemical conditioners are probably the best approach, besides being the technique which offers the most promise for the future. The use of adhesives, which have not been over popular or successful in the past, could also offer a great deal of scope when the technology of adhesives and adhesion has progressed further. Mechanical techniques are reliable and predictable but will obviously become obsolete when either or both of the first two approaches becomes more fruitful.

Of the remainder, thermal treatments and treatment by electrical and physical phenomena have yielded little as yet to excite the electroplater. Limited use is made of both in the vacuum metallising industry, their main outlet being in the printing and packaging field.

The last method in use is the incorporation of fillers, additives and similar materials. Generally speaking this is an indirect approach, since the addition of fillers is only effective after one of the aforementioned pre-treatments has been used. For example, the addition of calcium carbonate to epoxy resins improves bond strength considerably when the polymer is mechanically roughened. Also, one may cite the case of rubber particles in ABS; although these are added to obtain a polymer with specific properties, they still come within the scope of an additive. Here again, it is only on subsequent treatment that advantage can be taken of this.

Chemical Methods

These are the most desirable methods for preconditioning plastics, since they lend themselves to mass production techniques and blend in well with the general background and capabilities of the electroplating shop. Bond strengths obtained by using successful chemical conditioners are usually far superior to those obtained by other means. The chemical approach offers a great deal of promise in the future and is the sphere where most development work is concentrated at present.

A chemical conditioner may behave in different ways. In some cases it may condition the surface to enable the subsequently deposited metal film to adhere by a chemical mechanism, as is thought to occur with sodium treated PTFE.[1] In this context the term chemical bonding is being used in its widest sense since there is some dubiety about the theory of adhesion of metal films to plastics. Similarly, other current theories such as electrical double layers, interaction of dipole moments and such like may be classified in this category. In other words, this category includes metal-dielectric combinations where adhesion is due to chemical or physical means and not to mechanical means.

Another way in which chemical conditioners may act is to attack and dissolve one of the components of a heterogeneous system, thereby allowing a mechanical bond to be effected which is in line with the prevalent theory of the adhesion of metals to ABS.[2,3]

Yet another approach is that where the chemical merely roughens the surface of the polymer in a similar manner to mechanical roughening. However, even here there may be a slight difference in that a mechanically roughened surface is directional and not preferential. In the chemical technique the roughening may well be non-directional and preferential. Chemical roughening techniques in the past have normally resulted in very low adhesion values.

Solvent swelling techniques have also been employed prior to vacuum metallising particularly with polyethylene and polypropylene. Although this treatment has proved to be satisfactory, it is limited to these two polymers and vacuum metallising techniques and has found little use if any at present in the electroplating field.*

In some of the cases cited above, it is likely that both chemical and mechanical adhesion is taking place. How much either one contributes to the final figure still remains to be resolved.

The main advantages to be derived from the use of chemical conditioners are:—

1 Ease of application and ability to blend well with a plating shop line.
2 Generally speaking, etchants are economic and the process as a whole is cheaper since buffing operations can be dispensed with.
3 Higher bond strengths are attainable.

Disadvantages associated with the use of chemical conditioners are:—

1 Ingress of the chemicals may impair the properties of the polymer.
2 Creation of a surface on the polymer which will be amenable to metals adhering to it, may result in degradation of the surface.

Mechanical Methods

Mechanical methods used for preconditioning or surface roughening of plastics may be divided into two categories namely (1) tumbling (2) blasting. The first is normally used for small articles such as buttons and

---

* A recent Japanese report claims successful adhesion of electrodeposits on polypropylene using a solvent pretreatment.

lends itself to mass production since many thousands can be processed at the same time. However, treatment is usually prolonged, sometimes involving many hours. By way of contrast, blasting techniques are normally employed on larger objects and treatment takes only a few seconds. This does not really lend itself to mass production since it is normally a manual operation and only one article at a time may be processed. Although automated techniques may be practiced, there is no record of them being used in this sphere.

Tumbling

Wet tumbling is the process normally used for small parts, the abrasive being a slurry of pumice and water. The speed of the barrel, the size and shape of the abrasive used, the geometry and number of pieces processed and the time taken all help determine the result of the deglazing operation. Narcus[4] cites barrel speeds of about 40 to 50 r.p.m. and times of 1 to 5 hours. For some plastics, such as the thermosets and polystyrene, 12 to 15 hours may be required for the best results. As an alternative to wet tumbling, dry rolling in fine sea sand may be employed.

The abrasives used are not restricted to those quoted above, although they are quite commonly utilised. In general, even though no attention is required during this operation, the time taken is excessive; this would indicate that efforts will be made to replace it as soon as possible.

Blasting

The preferred method is by vapour blasting, or liquid honing as it is sometimes referred to. In this technique the abrasive is mixed with water and kept in a uniformly agitated suspension. The slurry is fed to the blasting gun by a motor-driven centrifugal pump. Compressed air introduced at the gun imparts the required velocity to the abrasive particles, consequently atomised water and abrasive particles moving at high speed abrade the surface being processed.

The pump on the machine delivers the slurry containing the required solids to liquid ratio partly to the gun with the remainder diverted back to the hopper. This circulation creates the agitation necessary to maintain the abrasive particles in suspension.

In practice various types of abrasive are used to attain the desired effects on a number of different materials, ranging from paint removal to the deburring of metals. Among the natural abrasives employed are the organic types (walnut shells, peach pips), silica, quartz and garnet. Artificial abrasives like the refractory materials are also used. Aluminium oxide is not only the preferred abrasive in this latter group, but the most satisfactory of all when using plastic substrates. As such, aluminium oxide is discussed in the text.

Other refractory materials used in this context include silicon carbide and beryllium oxide but their cost generally makes their use prohibitive. Other artificial materials available are spherical in nature, as opposed to the angular variety just discussed and are only suitable for obtaining matte finishes on materials. They are of no interest for preconditioning plastics.

Dry methods, such as grit and sand blasting are too aggressive and usually only result in an unclean surface on the plastic which is unacceptable for metallising.

Vapour Blasting Characteristics

As mentioned above, aluminium oxide is the preferred choice for the surface roughening of plastics. Not only does it remove foreign matter from the surface thereby leaving it perfectly clean but it is, in the present writer's opinion, a much more efficient cleaning medium than chemical cleaners, particularly as it is applicable to all plastics. Other advantages to be derived from the use of vapour blasting are that although thicknesses of the order of micro-inches only are removed from the surface, this is probably sufficient to remove the lower molecular layers present on the surface of plastics for these are intrinsically the source of weak bonding characteristics. Any other undesirable factions which have migrated to the surface during manufacture will also be removed. An example of this is that of the polyamide groups which are used as slip agents in the manufacture of polyethylene. A further advantage is that the process does not entail the absorption of undesirable chemicals into the bulk of the polymer which could possibly lead to trouble at a later date.

Vapour Blasting Parameters

By controlling the relevant parameters during vapour blasting, it is possible to exercise reasonable control over the resultant surface roughness of the polymer. The adhesion of a particular metallic film to any specific polymer is therefore predictable to within certain limits.

The variable factors in vapour blasting are (1) abrasive mesh size, (2) pressure at which the operation is carried out, (3) gun-substrate distance and (4) age of abrasive (the aggressive nature of the abrasive declines with use since the cutting edges become radiused). The angle at which blasting takes place also influences the final result.

Table 3.1
Effect of Vapour Blasting Conditions on Surface Roughness

Material	Nozzle Distance	New Abrasive		Old Abrasive	
		High Pressure	Low Pressure	High Pressure	Low Pressure
Polyvinyl chloride	3″	145	80	65	48
	12″	50	40	38	18
Polymethyl methyacrylate	3″	145	80	80	48
	12″	63	48	22	20

Values of surface roughness are expressed in micro-inches.

Generally, surface roughening of the polymer by mechanical means is not a popular technique. This is due to a number of reasons, among them being the necessity for buffing to obtain a decorative finish, thereby losing any initial economic advantage over zinc die castings, and the popular misguided belief that the metal-dielectric combination is completely unreliable unless very thick deposits are used and the substrate is entirely enveloped with the metal.

This technique has been put to considerable use in the electronics industry where reliability is essential. It is not suggested that this is a superior technique to the more sophisticated chemical conditioning treatments, it is just that there has been a tendency to frown upon it as a non-scientific approach to a scientific problem. Considering that a number of investigators had for many years been involved in this field prior to the advent of chemical conditioners, it is perhaps interesting to note that only one investigation to the writer's knowledge has been recorded[5] where surface roughness has been examined in any detail whatsoever.

Although this type of treatment will be superseded by chemical conditioners in the future, it must be pointed out that at the present state of the art one very good reason for using it is because of the absence of such treatments.

Electrical and Physical Phenomena

Although both electrical and physical phenomena have been widely investigated as possible means by which good bonding characteristics may be developed on a polymer surface, all of them to date (with one exception) have at the best yielded surfaces which are satisfactory only for printing inks and possibly a few vacuum metallising operations. All the results were totally inadequate for subsequent electroplating.

The one exception is that of the technique developed at the Bell Telephone Laboratories and is referred to as CASING[6] (cross-linking by activated species of inert gases). The process relies on the forming of a skin of large cross-linked molecules on the polymer which provides a better surface for adhesives.

Although the mechanism of adhesion using adhesives and metals obviously differs, experience in the past has shown that if one is improved there is every likelihood that an improvement will be obtained in the other. It is, for this reason that it is recorded here.

In this process the polymers (polyethylene and PTFE) are exposed to a flow of activated inert gases such as helium or neon in a glow discharge tube. Hydrogen, or fluorine, atoms at or near the surface are removed thereby forming free radicals which in turn react by cross-linking with each other. As a result, the surface becomes tougher and ideal for the formation of strong adhesive joints and for the acceptance of printing inks—yet another form of adhesion.

An important aspect of this treatment is that it does not affect the desirable chemical or physical properties of the polymers. Comparing the treatment to the sodium etchants used for PTFE, it is reported to produce no discoloration of the polymer surface.

Corona discharge, which is sometimes referred to rather vaguely as the "electronic treatment," has been used considerably for polyethylene in relation to printing inks. It is the most successful treatment available at present for 4-methyl pentene-1 prior to vacuum metallising, although it has been reported that a satisfactory etch primer has now been developed.[7]

A suitable device or apparatus includes an alternating current generator to provide the high voltage to the electrode; an electrode which serves as the implement to which the electric current is supplied and upon which the corona discharge is generated; a grounded back-up plate which serves to complete the electrical circuit and the dielectric that is interposed between the electrode and the back-up plate, which functions to spread the corona discharge along the length of the electrodes.

In the process, the dielectric and its surrounding medium are subjected to a voltage gradient sufficient to ionise the air at the dielectric interface, leading to a corona discharge current. The current is carried by the ionised particles produced. The pheomena which produces the surface effects on the polymer has been ascribed variously to ionic bombardment,[8] electron bombardment,[9] ozone attack and localised heating; the latter two factors are generally regarded as contributory rather than primary causes. Since polyethylene,[10] for example, is degraded far more rapidly by corona discharge from a negatively charged electrode than from a positive electrode, together with the theoretical arguments which may be presented concerning the relative energies of the ionised particles, they all serve to support the conclusion that electron bombardment is probably the chief factor involved.

The effect of electrical discharges on polymers (polyethylene seems to have received the most attention by far in this context) seems to result in unsaturation, formation of carbonyl groups and possibly cross-linking. Degradation will occur if the corona threshold voltage is reached, but initial degradation is probably synonymous with the attainment of a bondable surface. The voltage, treatment time, residual gas present, nature of the vacuum electrode system used and air gap will all influence the final result.

Other forms of energising the surface which have been used include gamma and neutron radiation.

Thermal Treatments

Thermal treatment is probably limited to the polyolefines, particularly polyethylene. It is normally used as a pretreatment prior to printing and on occasions prior to vacuum metallising but never in an electroplating sequence, since the adhesion, which is adequate for printing inks, is totally unacceptable for electroplating. Normally the polymer is in film form.

Two techniques are available, each of them being called after their respective inventors, Kreidl[11] and Kritchever.[12,13]

The Kreidl process is perhaps the more basic since it stipulates heat regardless of source and, therefore, finds extensive use in industry. As the process makes no provision for the exclusion of air and oxygen, polyethylene in the molten form is subject to oxidation and consequent degradation, this depending on the temperature and time of exposure. However, it has been reported by Kreidl and Hartmann[14] that the treatment is restricted to 10^{-5} in. maximum and no changes in properties occur.

The apparent effect here is that in addition to chemical changes such as the introduction of unsaturation and carbonyl groups, the heat releases surface tension and decreases the surface orientation of the film. It is also postulated that the crystalline structure will also be changed, at least in distribution. How much each of these three factors (oxidation, change in orientation and crystallinity) contribute to adhesion remains to be resolved.

In the Kritchever process a flame contact technique is used. Intense energy is caused to impinge upon the surface molecules, causing the hydrogen atoms to be removed, leaving a substantially unsaturated surface. As such it partly accomplishes the result achieved by the Kreidl process and although the approach is obviously different to that of electron bombardment, it is still basically similar in that both are energising the surface.

Miscellaneous

Adhesives

The use of adhesives has not been very much in evidence in the electroplating of plastics. Two processes have been reported to date but these do not appear to be in widespread use.

The first of these processes has been adopted by one large scale manufacturer of printed wiring boards in the United States and by a similar organisation in the United Kingdom. Although there are some differences in detail, the overall approach is probably somewhat similar.

In the process used in the United Kingdom,[15] a thermosetting resin of the nitrile phenolic type is sprayed onto the boards and given a "B" stage cure. Silver, or in some cases copper, is deposited by aerosol techniques and the circuit is built up to the required thickness by electroplating. The board is fully cured under heat and pressure and a top coat of an epoxy resin applied.

Good bond strengths have been reported and have proved to be reliable in the radio and television field. However, their success may be partly due to the top coat which is applied and also to the fact that adhesion will be improved because of the plating through holes incorporated into the circuit.

An interesting point worthwhile mentioning here is that silver migration problems have not been encountered even under stringent conditions which verifies that migration only occurs on certain substrates.

A second process is marketed by a supply house so comparatively few details are available. It is believed to be of an adhesive type where the actual electroless solution catalyses the polymerisation reaction. The reported benefit of using this " intermediate organic system " as it has been referred to, is that of its general applicability to a broad spectrum of polymers. Bond strengths of 20 lb/inch peel have been reported[16] for polyethylene terephthalate.

The use of adhesives has a number of disadvantages. For example, if the polymer is used primarily for its electrical properties, the use of an intermediate insulating system will obviously impair its efficiency. Another drawback is that adhesives very often deteriorate on ageing. While processing the articles it is likely that contamination of the electroplating solutions may take place.

Etch primers may be conveniently placed in this group since they are used to effect adhesion between the metal and the base material where difficulty is encountered in direct metallisation. Such primers are normally associated with vacuum metallising techniques and with polymers like polyacetal and 4-methyl pentene-1.

Fillers and Addition Agents

Fillers may be added to polymers, such as sand to PTFE and calcium carbonate, mica or quartz to epoxy resins. So too may be included addition agents in the form of anti-static substances like chlorosulphonic acid to polystyrene for example. All or any of these may improve adhesion when used in conjunction with other surface treatments like mechanical roughening.[5] On their own however, they will accomplish little if anything at all.

Although the properties of the dielectric are obviously affected by the inclusion of additives, they do not always impair the properties. In a number of cases a decided improvement is obtained.

REFERENCES

1 Goldie W., *Metal Finish.*, **62**, 12, 50 (1964).
2 Wiebusch K., Hendus H., Zahn E., " Metallic Coatings for Plastics," Hanser, Munich (1966).
3 Heymann K., Riedel W., Woldt G., Deutsche Gesellschaft für Galvanotechnik e.V, Bad Homburg (1965).
4 Narcus H., " Metallising of Plastics," Reinhold, New York (1960).
5 Goldie W., *Metal Finish. J.*, **11**, 127, 265 (1965).
6 *Plast. and Rubb. Wkly*, 117, 1 (1966).
7 Ford A. G., private communication.
8 Mason J. H., *Proc. Instn elect. Engrs*, 98, Pt I, 44 (1951).
9 Dakin T. W., Philofsky H. M., Divens W. G., *Trans. Am. Inst. elect. Engrs*, 73, Pt. I, 155 (1954).
10 Nail C. D., *Electron. Inds Tele-Tech.*, 17, 74 (1958).
11 Kreidl W. H., U.S.Pat., 2,632,921 (1953).
12 Kritchever M.F., U.S.Pat., 2,648,097 (1953).
13 Kritchever M.F., U.S.Pat., 2,683,894 (1954).
14 Kreidl W. H., Hartmann F., *Plast. Technol.*, **1**, 1, 31 (1955).
15 Mills R., private communication.
16 Riley M. W., *Plast. Technol.*, **10**, 9, 48 (1964).

BIBLIOGRAPHY

1 " Improvement of Bonding Properties of Polyethylene," K. Rossmann, *J. Polym. Sci.*, **19**, 141 (1956).
2 "Adhesive Bonding of Polyethylene," W. H. Schrader and M. J. Bodner, *Plast. Technol.*, **2**, 11, 988 (1957).
3 " Treating Polyethylene for Printing," S. F. Bloyer, *Mod. Plast.*, **32**, 11, 105 (1955).
4 " Adhesion of Printing Inks and Adhesives on Pretreated Polyolefine Surfaces," K. F. Büchel, *Br. Plast.*, **37**, 3, 142 (1964).
5 " Effects of Corona Discharge upon Polyethylene," R. F. Grossman and W. A. Beasley, *J. appl. Polym.Sci.*, **2**, 5, 163 (1959).

CHAPTER 4

ADHESION

What is adhesion? The definition proposed by Campbell,[1] who wishes to limit the use of the term strictly to its scientific sense, is " the attraction which exists between molecules at an interface." Adhesion is a very problematical subject indeed. Even allowing for the fact that some of the leading scientists have been engaged on this problem from time to time it is, nevertheless, a topic where many of the conclusions drawn may only be regarded as hypothetical, in spite of the vast amount of experimental work that has been performed.

There are a number of reasons for this. The methods of practically determining these values are subject to error, the estimation of the theoretical values often relies on a number of assumptions and finally, the large differential which invariably exists between the two.

In dealing with the problem of adhesion the background of the scientist investigating the phenomena often influences his approach to the subject. For instance, the rheologist feels that adhesion is closely allied to mechanical properties rather than interfacial forces. On the other hand, the chemist is biased towards the opposite view and seeks solutions involving contact angles, surface free energies and other parameters concerning thermodynamic functions. Whereas the rheologist is primarily concerned with the general overall picture of adhesion, being a somewhat disinterested party to atomic considerations, the chemist endeavours to explain the mechanism with reference to atomic structure and principles.

As a result, many hypotheses concerning the adhesion of electroplated plastics have been postulated and ascribed variously to chemical and physical phenomena at one end of the spectrum, to pure mechanical interlocking at the other. Within these very wide limits, hypotheses have been proffered which involve such familiar terms as covalent bonding, hydrogen bonding, Van der Waals forces, electrical double layers, interaction of dipoles and so on. On the mechanical side a new term has appeared in the literature to describe the mechanism of bonding electroplated metals to ABS namely, the " press stud " theory.

There are various categories of adhesion. The adhesion of printing inks to plastics is one type, whereas the use of adhesives on plastics is another.

The electroplating of plastics is yet another. However, there appear to be factors which are common to all. For example, when polyethylene is subjected to chemical, electrical or thermal treatments it is found that the subsequent adhesion of printing inks, many adhesives and vacuum metallised coatings is improved considerably and is, in general, quite satisfactory. Although the adhesion of electrodeposited metals is quite inadequate, there is obviously some improvement. Since it is possible that promoting adhesion in one category results in improved adhesion characteristics in others, examples, other than electroplated metal to plastic combinations, will be cited and referred to throughout this chapter.

It is not the writer's intention to attempt an explanation of the bonding mechanism of metals to plastics. Such an explanation has not yet been accomplished by experts in the field, primarily because of the complicated and complex mechanism involved and the number of factors which contribute to adhesion. It is intended here merely to draw the reader's attention to certain facts and hypotheses which have appeared in the relevant literature from time to time and to comment on these.

Theories of Adhesion

Since the approach of the rheologist and the chemist are poles apart, the mechanisms proffered by each of them are also of a divergent nature. Hence the appearance of the two prevalent schools of thought, aptly termed the rheology theory and the molecular theory.

Both the rheologist and the chemist now fully realise and appreciate that their individual approaches are complementary to each other since neither can satisfactorily explain the bonding mechanism without recourse to the other.

In order to elaborate on this point a few selected examples only of the many available are given by way of illustration.

In Support of the Rheological Theory

1   Bickerman[2] reports that when bonding metals to a brittle polar, brittle non-polar or a ductile non-polar material there is no similarity in the behaviour of the two non-polar materials whereas the two brittle materials behave in a similar manner. He also points out that metals will adhere to polyethylene despite the absence of dipoles.

2   Indium[3] adheres strongly to a wide variety of materials, both metallic and non-metallic such as glass. Experiments on plastics show relatively weaker bonding characteristics. Within this context the adhesion to polymethyl methacrylate is much superior to polyethylene. It has been pointed out that this is partly due to the marked elastic recovery in the polyethylene surface. With PTFE no adhesion is obtained. This is a hard plastic showing little elastic recovery and the absence of adhesion must be attributed to the nature of the polymer surface.

3   Heymann[4] suggests that theories of adhesion which depend on the formation of chemical covalent bonds or other types of chemical linkages can be discounted since the experimental bond strengths obtained are well below the probable theoretical values. On ABS for example, Heymann cites experimental values of less than 200 Kp/cm^2 (1 Kp representing 2·2 lb), whereas Van der Waals forces would mean adhesion values of around 800 to 2,000, hydrogen bonding 2,000 to 5,000 and chemical bonding 25,000 to 50,000 assuming an occupation density of 5×10^{14}/cm^2. Bickerman[2] also discounts chemical bonding for similar reasons.

4   Smith[5] cites the case of highly stressed ABS mouldings which have been etched for a short time. Even allowing for the fact that the peeled copper strip has a continuous layer of ABS adhering to it, bond strengths may be as low as 1 lb/inch. He feels that this confirms Bickerman's observations and that failure is caused by a weak boundary layer just below the surface which may be due to molecular orientation, low molecular weight species, hydrogen or even water, all having the necessary weakening effect. A prediction is made by Smith that in order to obtain good adhesion, weak boundary layers are to be avoided and the polymer should be ductile.

In Support of the Molecular Theory

Low energy surfaces such as polyethylene are hydrophobic and, as such, are not wettable. The wetting of a solid by a liquid results from the very high degree of attraction existing between the molecules of the liquid and those of the solid. When such an attraction is present the surface is regarded as being hydrophilic. The easier water flows on the surface, the greater the attraction and the lower the angle of contact (θ) is.

If the material is subjected to a preconditioning treatment as in chemical conditioning using chromic-sulphuric or sulphuric acid, the surface of the polymer will become hydrophilic because of the presence of polar carbonyl or sulphonic acid groups. As water now flows freely over the surface, it can be assumed that the forces of attraction exhibited by the new groups are much greater than the original and should therefore show some signs of improvement in adhesion.

This is, in fact, the case. Printing inks which would not normally adhere to the untreated polyethylene will now adhere satisfactorily. A similar statement may be made about vacuum metallised films. Although electrodeposits do not adhere adequately, an improvement is obtained.

Although wettability of the polymer surface is a necessary criterion in obtaining adhesion, it is not a sufficient requirement in itself. The need for adequate wetting probably lies at the basis of the compatibility rule of de Bruyne[6], namely that polar adhesives act for polar surfaces (which we are primarily interested in) and non-polar adhesives for non-polar surfaces.

Metals which readily form oxides (Al, Cr, Be) generally have a high degree of adhesion to glass surfaces whereas films of noble metals (Au,

Ag, Pd) are poorly adherent. Although Bateson[7] believes bonding to occur by chemical reaction, Weaver[8] points out that for most oxidisable metals with a reasonably high melting point, the adhesion of the metal to glass increases with time. The adhesion of a non-oxidisable metal such as gold, remains at a comparatively low value and the bonding can be attributed to Van der Waals forces. The final adhesion of an oxidisable metal is generally one or two orders of magnitude greater than the adhesion of a gold film and this can only be due to some form of chemical bonding.

This occurrence is attributed to the action of oxygen. By depositing iron films with different oxygen concentrations in a vacuum chamber, high concentrations tend to result in maximum adhesion being attained before withdrawal from the chamber, whereas with low oxygen concentrations adhesion rises after deposition. It is said that this is due to atmospheric oxygen and the rate of rise suggests that oxygen diffuses through faults or grain boundaries in the film structure to the metal-glass interface.

In all instances where adhesion rises slowly enough for observation, the adhesion seems to start at a low level, roughly corresponding to the adhesion of gold and this suggests that all bonding in the initial stages may simply be due to Van der Waals forces, which is then more or less followed by oxide formation. That this is what actually happens has not been definitely established but figures obtained for the bonding energy by critical condensation methods tend to support the idea.

Holland[9] observes that evaporated platinum which adheres poorly to glass, shows improved bonding characteristics when sputtered in oxygen because of contamination by PtO_2. It is further pointed out that adhesion of metals to phenolics may be improved by vacuum depositing an initial film of nichrome.

This preoccupation with oxide films to achieve adhesion has also been observed in a number of other ways. Copper, which normally bonds very poorly to polyethylene, can be made to produce a good bond to the polymer by chemically oxidising the copper surface to produce a thin layer of black cupric oxide. Such a technique has also been used to promote the bonding of copper to other polymeric materials.

Up till now the solutions used mostly as conditioners for plastics have been oxidising solutions, by far the most successful being chromic-sulphuric mixtures. It may well be stated that where chromic-sulphuric mixtures have proved to be satisfactory, other oxidising solutions have had little or no effect in promoting adhesion. In the plating of ABS it has been reported that the ratio of H_2O to H_3PO_4 to H_2SO_4 is critical but the concentration of chromium ions is not—always provided that they are present. Smith[5] using radio tracer techniques, has observed the presence of chromium on the surface of ABS as well as palladium and tin. It is possible evidence of this nature which leads Saubestre[10] to suggest that perhaps chromium complexes or co-ordination compounds are formed and that these facilitate good adhesion.

It is perhaps as well to recall that chromic-sulphuric mixtures have been used as preconditioners for polyacetals, polyethylene, polypropylene, ABS and polyethylene terephthalate. Admittedly, all have not been successful as preconditioners prior to electroplating but they have proved to be sufficiently active in promoting the adhesion of printing inks and vacuum deposited films.

Evidence that good adhesion of metals to enamels is largely a chemical phenomenon has been reported by King, Tripp and Duckworth[11]. Originally it was thought that the adhesion of enamel to steel was due to mechanical interlocking since better bond strengths had been achieved when the metal was surface-roughened prior to enamelling. It was, therefore, generally believed that a rough surface was necessary for good bonding between metal and enamel.

Nature of Bond Failure

Although the mechanism by which adhesion occurs is of the utmost importance, not only from the academic standpoint, but in order to reach a better understanding which might result in a more direct approach to the problems encountered, the reason why failure occurs is perhaps of more practical and immediate significance.

According to Bickerman[2] failure rarely occurs at the interface, a conclusion based on considerations of crack propagation. Saubestre[12] and colleagues are in agreement and, citing the Jacquet Test, they illustrate by dimensional analysis that the break cannot occur at the plastic metal interface. It is maintained that this will actually occur in any one of three places (a) within the metal, (b) within the plastic, (c) along a relatively weak boundary layer between the two which forms at one stage or another within the body of the plastic. In consideration of the tensile strength and Youngs modulus, a break within the metal itself can generally be discounted.

Bickerman refers to bonds that break within the plastic as proper bonds and those that fail along the weak boundary layer as improper bonds. Saubestre[12] and his collaborators transpose this into good adhesion of metal to plastic and poor adhesion of metal to plastic.

It is well known that weak boundary layers exist on most plastics and that this is due to low molecular weight fractions being present, migration of addition agents to the surface during manufacture, highly stressed surfaces and so on. It should be realised that the preconditioning stage often introduces weak boundary layers or further weakens those already present, since the plastic may be degraded or in the initial stages of degradation, depending on the treatment parameters and the polymer involved. Although this might well facilitate adhesion of the subsequently deposited metal to the plastic, it is also the cause of the cohesive strength being reduced which results in a fine plastic film being observed on the underside of the peeled off metal. In this instance the adhesion is greater than the cohesion and the break will occur at the weakest point, that is along the weak boundary layer.

It is probably a mechanism like this that operates in the case of electroplated PTFE, the black carbonaceous film being detached with the metallic deposit on peeling.

The writer is not in agreement with the supposition that the break cannot occur at the interface of the metal and plastic surface. When, for example, metals are deposited on to surface-roughened polymers the break will take place at this point. The effect is probably due to various factors, such as vapour blasting causing the removal of weak molecular layers already present because of the manufacturing conditions, or the omission of chemical conditioning agents which in most cases will either introduce weak molecular layers or aggravate those already present and lastly, the fact that bond strengths are generally of a lower order which indicates that the adhesion of the metal to plastic is less than the cohesive forces acting within the body of the plastic.

According to Skinner[14] and colleagues when an adhesive is stripped from a metallic surface an appreciable separation of electrostatic charge occurs if the break takes place at the adhesive-adherend interface which tends to support the writer's objection.

Comment

In the foregoing it can be seen that anomalies do exist. Theories proposed are of a contradictory nature, although this merely seems to underline the fact that a complicated and complex mechanism is involved and that there are a number of contributory factors to be considered.

One point of contention which strikes the writer is the amount of supposition and conjecture involved in attempts to explain certain theories of adhesion in the literature. The use of specific terms in these theories appears to be interpreted somewhat differently by different investigators. The reasons offered to explain the vast differences sometimes obtained between the experimental results and theoretical considerations invariably refer to "ideal" states and "ideal" conditions. Not infrequently a theory which is based on various assumptions is rejected by another, also based primarily on assumptions, neither having any regard to the experimental results obtained.

An example, which may seem inexplicable to the non-specialist in adhesion studies, may well be cited to illustrate the interpretation of a common term by two investigators working in different fields.

In the first case Heymann[4], whose name is associated with Wiebusch[13] as the co-originator of the "press stud" theory in the electroplating of ABS, quotes the following theoretical values assuming an occupation density of the bonds of $5 \times 10^{14}/cm^2$ (a) Van der Waals forces 800 to 2,000 Kp/cm^2 (b) hydrogen bonding, 2,000 to 5,000 Kp/cm^2 (c) chemical bonding 25,000 to 50,000 Kp/cm^2. He underlines the fact that these values should be accepted with considerable reserve since there is a great deal of uncertainty regarding the above value of the bonds per cm^2. From his experimental work he obtains results of the order of less than 200 Kp/cm². and concludes, not unreasonably, that chemical bonding may be disregarded as the source of adhesion.

In an attempt to explain the large differential, Sykes and Hoare[12] point out that bond strengths are not as high as might be expected in terms of intermolecular forces because of the large size of the long chain molecules which sterically hinder other molecules from attaching themselves to the surface, thereby limiting the amount of surface available for bonding. Although this is an assumption, once again it is not unreasonable since it is based on known and proven facts concerning the structure of high polymers. A similar view is shared by de Bruyne[6] who maintains that theoretical values are all immensely higher than those observed in practice.

A flaw which is detectable in the Heymann theory however, is the comparison made between the experimental results and the theoretical values. Since the failure generally occurs in the plastic subsurface it may be concluded that the experimental value obtained is that of the cohesive force between the weak top molecular layer and the body of the plastic, not the adhesion between the metal and plastic which obviously must be greater than the values quoted.

Returning to the main theme, the second case to be cited by way of comparison lies in the field of thin film technology. Weaver[8] states that oxidisable metals will adhere well to glass and non-oxidisable metals will exhibit poor adhesion to glass on vacuum deposition. For example, gold deposited on glass by normal techniques is so poor that it would be difficult to obtain adhesion values. Furthermore any attempt to electroplate the film in an almost stress free bath invariably ruptures the film, the adhesion is so poor. Consequently aluminium or some similar metal is normally deposited onto glass prior to gold in order to effect adhesion. Weaver continues by stating that obviously a couple of orders of magnitude exist between them, which is another generally accepted point. Although he cites values for Van der Waals forces as being in the region of 10^9 dynes/cm², he maintains that the adhesion of gold to glass may be attributed entirely to Van der Waals forces and that of aluminium to glass as being due to some form of chemical bonding.

As the two investigators base their figures on different experimental techniques, a direct comparison is not possible because of the number of factors which influence each test. They do not generally appear to contradict each other. The experimental figures obtained in practice for the adhesion of aluminium to glass also fit into this pattern. The one exception is Weaver's statement that the adhesion of gold to glass is due to Van der Waals forces. If we accept the theoretical figures proffered by Heymann, together with those of Weaver, and also the experimental observations of a number of investigators, there would appear to be some discrepancy.

REFERENCES

1 Campbell W. G., Adhesion and Adhesives Symposium, Case Inst. Technol., Cleveland (1954).
2 Bickerman J. J., "The Science of Adhesive Joints," Academic Press, New York (1960).
3 Moore A. J. W., Tabor D., *Brit. J. appl. Phys.*, 3, 229 (1952).
4 Heymann K., Riedel W., Woldt G., Deutsche Gesellschaft für Galvanotechnik e.V, Bad Homburg (1965).
5 Smith R. R., "Metal Plating of ABS and other Plastics," Plast. Inst. Conf., London (1966).
6 De Bruyne N.A., *J. Scient. Instr.*, 24, 29 (1947).
7 Bateson S., *Vacuum*, 3, 1, 35 (1953).
8 Weaver C., *Chemy Ind.*, 370 (1965).
9 Holland L., "Vacuum Deposition of Thin Films," Chapman and Hall, London (1960).
10 Saubestre E. B., *Chem. and Engng News*, June 13th (1966).
11 King B. W., Tripp H. P., Duckworth W. H., 58th Ann. Meeting of the Am. Ceramic Soc. (1957).
12 Saubestre E. B., et al, *Plating*, 52, 10, 982 (1965).
13 Wiebusch K., Hendus, H., Zahn E., Deutsche Gesellschaft für Galvanotechnik e.V, Bad Homburg (1965).
14 Skinner M. S., Savage R. L., Rutzler J. E., *J. appl. Phys.*, 24, 438 (1953); 25, 1055 (1954).

BIBLIOGRAPHY

1 "Adhesion," D. D. Eley, Ed., University Press, Oxford (1961).
2 " Adhesion," A.S.T.M. Special Tech. Publ. No. 360 (1964).
3 " Adhesion and Adhesives," A.S.T.M. Special Tech. Publ. No 271 (1959).
4 " The Adhesion of Electrodeposits to Plastics," E. B. Saubestre et al, Plating, 52, 10, 982 (1965).
5 " On the Theory of the Adhesion of Galvanic Deposits on ABS Graft Polymers," K. Heymann, W. Reidel and G. Woldt, Deutsche Gesellschaft für Galvanotechnik e.V, Bad Homburg (1965).
6 "Metal Plating of ABS and other Plastics," R. R. Smith, Plast. Inst., Conf., London (1966).

CHAPTER 5

SENSITISERS AND ACTIVATORS

After preconditioning and prior to electroless deposition, the polymer is usually subjected to a pretreatment stage, consisting normally of two steps. The first of these is commonly referred to as sensitising, although the term priming has also been used. The second step, activation, has sometimes in the past been referred to as seeding. Confusion has, therefore, arisen through lack of standard nomenclature and the fact that either or both steps may be omitted, combined, or even interchanged. As some doubt exists concerning the function and mechanism of sensitisers and activators, this has not helped to clarify the situation. The terminology used in this chapter is believed to be the standard likely to be officially adopted in the near future.

Sensitisers

By far the most commonly used sensitisers are those based on stannous compounds, particularly the chloride. Hydrochloric acid is normally added to prevent hydrolysis. Solutions with concentrations as low as 0·16 gm/l stannous chloride and 0·8 ml/l hydrochloric acid have been reported by Pearlstein[1] to be satisfactory in the electroless nickel process. At the other end of the scale, a stannous chloride concentration of 100 gm/l with a hydrochloric acid content of 200 ml/l has been recorded by Chakraborty and Banerjee.[2] Other stannous compounds which have been used in the past include the fluoroborate, which Narcus[3] claims to be an improvement over the chloride in that a more rapid coverage of electroless nickel is obtained, and the sulphate.[4] Addition agents such as hydroquinone[5] have been used to effect more uniform coverage. The incorporation of wetting agents has also found widespread use. Non-aqueous solutions of stannous chloride and lower aliphatic alcohols have also been employed.[6]

Stannates have been examined by Upton[7] and found to be none too successful, whereas Saubestre[5] claims that stannites should be preferred to stannous chloride in electroless copper processes. This is based on the fact that when an activator is omitted, stannites are capable of reducing cupric ions to the corresponding metal in alkaline solutions but not in acid solutions, whereas stannous chloride is incapable of effecting this in either solution. This is verified by reference to the standard potentials.

$$Sn^{++} \rightarrow Sn^{++++} + 2\epsilon \qquad\qquad E° = -0.15V$$
$$HSnO_2^- + 3OH^- + H_2O \rightarrow Sn(OH)_6^{--} + 2\epsilon \quad E° = +0.93V$$

Because of the very rapid deterioration of the stannite solution, it is necessary to add an addition agent to retard the reaction. Tartrates are recommended in this context.

Stannous chloride	100 gm/l
Sodium hydroxide	150 gm/l
Sodium potassium tartrate	172 gm/l

It is suggested that an alkaline sensitiser such as this is advantageous when plating from an alkaline electroless solution.

MacNeill[8] has examined the possibilities of using silver nitrate as a sensitiser in place of stannous chloride, prior to activation by palladium chloride in the electroless deposition of copper, but finds it noticeably inferior. Saubestre[9] feels that precious metal sensitisers are to be recommended. In this case, an activator is used which is the reducing agent in the electroless solution, e.g. formaldehyde (electroless copper), or hypophosphite (electroless nickel). Since the metal catalyst should be in the most suitable state to effect easy reduction, the aurate, platinate and palladate are suggested. Saubestre finds gold to be more effective than platinum or palladium. Although the platinate is as good as the aurate in nickel solutions, it is inferior in electroless copper systems.

Although Saubestre[10] classifies these compounds as sensitisers they could equally be referred to as activators since it could be argued that it is the sensitiser which is omitted. Perhaps this is where some misunderstanding arises, in that stage one is the sensitiser whether or not it involves the catalytic metal. This point is extremely vague at the moment and may only be resolved when the mechanism and function of sensitisers and activators are fully appreciated.

Saubestre[10] points out that since the sensitiser (stannous chloride) is oxidised by the noble metal catalyst activator, this is the reason why sensitised glass surfaces can readily be plated with silver without a subsequent activation step.

$$Sn^{++} \rightarrow Sn^{++++} + 2\epsilon$$
$$2Ag^+ + 2\epsilon \rightarrow 2Ag$$
$$\overline{}$$
$$Sn^{++} + 2Ag^+ \rightarrow 2Ag + Sn^{++++}$$

Titanous salts have found favour among some workers,[11,12] but there is general agreement amongst most investigators that they are inferior to stannous compounds. The following solution has been reported:—

Titanium trichloride	50 gm/l
Hydrochloric acid	50 ml/l

Others mentioned as sensitisers are compounds of zirconium, thorium and silicon. However, Levy[13] points out that these function merely as polar adsorbates rather than reductants. A vast number of other sensitisers used has been reported in a bibliography by Wein.[14]

Generally speaking, stannous chloride is the preferred sensitiser. A typical formula is:—

Stannous chloride	10 gm/l
Hydrochloric acid	40 ml/l
pH	>1
Temperature	Room
Time	1-2 minutes

Good class reagents should be used throughout. Distilled or deionised water should also be employed. A tin anode may be suspended in the solution to prevent oxidation of the stannous ion by atmospheric oxygen.

The present writer[15] has found that in the electroless copper deposition process using a large number of plastics, a stannous chloride solution was satisfactory over a wide range of concentrations and periods of immersion, ranging from 1 minute to 72 hours. No variation in the results obtained was observed. The initiation period in the copper solution, rate of deposition, covering power of the copper and subsequent peel strengths remained substantially constant.

Activators

Between the sensitising and electroless deposition stages the surface of the polymer is exposed to a solution containing a noble metal to ensure the presence of a thin, catalytic layer on the surface. Among those used for this purpose, which are sometimes referred to as reduction catalysts, are members of the platinum group, particularly palladium and to a lesser extent platinum, gold and silver. Normally, an acidified solution of the chloride is used, except in the case of silver where an ammoniacal solution of the nitrate is used.

Saubestre[9] states a preference for the use of the hydroxide complexes of gold ($HAuO_3^{--}$), platinum ($Pt(OH)_6^{--}$) and palladium ($Pd(OH)_6^{--}$) when the metal to be deposited is copper. Although he agrees that the acidified chlorides are effective when nickel, cobalt, silver, chromium and iron are deposited, he feels that the hydroxide complexes are more efficient when depositing copper. He bases his argument on the fact that the ease with which a metal cation is reduced is often dependent upon the nature of the anion present. In this case the chloride is not fully dissociated from the catalytic metal but another chloride complex such as palladium hexachloride, platinum hexachloride or aurate tetrachloride is formed and such complexes are relatively stable. When a metal such as silver is deposited, the stability of these complexes is not an important factor since the metal is easily reduced from the ionised state to the metal. However, copper is not so easily reduced and therefore the chloride complexes tend to exhibit an inhibiting action. Saubestre states that concentrations as low as 0·001 % Au have proved satisfactory. A typical example cited contains 0·1 %Pt, and is prepared by dissolving the appropriate amount of platinum chloride in sodium hydroxide solution, the hydroxide content being somewhat in excess of the appropriate stoichiometric content by weight. Potassium or ammonium hydroxide may be used in place of sodium hydroxide. Silver hydroxide, being insoluble, does not form such a complex and cannot therefore be used.

Platinum

Platinum is very rarely used as a catalyst. This is probably due to the fact that it is the most expensive of the metals used in this context. Furthermore, no information has been published to suggest that it has any outstanding qualities or characteristics not found in other metals discussed in this chapter. The same may be said for the remainder of this group, ruthenium, rhodium, osmium, and iridium.

Silver

One of the advantages attributed to the use of silver as a catalytic material is its price, which is considerably less than other members in this category. However, the advantage is not quite so marked when one considers the dilute solutions used. Generally, silver is not as effective a catalyst as gold or palladium, much stronger solutions being required, which is a further subtractive factor from its initial economic advantage. A typical solution contains:—

Silver nitrate	1-10 gm/l
Ammonium hydroxide (0·880)	10-20 ml/l
pH	>10
Temperature	15-25°C
Time	1-3 minutes

A characteristic exhibited by silver as a catalytic material is its ability to act, in some cases, as a visual control, since a uniform, light brown film is formed on the surface of the polymer. This is noticeable, for example, on the off-white grades of ABS. Uniformity of such a film is indicative of proper sensitising and activation. This visual control is obviously an asset to the plater since faulty work can be retrieved at an early stage.

Silver activators are generally not recommended for use in the electronics industry, this being due to the possibility of migration (see chapter 8).

Palladium

Although palladium has long been associated with the reducing characteristics of phosphorous acids, their salts and derivatives (Sieverts,[16] Sieverts and Loessner[17]), the first report of its catalytic role in electroless techniques was recorded by Paal and Friederici.[18] They attempted to separate palladium from a mixed catalyst containing nickel and a small amount of palladium by means of hypophosphite. The attempt was based on the data of Sieverts,[16] according to which the nickel is not reduced by hypophosphite in solution, while the palladium is reduced. The catalyst sample was dissolved in hydrochloric acid containing a small amount of nitric acid, ammonia was added until the solution was alkaline, and then the hypophosphite was added. Contrary to expectations, heating the solution caused an almost quantitative reduction of the nickel together with the evolution of hydrogen. Brenner,[19] in his classic researches into electroless nickel, favoured palladium. This background, together with the fact that palladium is reputed to be a much more efficient dehydrogenator than the other metals discussed, led to its widespread use in electroless techniques.

A number of workers have examined and reported on the variable factors which influence the efficiency of palladium chloride as an activator. Parameters such as temperature, concentration, immersion time, pH and state of the surface have been the principal parameters investigated. Some of the more pertinent points disclosed in these investigations are discussed in the following paragraphs.

Pearlstein[1] found that, in the electroless nickel plating of polystyrene, activation without previous sensitising was quite successful, but limitations were imposed in that the permissible pH range was extremely narrow at the lower temperature to ensure satisfactory coverage of the polymer. Increasing the working temperature of the activator resulted in a wider range of permissible pH values to accomplish adequate coverage. These results are recorded in table 5.1. By incorporating a sensitising stage into

Table **5.1**

Effect of pH and Temperature

pH of PdCl₂ solution	Percentage of Area Coated with Nickel			
	27°C	43°C	52°C	74°C
3·0	0	0	2	10
3·4	0	15	25	100
3·8	0	99	100	100
4·4	40	99	100	100
4·8	90	100	100	100
5·8	0	2	5	—

Concentration of $PdCl_2 = 0.1$ gm/l.

the process, Pearlstein found that the activator need not be heated and, at room temperatures, a much broader range of pH values could be employed (table 5.2). It was also found that as the palladium concentration decreased so did the effective pH range (table 5.3). The minimum concentration of both sensitiser and activator, when used in sequence, was also investigated by the simple expedient of dilution to ascertain the minimum concentration necessary to effect proper coverage of polystyrene with electroless nickel. At room temperatures, concentrations as low as 0·16 gm/l SnCl$_2$ (0·8 ml/l HCl) and 0·02 gm/l PdCl$_2$ (0·02 ml/l HCl) were found to be successful. When concentrations as low as 0·004 gm/l PdCl$_2$ (0·04 ml/l HCl) were used, satisfactory results were obtained by increasing the temperature to 82°C.

Table 5.2		Table 5.3	
Effect of Stannous Chloride Sensitising		Effect of Palladium Concentration	
pH of PdCl$_2$ solution	Percentage of Area Coated with Nickel	pH of PdCl$_2$ solution	Percentage of Area Coated with Nickel
0·9	100	1·0	0
1·7	100	3·0	70
4·2	100	4·1	100
8·8	0	6·4	0

Concentration of PdCl$_2$=0·1 gm/l
Temperature—room

Concentration of PdCl$_2$=0·01 gm/l

An earlier investigation by Bayens[20] corroborates the facts already presented in that as the concentration of palladium decreases, so does its effectiveness at lower temperatures. The differential, however, can be reduced considerably by increasing the temperature. Concentrated solutions of palladium chloride are quite indifferent to temperature changes. In an investigation by the present writer,[15] the concentration was varied over the range of 2 to 30 ml/l (2% solution) and immersion times of 15 seconds to 72 hours used. No variations in results were detected.

The palladium activators discussed so far have been in the form of an acidified aqueous solution of the chloride. Exceptions to this are the hydroxide complexes (Pd(OH)$_6^{--}$) previously mentioned, and the use of palladium in organic solvents such as acetone.[21]

Palladium chloride	0·1-0·2 gm/l
Hydrochloric acid	1 ml/l
Acetone	1 litre

Summing up the data accumulated to date on palladium chloride, it is apparent that the palladium concentration must not be too low although some of the limitations can be overcome by using it at higher temperatures. This conclusion may well hold good for other palladium complexes. However, since the effective pH range also decreases with dilution, it is obviously unwise to use low concentrations of palladium. The sensitising step should also be included in any electroless process.

A typical solution is:—

Palladium chloride	0·1-1 gm/l
Hydrochloric acid	5-10 ml/l
Temperature	18-25°C
Time	½-2 minutes

Gold

The use of gold as a catalyst has been advocated by a number of workers but a great deal of disagreement exists about the relative merits of gold and palladium in this sphere. Wein[14,22,23] lists all of the catalysts used but offers no preference. Saubestre,[9] as previously mentioned, selects gold specifically for electroless copper processes because of the reasons already outlined. In direct contrast, MacNeill[8] shows a preference for palladium in electroless copper processes, claiming that the difference in the deposition rate of copper is visibly discernible. This view is shared by the writer in as much that lag time (the time between immersing the specimen and the onset of copper deposition) was found to be quite definitely reduced. This was also found to be the case when using aerosol techniques for copper.

Narcus[3] claims that gold is superior to palladium in electroless nickel processes. On investigation of the temperature, concentration and pH of both activators he reaches the following conclusions.

1 While an increase in the operating temperature of palladium chloride increases the permissible pH range which can be satisfactorily employed, the activation with gold chloride works efficiently at all pH values up to approximately 6·0 and at all temperatures up to 66°C.

2 The permissible pH range of palladium chloride is decreased when there is a decrease in the palladium concentration, while gold chloride gives equally good results at all concentrations and pH values.

3 The adhesion of the electroless nickel deposit in the case of ceramic based materials is about 50% higher when using gold chloride activators.

Narcus[3] on comparing the relative merits of palladium and gold chloride has covered some of the ground previously reported by Pearlstein. In observing the effect of pH and temperature his conclusions are, broadly speaking, similar to those of Pearlstein.[1] The results reported by Narcus are, however, not quite so promising, as poorer coverage by electroless nickel was obtained in spite of using more favourable conditions, such as a higher concentration of palladium chloride, longer immersion periods and a ceramic substrate that had been liquid honed.

A typical gold activating solution contains:—

Gold chloride	0·5-1·0 gm/l
Hydrochloric acid	10 ml/l
Temperature	room
Time	2 minutes

Miscellaneous Sensitisers and Activators

Two other techniques have been reported in the past which are some-what different in their approach to those already discussed. The first of these, by Eisenberg and Schneider,[24] utilises the reducing agent used in the electroless system as a pre-dip. By immersing a ceramic substrate in a solution of hypophosphite, the reducing agent is absorbed in the pores of the non-conducting material. On transferring this to a typical Brenner bath,[19] these localised, highly concentrated areas effect spontaneous reduction of nickel, which then proceeds autocatalytically.

The second method, which is attributed to Saubestre,[5] makes use of the fact that the effectiveness of formaldehyde as a reducing agent is very dependent on pH; the higher the pH the more effective it is. By immersing a phenolic laminate in a highly alkaline solution prior to transferring it to an electroless copper solution, causes the formaldehyde to reduce copper initially on to the highly alkaline areas of the laminate. When the initial film is deposited, the reaction proceeds autocatalytically. Deposition tends to be on the slow side and is non-uniform. It will not work unless the electroless copper solution is adjusted to the comparatively high level of pH13.

Mechanism

Although theories have been proffered from time to time outlining the possible overall mechanism of sensitising and activation, the detailed mechanism is somewhat obscure. This is probably due to the confusion arising from the number of diversified reports appearing in the technical literature proclaiming the necessity, or desirability, of using sensitisers and activators. The use of combined sensitiser-activator collodial suspensions, the use of two noble metal solutions in sequence, and the occasional omission of both sensitiser and activator has tended further to confuse the issue.

A number of reasons for this situation exist. The first has already been dealt with and illustrates that the parameters are all important. It is quite feasible that some investigators, having overlooked the importance of some of these parameters, may well have found that, by omitting one of the stages, results were obtained that were at least equal to those obtained by including it; this was possibly due to the fact that they were operating under unfavourable conditions. Other factors which must be considered are the metal being deposited, the reducing system used and the operating conditions of the electroless bath, particularly pH, temperature and concentration. The surface on which deposition is to take place is also a contributing factor. It is also quite feasible to suppose that the method of application (aerosol, immersion) will influence the mechanism.

In addition to the examples discussed throughout this chapter, some others are cited to illustrate the preceding points. For example, in the aerosol deposition of copper, Swanson[25] dispenses with sensitising but includes a silver nitrate activation step. Carlson and Prymula[26] find that, in aerosol nickel deposition, a stannous chloride and palladium chloride stage are essential when the nickel solution is operated at temperatures up to 38°C. When the temperature is increased further, sensitising can be omitted. Chakraborty and Banerjee[2] also find that in the nickel sulphate-pyridine-hydrosulphite immersion system the sensitising and activation steps can both be dispensed with when treating glass substrates. A number of other examples may be quoted but it is felt that the point has been made.

Table 5.4

Comparison of Sensitiser-Activator Systems

Sensitiser	Activator	Electroless Solution	Technique	Substrate	Reference	Remarks
SnCl₂ 40 gm/l HCl 10 ml/l Temp. room Time 5-6 min.	PdCl₂ 0·3 gm/l HCl 10 ml/l Temp. room Time 5-7 min.	CuSO₄.5H₂O 3-5 gm/l NiCl₂.6H₂O 1·0 gm/l NaKC₄H₄O₆.4H₂O 34·2 gm/l NaOH 6·7 gm/l Na₂CO₃ 3·1 gm/l HCHO 13·3 ml/l Temp. room	Immersion	Plastics in general	MacNeil[8]	Investigation included other sensitisers, activators and electroless copper solutions. This sequence yielded the most favourable results
SnCl₂ 100 gm/l HCl 200 ml/l Temp. room Time 4 min.		NiSO₄.7H₂O 10 gm/l Pyridine 5 ml/l Na₂S₂O₄ (62%) 60 gm/l pH 7-6 Temp. 30°C	Immersion	Soda Glass	Chakraborty and Banerjee[2]	Sensitising was found to be unnecessary but its use yielded slightly greater deposition rates
SnCl₂.H₂O 4.5 gm/l HCl 11 ml/l	AgNO₃ 1 gm/l	(a) Cu(C₂H₃O₂)₂.H₂O 20 gm/l wetting agent 0·2 gm/l (b) Na₂S₂O₄ 5·5 gm/l NaOH 1·8 gm/l	Aerosol	Printed wiring boards. probably phenolic and epoxy glass laminates	Swanson[26]	
SnCl₂ 70 gm/l HCl 40 ml/l Temp. 27°C Time 1 min.	PdCl₂ 0·1 gm/l HCl 1 ml/l pH 0·9-4·2 Temp. 27°C Time 1 min.	NiCl₂.6H₂O 30 gm/l NaH₂PO₂.H₂O 10 gm/l Na₃C₆H₅O₇.5½H₂O 10 gm/l	Immersion	Polystyrene	Pearlstein[1]	For further information refer to text
SnCl₂.2H₂O 5 gm/l HCl 40 ml/l	PdCl₂(2%) 2.5 ml/l HCl 1 ml/l	CuSO₄.5H₂O 5 gm/l NaOH 7 gm/l NaKC₄H₄O₆.4H₂O 25 gm/l HCHO (37-41% w/v) 10 ml/l	Immersion	Broad range of polymers, ceramics and glasses	Goldie[14]	For further information refer to text

Table 5.4 (continued)

Comparison of Sensitiser-Activator Systems

Sensitiser	Activator	Electroless Solution	Technique	Substrate	Reference	Remarks
$SnCl_2.2H_2O$ 5 gm/l HCl 40 ml/l		(a) HCHO 80 ml/l HCl 2 ml/l $PdCl_2$(1%) 4-30 ml/l (b) $CuSO_4$ 80 gm/l NaOH 80 gm/l $NaKC_4H_4O_6.4H_2O$ 80 gm/l	Aerosol	Broad range of polymers, ceramics and glasses	Goldie[16]	For further information refer to text

$Sn(BF_4)_4$ (47%)
      20 gm/l
HBF_4 (42%) 50 ml/l
HF (52%) 10 ml/l
*Triton N. E.
(1% w/v) 10 ml/l
Temp.   room
Time   2 min.
	$AuCl_3$ (50%)
	       0·1 gm/l
	Temp. room
	Time 2 min.
		$NiSO_4$ 35 gm/l
		$Na_3C_6H_5O_7$ 10 gm/l
		CH_3COONa 10 gm/l
		
		NaH_2PO_2 15 gm/l
		$MgSO_4$ 20 gm/l
		**Duponol(1% w/v) 10 ml/l
		Temp. 85°C
		pH 5·6-5·8
			Immersion	Barium Titanate	Narcus[3]	This system is claimed to be an improvement over $SnCl_2$-$PdCl_2$

$SnCl_2.H_2O$ (1%) (in isopropyl alcohol)	2-10 gm/l $AgNO_3$	(a) $AgNO_3$(ammon.) 19 gm/l (b) CHO.CHO 7·5 gm/l $(HOCH_2CH_2)_3N$ 6 gm/l	Aerosol	Glass	Kantrowitz et al[6]	
$SnCl_2$ 2-10 gm/l Sodium lauryl sulphate 0·5-2·0 gm/l	2-10 gm/l $AgNO_3$	(a) $NiSO_4.6H_2O$ 20 gm/l Citric Acid 10 gm/l (b) NaOH 8 gm/l $NaH_2PO_2.H_2O$ 10 gm/l $Na_2S_2O_4$ 50 gm/l	Aerosol	Plastics	Carlson and Prymula[26]	Sensitising step may be omitted when solutions are sprayed hot.
$SnCl_2$ 0·25 gm/l $AgNO_3$ 6 gm/l		Copper-hydrazine system	Aerosol	Borosilicate glass	Levy[13]	

Table 5.4 (continued)

Comparison of Sensitiser-Activator Systems

Sensitiser	Activator	Electroless Solution	Technique	Substrate	Reference	Remarks
$PdCl_2$ HCl $SnCl_2$ pH	1·1 gm/l 333 ml/l 55.5 gm/l 1	$CuSO_4.5H_2O$ 31 gm/l NaOH 45 gm/l $NaKC_4H_4O_6.4H_2O$ 152 gm/l HCHO 120 ml/l	Immersion	Printed wiring boards. Probably phenolic and epoxy glass laminates	Shipley[20]	Electroless nickel and cobalt are also satisfactory. Platinum and gold may replace palladium
$NaH_2PO_2.H_2O$ Temp.	150 gm/l 90°C	$NiSO_4.7H_2O$ 30 gm/l CH_3COONa 10 gm/l $NaH_2PO_2.H_2O$ 10 gm/l pH 4-6 Temp. 80-90°C	Immersion	Alumina type ceramics	Eisenberg and Schneider[24]	

The non-conductors listed here are those quoted by the investigators themselves although it is obvious that other non-conductors can be added to the respective lists. Formulae tabulated are those reported by the authors. There appears to be a general laxity in quoting water of crystallisation figures. For example, in all probability the stannous chloride cited in these tables should be the dihydrate throughout.

*—Triton N. E. Product of Rhom & Haas.   **—Dupanol. Product of E. I. du Pont de Nemours.

The most popular concept of the mechanism is based on a redox reaction. The sensitiser is normally a stannous or titanous compound; that is, one which is easily oxidisable. This, in turn, means that the activator must be easily reduced, which is true of the noble metals in general.

$$Sn^{++} + Pd^{++} \rightarrow Sn^{++++} + Pd^{\circ}$$

When sensitisers are omitted the reduction of palladium ions is carried out by the reducing agent present in the electroless solution. The following conclusions were drawn by the writer in a previous paper.[15]

1 Sensitising is unnecessary unless dilute (low pH) electroless copper solutions are used.
2 Nylon 6 can be successfully metallised in dilute copper solutions, whereas other non-conducting materials require sensitising.
3 A black film is obtained initially before copper is deposited as metal on the substrate.
4 The initiation period varies considerably with concentration of electroless copper solution. Except where baths are used which result in instantaneous deposition, a black film is always obtained on the substrate before copper is deposited. This appears to be metallic palladium, present in the colloidal (active) form.
5 No deposition takes place when activating solutions are omitted.

A possible mechanism assumes that the black film is palladium, present in the colloidal state. This is responsible for the breakdown of formaldehyde, the hydrogen evolved reducing the copper ions to metallic copper at the interface of the solution and substrate, metallising taking place only on the substrate. When the initial layer of copper is deposited, the reaction proceeds autocatalytically.

Activating solutions are essential, for without them the process will not function. As it is believed that the reaction $Pd^{++} \rightarrow Pd^{\circ}$ takes place, causing the breakdown of formaldehyde with the evolution of hydrogen, the theory that stannous ions are responsible for the reduction of Pd^{++} may be only partly true, since the reaction can proceed in their absence. The probability is that alkaline formaldehyde in the electroless copper solution is reponsible for the reaction. This may be verified to a certain extent by the fact that, below about pH 2·8, formaldehyde has no effect on palladium chloride. However, when this figure is reached, the reaction is very slow but increases with increasing pH until black palladium is deposited instantaneously in the alkaline region. The effect can be seen happening when a glass slide with palladium chloride on the surface is immersed in an alkaline electroless bath; black palladium is formed on the surface and catalyses the reaction,

$$HCHO \rightarrow \overset{\uparrow}{H_2} + CuSO_4 \rightarrow Cu^{\circ}$$

the initiation period decreasing with increased NaOH content. This, of course, is in agreement with the fact that formaldehyde becomes a more efficient reducing agent with increasing pH.

A role which stannous ions may be partly filling is that of a "fixing" agent, holding the palladium ions long enough to enable weakly alkaline solutions to reduce them to metallic palladium. The " fixing" may be due to the formation of an addition compound, adsorption of the palladium ions (adsorption is a characteristic exhibited by stannous compounds) or some similar mechanism. When highly alkaline copper solutions are used, this favours the reducing properties of formaldehyde and under these conditions the reaction $Pd^{++} \rightarrow Pd^{\circ}$ takes place much more rapidly. Consequently, fixing is not essential and therefore the sensitising solution can be dispensed with.

Nylon 6 is a notoriously water absorbent material. When it is immersed in the palladium solution, the palladium ions are probably absorbed by the material. After immersion in the copper solution these ions may diffuse slowly to the surface, accounting for the subsequent deposition. This also explains the use of alkaline pre-dips of formaldehyde and hypophosphite following activation and prior to immersion in electroless baths. Reduction to the noble metal takes place in the pre-dip and prevents the noble metal salt being carried into the electroless solution.

When activators are omitted, the stannous ions reduce the metal ions in the electroless solution to the metal. As previously mentioned, this takes place in the reduction of easily reducible, noble metals, such as silver, but not with copper or nickel, since the driving force of the redox reaction is not sufficient. The use of activators is, therefore, recommended for these two metals. From this it may be seen why noble metal catalysts are normally used.

Returning to the use of silver, which is more often than not deposited on to glass substrates, it is postulated by Volmer[27] that SnO_2 ions are adsorbed at the glass surface, facilitating the adsorption of colloidal silver hydroxide, which is subsequently reduced to metallic silver in the presence of a reducing agent. An alternative theory put forward by Volmer is that the presence of a film of stannous hydroxide results in the formation of a film of coagulated silver.

Smith[28] has shown by radioactive tracer techniques that tin remains on the surface of ABS after activation with palladium. He discloses the fact that 1 to 2 mgm/cm^2 of stannous chloride is adsorbed during sensitising. An ion exchange reaction with carboxyllic groups in the polymer has been proposed but it is felt that this is unlikely to occur at the low pH of the sensitiser. The concentration of stannous chloride adsorbed is dependent on the moulding conditions used. The adsorption is not specific to ABS but occurs to a lesser extent with polystyrene and styrene acrylonitrile.

Summarising the data presented above, a brief outline of the reactions taking place may be regarded as follows:—

1 A stannous chloride sensitiser is successful on its own when the metal to be deposited is easily reducible, such as a noble metal. Silver is a good example since the redox conditions are favourable.

2 When the redox conditions are unfavourable, as in the case of copper, use is made of the above information and an easily reducible noble metal activator, which also happens to have catalytic properties, is used as an intermediate step to render conditions more favourable. If the stannous ions do not fully reduce the noble metal ions to the metallic state, this will be completed by the reducing agent in the electroless solution.

3 Activation can be used quite successfully, without sensitising, since the reducing agent in the electroless solution effects reduction to the metallic state.

4 The adsorptive powers of stannous compounds enable them to be readily adsorbed on to the surface, in turn adsorbing the noble metal ions, preventing them from diffusing away on entering the electroless solution.

REFERENCES

1   Pearlstein F., *Metal Finish.*, **53**, 8, 59 (1955).
2   Chakraborty K., Banerjee T., *J. Scient. ind. Res.*, **13B**, 433 (1954).
3   Narcus H., *Proc. Am. Electropl. Soc.*, **43**, 157 (1956).
4   Schreiber E. P., U.S. Pat., 2, 025, 528 (1933).
5   Saubestre E. B., *Proc. Am. Electropl. Soc.*, **46**, 264 (1959).
6   Kantrowitz M. S., Gosnell E. J., General B., U.S. Pat., 2, 602, 757 (1952).
7   Upton P. B., *J. Electrodep, tech. Soc.*, **22**, 45 (1947).
8   MacNeill C. E., *Proc. Am. Electropl. Soc.*, **48**, 190 (1961).
9   Saubestre E. B., U.S. Pat., 2, 872, 359 (1959).
10 Saubestre E. B., *Metal Finish.*, **60**, 6, 67 (1962).
11 Narcus H., *Metal Finish.*, **45**, 9, 64 (1947).
12 Pridal O., *Sklár. Rozhl.*, **20**, 61 (1943).
13 Levy D. J., *Proc. Am. Electropl. Soc.*, **51**, 139 (1964).
14 Wein S., "Silver Films," PB111236, OTS, U.S. Dept. Commerce (1953).
15 Goldie W., *Plating*, **51**, 11, 1069 (1964).
16 Sieverts A., *Z. anorg. allg. Chem.*, **64**, 29 (1909).
17 Sieverts A., Loessner F., *Z. anorg. allg. Chem.* **76**, 1 (1912).
18 Paal C., Friederici L., *Ber.*, **64**, 1766 (1931).
19 Brenner A., Riddell G., *J. Res. natn. Bur. Stand.*, **37**, 31 (1946).
20 Bayens P., Brit. Pat., 749, 824 (1956).
21 Belg. Pat., 648, 589 to Sperry Gyroscope (1964).
22 Wein S., " Metallizing Non Conductors," Metal and Plastics Publ., New Jersey (1945).
23 Wein S., " Copper Films," PB 111237, OTS, U.S. Dept. Commerce (1953).
24 Eisenberg P. H., Schneider H. C., *Proc. Am. Electropl. Soc.*, **42**, 155 (1955).
25 Swanson D. W., U.S. Pat., 3, 122, 449 (1964).
26 Carlson A. M., Prymula C. E., U.S. Pat., 2, 956, 900 (1960).
27 Volmer M., *Glastech. Ber.*, **9**, 133 (1931).
28 Smith R. R., " Metal Plating of ABS and other Plastics," Plast. Inst. Conf., London (1966).
29 Shipley C. R., U.S. Pat., 3, 011, 920 (1961).

PART II

ELECTROLESS DEPOSITION TECHNIQUES

INTRODUCTION TO PART II

ELECTROLESS DEPOSITION TECHNIQUES

This part, which includes chapters 6 to 11, discusses those metals and alloys which can be deposited from solutions without the aid of an externally applied field or galvanic couple. Excluded from this part are immersion processes wherein one metal is deposited on another by a simple replacement mechanism and where a very limited thickness is obtained. The remaining processes include electroless deposition, chemical deposition and processes where deposits are built up on a metallic base, the thickness exceeding by many times that which would be expected from a simple replacement process. These latter methods are included because they appear to be autocatalytic in nature and it is felt that deposition on non-conductors may be possible provided the correct catalytic system is used.

In some of the chapters, the terminology " metals and alloys " is employed, implying that the remaining chapters refer to unalloyed deposits. To avoid any misunderstanding, it should be pointed out that metals of Group VIII, iron, cobalt and nickel, using a hypophosphite or borohydride type of reducing agent, will produce alloys containing appreciable amounts of phosphorus or boron, although the chapter heading under which they appear does not indicate this.

Some difficulty was encountered when attempting to classify the metals and alloys. It is, therefore, unavoidable that some anomalies exist in the text. For example, nickel is not classified as a ferromagnetic material although it exhibits ferromagnetic properties when deposited from a solution containing hydrazine as the reducing agent. Even so, it is felt that a case can be made out for its exclusion from the group in question, since nickel is normally co-deposited with phosphorus or boron, in which case the deposit is virtually non-magnetic. Furthermore, because of high eddy current losses there is little interest at present in using nickel as a ferromagnetic material.

Standard nomenclature usually decrees that alloys should be referred to by the major constituent present. This has been ignored on one or two occasions, particularly when dealing with alloys of vanadium, although this metal is the minor constituent present. The explanation for this is purely one of convenience, since the same investigators carried out all of the work on these alloys and a direct comparison is therefore possible, avoiding a great deal of cross referencing and unnecessary repetition.

Electroless deposition is a term applied by Brenner and Riddell[1] with reference to their work on nickel solutions. As the metallic deposit forms on a catalysed surface it has also been referred to by these investigators as preferential deposition. Gutzeit[2] is more explicit and calls it " selective deposition by catalysed reduction on metallic substrates from aqueous solutions." Some people accept the terminology " chemical deposition " as being synonymous with " electroless deposition." There are, however, differences. A true electroless solution should, according to Saubestre,[3] fulfil the following requirements: (a) the thickness should be capable of being built up, and (b) the reaction should be autocatalytic, allowing for controlled continuous plating.

Nickel and cobalt from standard Brenner baths are typical electroless solutions, whereas silver, using the solutions available, is excluded from this category since the reaction does not proceed autocatalytically. The latter may be classified as chemical deposition. It might be added that a further characteristic is that electroless solutions are theoretically regenerable but chemical deposition solutions are not, being essentially batch processes in which the solutions have to be discarded when the reaction has gone to completion.

A limited number of metals can be reduced to the metallic state by chemical means from solutions of their salts. These are gold, silver, chromium, iron, nickel, cobalt, copper, antimony and palladium. The reduction of alloys such as nickel-tungsten and arsenic-zinc has been reported in the literature. In the plating of plastics, this technique is the one most commonly used, since it is the most economic and the easiest to monitor.

Principles of Electroless Deposition

Electroless deposition is a process wherein metal ions in aqueous solution are reduced to the metallic state by a suitable reducing agent which is simultaneously oxidised in the course of the reaction. Expressed in ionic form, the reactions taking place are:—

$$Cu^{++} + 2\epsilon \rightarrow Cu^{\circ}$$

$$HCHO + 3OH^- \rightarrow HCOO^- + 2H_2O + 2\epsilon$$

$$Cu^{++} + HCHO + 3OH^- \rightarrow Cu^{\circ} + HCOO^- + 2H_2O$$

The solution is carefully formulated and conditions chosen so that random reduction does not occur in the bulk of the solution, but only on specially prepared, catalysed surfaces. The metal being deposited will itself be a catalyst for the particular reducing system employed, so that the reaction proceeds autocatalytically, the thickness of deposit increasing with time.

Although there are many factors to consider in electroless systems, the three which exert the most influence are (a) complexing agent, (b) reducing agent and (c) hydrogen ion concentration. (In this context it is accepted that temperature exerts an enormous effect on deposition rates.)

Complexing Agents

These are normally present to prevent metal hydroxide precipitation in alkaline media and to serve a multitude of purposes in the acid range, such as preventing sludge formation from insoluble metal salts, acting as a buffer and so on. In both the acid and alkaline ranges they control the rate of plating. Complexing agents may also be used to dissolve an insoluble compound at a controlled rate so that the newly formed complex may be reducible.

$$AgCN + KCN \rightarrow KAg(CN)_2$$

The stability of the complex is important. If it is exceptionally stable, weak reducing agents will have no effect on it. On the other hand, if a fairly unstable complex is used, particularly with a strong reducing agent, the reaction is not properly harnessed and spontaneous decomposition is favoured.

The effectiveness of a given reducing agent at a fixed hydrogen ion concentration, is dependent on the state in which the metal is present. The reduction potential of copper changes considerably as illustrated in the following example:—

$$Cu^+ + \epsilon \rightarrow Cu \qquad\qquad E° = +0.521V$$
$$Cu^{++} + 2\epsilon \rightarrow Cu \qquad\qquad E° = +0.337V$$
$$Cu(NH_3)_4{}^{++} + 2\epsilon \rightarrow Cu + 4NH_3 \qquad E° = -0.07V$$

Reducing Agents

The effectiveness of a reducing agent is normally pH dependent. Hypophosphites, for instance, are much stronger reducing agents in the acid than alkaline range. There is also the classic case of formaldehyde which is a powerful reducing agent in alkaline solution but possesses no reducing characteristics in acid solution.

$$pH 14 \qquad HCHO + 3OH^- \rightarrow HCOO^- + 2H_2O + 2\epsilon \qquad E° = +1.072V$$
$$pH\ O \qquad HCHO + HOH \rightarrow HCOOH + 2H^+ + 2\epsilon \qquad E° = -0.06V$$

Careful thought should be given to the selection of the complexing agent/reducing agent combination, and to the pH range in which it is intended to operate. A study of the redox potentials gives sufficient information for screening purposes. An overall net positive result should be obtained. If this is too high, decomposition may occur; if too low or negative, reduction may not take place.

$$Ni^{++} + 2\epsilon \rightarrow Ni° \qquad\qquad\qquad E° = -0.25V$$
$$H_3PO_2 + HOH \rightarrow H_3PO_3 + 2H^+ + 2\epsilon \qquad E° = +0.50V$$

$$\overline{Ni^{++} + H_3PO_2 + HOH \rightarrow Ni° + H_3PO_3 + 2H^+ \qquad E° = +0.25V}$$

Hydrogen Ion Concentration

This is an extremely important factor in the mechanism of electroless plating. As already mentioned, the reducing agent is very pH dependent. Furthermore, formaldehyde has no reducing properties in acid solutions. In the alkaline range, it becomes more powerful with rise in pH value, whereas hydrazine which is a strong reducing agent in alkaline solution possesses oxidising properties in acid media.

Metal complexes are very dependent on the hydrogen ion concentration for this affects the solubility product and hence the free ion concentration.

In the field of magnetic film deposition, the hydrogen ion concentration exerts the largest single influence on the magnetic properties of the deposit, with the result that finite tolerances are required and the control exercised over this parameter is much greater than in any other electroless process.

Other parameters which directly affect the efficient working of electroless solutions are:—

Absolute and relative concentration of the constituents
Addition agents incorporated in the solution such as stabilisers, exaltants, wetting agents
Catalytic surface used
Agitation and type used[4]
Hydrostatic pressure[5]
Ratio of volume of solution to area plated.

REFERENCES

1 Brenner A., Riddell G. E., *J. Res. natn. Bur. Stand.*, **37**, 31 (1946).
2 Gutzeit G., *Plating*, **46**, 10, 1158 (1959); **46**, 11, 1275 (1959); **46**, 12, 1377 (1959); **47**, 1, 63 (1960).
3 Saubestre E. B., *Metal Finish.*, **60**, 6, 67 (1962); **60**, 7, 49 (1962); **60**, 8, 45 (1962); **60**, 9, 59 (1962).
4 Walton R. F., *J. electrochem. Soc.*, **108**, 8, 767 (1961).
5 Sallo J. S., Swenson J. I., Carr J. M., *J. electrochem. Soc.*, **109**, 5, 389 (1962).

BIBLIOGRAPHY

1 " Ionic Reactions," E. R. Alexander, John Wiley, New York (1950).
2 " Chemistry of the Metal Chelate Compounds," A. E. Martell and M. Calvin, Prentice-Hall, New York (1952).
3 " Oxidation Potentials," W. M. Latimer, Prentice-Hall, New York (1952).
4 " Stability Constants," Parts I & II. J. Bjerrum, G. Schwarzenbach and L. G. Sillén, The Chemical Society, London (1957 & 1958).
5 " The Chemical Elements and their Compounds," Vols. I & II, N. V. Sidgwick, Clarendon Press, Oxford (1950).
6 " Metalizing of Plastics," H. Narcus, Reinhold, New York (1960).
7 " Strengths of Chemical Bonds," T. H. Cottrell, Butterworth, London (1958).
8 " Electroless Plating Today," E. B. Saubestre, *Metal Finish*, **60**, 6, 67 (1962); **60**, 7, 49 (1962); **60**, 8, 45 (1962); **60**, 9, 59 (1962).
9 " Aspects of the Autocatalytic Plating Reaction," D. J. Levy, *Proc. Am. Electropl. Soc.*, **50**, 29 (1963).

CHAPTER 6

ELECTROLESS DEPOSITION OF COPPER

Background

The growth of the electronics industry and the arrival of the printed circuit bestowed a great deal of importance on this metal and the need arose to devise satisfactory means by which it could be electrolessly deposited. Although methods for manufacturing copper mirrors had been known for some considerable time, the metal was completely overshadowed by silver in this specific application. As such, it lay dormant for many years.

When the problem of interconnecting both sides of a printed circuit arose, the first approach was by mechanical means such as riveting and eyeleting. This did not prove altogether satisfactory because it was expensive, and not particularly reliable. Furthermore, it was envisaged that, as the technology of printed circuits advanced, requirements would necessitate the need for more holes per unit area in the board. As a result, mechanical methods of interconnection would become increasingly costly. An alternative method had to be found.

Attention was turned to electroless deposition techniques as other methods explored were found to be unsatisfactory. Silver was the obvious choice but the problems of silver migration overruled it. The only other process employed commercially was that of nickel deposition. This, however, was not satisfactory due to:—

    (a) poor solderability
    (b) high contact resistance
    (c) its ability to deposit only at high temperatures.

The laminates tended to warp at high temperatures and, as they were also susceptible to ingress of moisture, this would be further accentuated.

Interest was then focussed on copper. After all, it was an ideal choice since its conductivity was high, it possessed excellent solderability characteristics and was capable of being deposited at room temperature. The result was that many electronics companies started research programmes to obtain workable solutions, most of the then available processes being outdated, unstable and completely unsuitable. In the past few years rapid progress has been made and, today, baths which are stable over long periods are in commercial use.

Typical Solutions

Most of the solutions used today are based on a modified Fehlings solution, sometimes referred to as the Fehling-formaldehyde bath. A typical solution[1] is:—

Copper sulphate, pentahydrate	10 gm/l
Sodium hydroxide	10 gm/l
Formaldehyde (37-41% w/v)	10 ml/l
Sodium potassium tartrate, tetrahydrate	50 gm/l
Temperature	room

If proper precautions are taken and careful control exercised over this bath, the solution is stable for prolonged periods. Analysis should be carried out daily and regular additions made. It is not generally appreciated that particles of dust are one of the main sources of breakdown of electroless solutions. If a 2-micron filter is used, nearly all dust particles are removed so that nucleation takes place inside the filter. Particles which are smaller than this will be removed as soon as they reach 2-microns and before decomposition starts in the bulk of the solution. Normally, very little decomposition takes place inside the filter, but when necessary the filter can be disconnected and flushed with a suitable solvent, for example HNO_3 or $(NH_4)_2S_2O_8$, followed by further flushing with water. All dust and copper particles are thus removed and the solution is maintained in its initial condition.

The process is best carried out in a polyethylene tank, that is one with a hydrophobic surface, so as to minimise any possible deposition on the sides of the tank. For this reason, a two tank system should be used, the second tank being empty. Periodically the solution should be transferred and any metallic decomposition products removed from the first tank.

Anionic wetting agents which are sometimes added to these solutions should be avoided. Their prime function is to lower surface tension and permit wetting of the substrate by decreasing the angle of contact. As the substrate should be hydrophillic when immersed in the solution, all that will be accomplished is superior wetting of the low energy surface, which is the sides of the polyethylene tank in this case, thereby leading to deposition on the tank walls.

The solution has a relatively slow plating rate, taking between 20 and 25 minutes to deposit a film sufficiently thick to build up by electroplating. However, as the prime object is to obtain a film suitable for electroplating, this is not considered to be a serious drawback considering the advantages gained, namely (a) low cost operation compared to batch processes (b) longer life.

In order to prolong the life of electroless copper solutions, the pH may be lowered at the end of the working day, using sulphuric acid. The reason for this is that electroless copper solutions using formaldehyde as the reducing agent are pH sensitive and will not operate below a pH of 7. In the morning, the solution is made up with the equivalent of sodium hydroxide. Although this has worked satisfactorily in the past, the need does not arise now since commercial solutions are available on the market incorporating suitable stabilisers, which have a life in excess of six months without resorting to this technique. Furthermore, the effect that a build up of salts has on the bath over a period is still an unknown quantity.

Parameters

Temperature

The effect of temperature may be seen in fig. 6.1. Increasing the temperature results in a higher deposition rate but it also accelerates the rate of decomposition. Blistering of the deposit occurs rather easily, and is probably caused by hydrogen occlusion in the deposit due to the rate at which the reaction proceeds. It will be seen that at 53°C, decomposition is rapid, and the rate of deposition decreases very quickly, since the preference is to form cuprous oxide in the bulk of the solution at this temperature.

Absolute Concentration

When relatively weak solutions are used, no change in the deposition rates are obtained by increasing the tartrate or formaldehyde concentration (fig. 6.2 and 6.3). The solutions are also very stable. It may be assumed that, under these conditions, only two predominant parameters exist in the solution, metal content and pH. When the absolute concentration is increased, both the tartrate and formaldehyde concentration affect deposition rates markedly (fig. 6.4 and 6.5).

Increasing the copper concentration will increase the rate of deposition. In fig. 6.6 it will be seen that the deposition rate decreases around 9-10 gm/l. This is due to a drop in the pH level so that the reducing agent becomes less effective.

All other parameters remaining constant, increasing the NaOH content results in increased deposition rates (fig. 6.7). This is probably due to the increased efficiency of the reducing agent which, we may remember, is very pH dependent.

Volume—Area

If too great a catalysed surface area is exposed per unit volume, decomposition is facilitated. Increasing the area results in increased rate of decomposition. About 250 cm² per litre is the maximum that can be used with safety. When too much catalysed surface area is exposed, too much hydrogen is evolved, consequently the reaction rate increases greatly and favours bath decomposition.

It will be seen later that this is a diametrically opposite observation from that reported with electroless nickel deposition.

Complexing Agents

Complexing agents prevent the precipitation of copper hydroxide by alkalies from cupric solutions by depressing the free cupric ion below

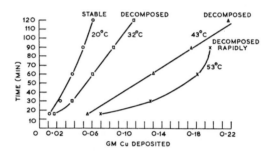

Fig. 6.1 Effect of temperature on the deposition rate of electroless copper. $CuSO_4.5H_2O = 10$ gm/l; HCHO (37-41% w/v) = 10 ml/l; NaOH = 7 gm/l; sodium potassium tartrate = 50 gm/l; area = 39 cm²; substrate glass. [Goldie]

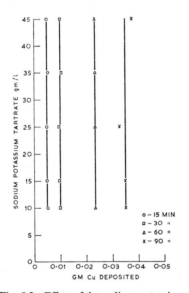

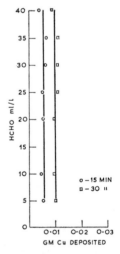

Fig. 6.2 Effect of the sodium potassium tartrate concentration on the deposition rate of electroless copper in weak solutions. $CuSO_4.5H_2O = 5$ gm/l; NaOH = 5 gm/l; HCHO (37-41% w/v) = 10 ml/l; temperature 20°C; area = 39 cm². [Goldie]

Fig. 6.3 Effect of the formaldehyde concentration on the deposition rate of electroless copper in weak solutions. $CuSO_4.5H_2O = 5$ gm/l; NaOH = 5 gm/l; sodium potassium tartrate = 25 gm/l; temperature = 20°C; area = 39 cm². [Goldie]

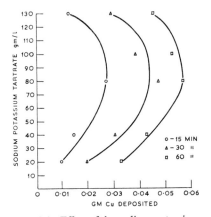

Fig. 6.4 Effect of the sodium potassium tartrate concentration on the deposition rate of electroless copper in strong solutions. $CuSO_4.5H_2O$ = 15 gm/l; NaOH = 7 gm/l; HCHO (37-41 % w/v) = 10 ml/l; temperature = 20°C; area = 39 cm². [Goldie]

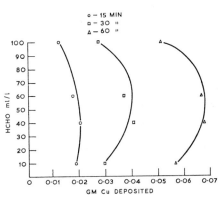

Fig. 6.5 Effect of the formaldehyde concentration on the deposition rate of electroless copper in strong solutions. $CuSO_4.5H_2O$ = 10 gm/l; sodium potassium tartrate = 20 gm/l; NaOH = 12 gm/l; temperature = 20°C; area = 39 cm². [Goldie]

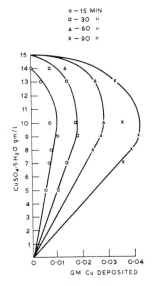

Fig. 6.6 Effect of the copper ion concentration on the deposition rate of electroless copper. NaOH = 5 gm/l; HCHO (37-41 % w/v) = 10 ml/l; sodium potassium tartrate = 25 gm/l; temperature = 20°C; area = 39 cm². [Goldie]

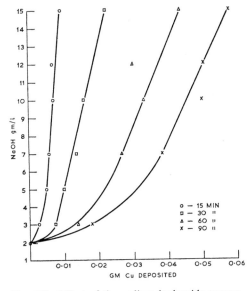

Fig. 6.7 Effect of the sodium hydroxide concentration on the deposition rate of electroless copper. $CuSO_4.5H_2O$ = 5 gm/l; HCHO (37-41 % w/v) = 10 ml/l; sodium potassium tartrate = 25 gm/l; temperature = 20°C; area = 39 cm². [Goldie]

that corresponding to the solubility product of copper hydroxide. The free ion concentration will depend primarily on the complexing agent used. Copper tends to form complexes rather easily, as one would expect from its position in the electrochemical series. Two types of complex are obtainable, the first being open chain, the second being closed ring, or chelate. In the first type both Cu^+ and Cu^{++} tend to form co-ordination compounds rather easily and, as would be expected, the Cu^{++} shows a greater tendency to do so, due to the double charge. Although some of these complexes are very stable, for example with cyanide or ammonia, they are not generally as stable as the closed ring compounds. In both cases, the most stable compounds usually have a co-ordination number of four.

In the second type, chelate complexes with cuprous compounds are not abundant, but those obtainable have the copper co-ordinated through oxygen, a sulphur, or both, but never through nitrogen. On the other hand, the cupric ion forms innumerable chelates and these are renowned for their stability. They may be formed by the attachment of oxygen, sulphur or nitrogen to the copper atom.

In acid solutions, where the copper ion can exist entirely in the free state and complexing agents are omitted, reduction of copper ions to metallic copper is comparatively easy. This is, of course, of no value with immersion techniques since random deposition takes place. Complexing agents are therefore added to harness the reaction.

Cupric salts are preferred in electroless copper solutions for a number of reasons, such as (a) the limited number of cuprous compounds obtainable and their insolubility, (b) the greater stability of cupric complexes, their stronger tendency to form complexes and the number available, (c) the relative instability of the free cuprous ion. Some of the well known copper complexes are discussed in the following paragraphs.

Cyanides

These are never used because of the stability of the complexes formed in both the cuprous and cupric state. It has already been mentioned that the most stable state exhibits co-ordination numbers of 4* giving rise to typical compounds such as $K_3[Cu(CN)_4]$ and $K_2[Cu(CN)_4]$ respectively. The 4 covalent ion is remarkably stable, the dissociation constant to $Cu^+ + 4CN^-$ being 2×10^{-27}. Complexing is so complete that the free ion concentration is almost negligible; for example, a solution in which KCN is normal and the Cu^+ concentration decinormal has a free cuprous ion concentration of 5×10^{-29}.

Ammonia

Ammonia, alkyl and arylamines, have a marked tendency to form co-ordination, or Werner type compounds with cupric ions. The complexes are very stable and there are very few free cupric ions present in solution.

---

*—Some disagreement exists over the co-ordination number of the cuprous ion. Among the references consulted on this subject, the majority of workers favour a co-ordination number of 2 giving rise to the complex K Cu (CN)$_2$.

Increasing the ammonia content results in decreased deposition rates but an increase in OH^- from alkali hydroxides counteracts this and results in increased deposition rates. This is in general agreement with the views of Kohlschütter[2] on silver reduction and with the observations of Chattaway[3] on copper using phenylhydrazine as the reducing agent.

Ethylenediaminetetra-acetic Acid

This sequestering agent forms very stable complexes with cupric ions probably of the type:—

$$
\begin{array}{l}
CH_2—NH_2 \diagdown \\
\quad | \qquad\qquad \diagup Cu \\
CH_2—NH_2 \diagup
\end{array}
$$

The free cupric ion present is once again almost negligible which leads Lukes[4] to raise the following points.

1 If the rate of reaction is a function of the free cupric ion concentration which is accessible to reducing agents, the overall reaction should not be discernible due to the amount of free cupric ions present.

2 Alternatively, the chelating agent supplies the complex cupric ion with sufficient electrons and should therefore require a reducing agent of greater reducing power than formaldehyde. As the reducing reaction proceeds at a reasonable rate, it is concluded that the mechanism is much more complicated than the basic equations would indicate.

A mixture of EDTA and triethanolamine, known as Versene T[5] has been added to Fehling-formaldehyde solutions along with carbonates to improve stability and increase the plating rate. It may be seen that the term " addition agent," with respect to electroless solutions, is a very broad term indeed and emphasises once again the interchangeability of these compounds. In this particular example we have four compounds present which are known to effectively form complexes with copper, namely tartrate, carbonate, EDTA and triethanolamine.

Tartrates

This is probably the commonest complexing agent used in electroless copper solutions. Wark[6-9] suggests the following structural formula, a five membered ring complex being formed, a characteristic that other $\propto$-oxy-acids exhibit:—

$$
\begin{array}{l}
\qquad\qquad COOH \\
\qquad\qquad | \\
\qquad\quad H—C—OH \\
\qquad\qquad | \\
\qquad\quad \diagup O—C—H \\
Cu \diagdown \qquad | \\
\qquad\quad \diagdown O—C=O
\end{array}
$$

The more general interpretation of the reaction however is:—

$$
\begin{array}{ccc}
\text{COOH} & & \text{COOH} \\
| & & | \\
\text{H—C—OH} & & \text{H—C—O} \\
| & +\text{Cu}^{++}+2\text{OH}^- \rightarrow & | \quad\quad\rangle\text{Cu}+2\text{H}_2\text{O} \\
\text{H—C—OH} & & \text{H—C—O} \\
| & & | \\
\text{COONa} & & \text{COONa}
\end{array}
$$

The effect of complexing agents on copper ions is illustrated as follows:—

Cu^{++}	$+2\epsilon \rightarrow Cu$	$E° = +0\cdot337V$
$Cu(T)_3^{----}$	$+2\epsilon \rightarrow Cu+3T^{--}$	$E° = +0\cdot154V$
$Cu(CO_3)_3^{----}$	$+2\epsilon \rightarrow Cu+3CO_3^{--}$	$E° = +0\cdot001V$
$Cu(NH_3)_4^{++}$	$+2\epsilon \rightarrow Cu+4NH_3$	$E° = -0\cdot070V$
$Cu(EDTA)^{--}$	$+2\epsilon \rightarrow Cu+EDTA^{----}$	$E° = -0\cdot203V$

It may be seen that the lower the value of E°, the stronger the complex. When Cu^{++} is entirely in the free state, E° is very high, a high figure facilitating reduction.

Reducing Agents

Wein[10] has published a comprehensive, non-critical review of reducing agents used in electroless copper solutions. Saubestre,[5] on the other hand, has published a critical review of the most promising reducing agents, this being supported by experimental evidence and from theoretical considerations of redox potentials.

The most important characteristic that the reducing agent should possess when used in electroless copper solutions is that copper itself should be an effective catalyst for it, thus enabling the reaction to proceed auto-catalytically. It may well be pH dependent. It should be capable of reducing divalent copper to metallic copper ($Cu^{++} \rightarrow Cu°$) and not merely reduce it to an intermediate compound, cuprous oxide. The more important reducing agents are discussed below.

Tartrates

They are used as reducing agents for silver and gold. In copper solutions it would appear that only partial reduction takes place, the intermediate red cuprous oxide being precipitated and this usually on heating. The primary use of tartrate is to complex the copper ions, preventing copper hydroxide precipitation in alkaline solution.

Aldehydes

Aliphatic aldehydes, particularly formaldehyde, are the most common reducing agents used in electroless copper solutions. They are very dependent on pH, their effectiveness increasing with increasing pH. In the acid range they do not function as reducing agents.

Hypophosphite

As already stated, this is an effective reducing agent in both acid and alkaline solutions. Only one solution, however, has come to light which uses hypophosphite as a reducing agent for copper, this operating at 93°C. Brookshire[11] is the investigator and his solution functions on the same principle as his hypophosphite electroless silver and gold discussed in chapter 8.

Cupric oxide	3·0 gm/l
Sodium hypophosphite, monohydrate	10·0 gm/l
Ammonium chloride	0·1 gm/l
pH	3·0
Temperature	93°C
Rate of deposition	136 mgm/cm²/hr.

The insoluble compound, CuO, is dissolved by the complexing agent, NH_4Cl, to form a readily reducible soluble complex. When the copper ions are reduced to metallic copper, this releases the complexing agent to dissolve a further amount of the insoluble compound. The reaction is thus controlled in this manner.

Hydrazine

Hydrazine and its compounds have been successfully used by some investigators as a reducing agent for copper. Wein[12] states a preference for this compound since no fumes are evolved as in the case of formaldehyde. Bamberger and Schweitzer,[13] Eyber[14] and French[15] are others who have employed this reducing agent. Hydrazine hydrate is the preferred compound to use.

Derivatives of hydrazine such as phenylhydrazine have been investigated by Volmer[16] and Chattaway.[3] The optimum conditions for the method were ascertained by French,[15] but the process has the disadvantage of depositing tarry by-products and is therefore rarely used.

Stabilisers

In order to reduce the decomposition potential of electroless copper solutions, workers have investigated means by which they can stabilise these baths. Agens[17] found that passing air or oxygen through the solution prevented the formation of Cu_2O, a soluble cupric salt being formed on reoxidation, which prolonged the life of the bath.

A method has been described[18] in which 2 mercaptobenzothiazole was added to the solution and proved to be a successful stabiliser. Too high a concentration increases stability with a subsequent lowering of the

67

deposition rate. A compromise has therefore to be reached. The recommended solution is:—

Copper sulphate, pentahydrate	13·8 gm/l
Sodium potassium tartrate, tetrahydrate	69·2 gm/l
Sodium hydroxide	20 gm/l
Formaldehyde (36% w/v 12½% CH₃OH)	40·0 ml/l
2 mercaptobenzothiazole	0·003%
Temperature	25°C

Fig. 6.8 illustrates the rate of deposition using the above bath. Increasing the temperature to 31°C results in slow decomposition of the solution but increasing the MBT content counteracts this. Further work is necessary on the relationship between temperature and MBT concentration. This initial investigation showed that deposition rates were better than proprietary solutions tested at the time and, moreover, stability was considerably enhanced. Life in excess of eight days is reported.

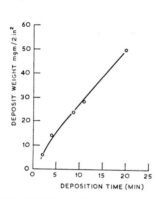

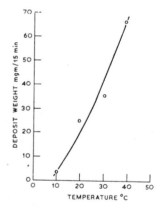

Fig. 6.8 Effect of immersion time on weight of deposit. [Pearlstein et al]

Fig. 6.9 Effect of various temperatures on deposition rate. [Pearlstein et al]

Cahill[19] claims the use of carbonates as stabilising agents. Copper is known to form carbonate complexes such as $Na_2[Cu(CO_3)_2]$. Cahill suggests that the copper complex formed, $Cu(CO_3)_3^{----}$ prevents decomposition taking place and facilitates the build up of heavy deposits by employing a quick deposition rate. Although carbonates are used in electroless solutions, the production of thick deposits from stable baths has not yet been achieved. Saubestre,[5] in an examination of this process, states that bath stability is obtained with increasing carbonate content but only at the expense of decreasing deposition rates. Another disadvantage is the strong tendency for the deposits to blister, probably due to the conversion of carbonate to carbon dioxide which is trapped beneath the copper film.

Alkanolaminacetic acid[20] and thiourea[21] have also been used as stabilisers.

Heavy Deposits

There is an obvious requirement in the electronics industry for thick deposits of electroless copper (of at least 1 mil per hour). Such applications as plated-through holes in printed circuitry are the outstanding application at the present time.

Ideally, the copper deposited inside a hole in printed circuitry should be of uniform thickness and about 1 mil thick to facilitate soldering of components, since a good fillet of solder is essential. At present, a thin deposit is reinforced by electroplating. Uniformity, or non-uniformity as is the case, is dependent on (a) throwing power of the plating solution, (b) depth of hole, and (c) diameter of hole. Specifications suggest a minimum thickness of 1 mil with a tolerance of 100% which means that at the lip of the hole the thickness is 2 mil and a reduction in diameter is obtained of 4 mil. This is in consideration of the hole diameters being 42 mil but it is obviously unsatisfactory where smaller diameter holes, such as 10 mil are coming into vogue. One solution to the problem is to use very thin substrates, but this is not always possible in conventional printed wiring.

The only high speed electroless copper process found in the literature is attributed to Saubestre[5] who obtained plating rates of 1 mil/hour. The solutions, however, are unstable, having a life of just over two hours.

Solution "A"	Copper sulphate, pentahydrate	35 gm/l
	Sodium hydroxide	50 gm/l
	Sodium carbonate	30 gm/l
	Sodium potassium tartrate, tetrahydrate	170 gm/l
	Versene T	20 ml/l
Solution "B"	Formaldehyde (37% w/v)	

Use 5 parts "A" to 1 part "B." Mix immediately prior to use. Operate at room temperature.

Mechanism

The overall reaction taking place may be represented in the following simplified form:—

$$Cu^{++} + 2\epsilon \quad \rightarrow Cu^{\circ}$$
$$HCHO + 3OH^- \rightarrow HCOO^- + 2H_2O + 2\epsilon$$

$$Cu^{++} + HCHO + 3OH^- \quad \rightarrow Cu^{\circ} + HCOO^- + 2H_2O$$
$$\text{or} \quad CuSO_4 + HCHO + 3NaOH \rightarrow Cu^{\circ} + HCOONa + Na_2SO_4 + 2H_2O$$

In order to illustrate the complete reaction, however, from beginning to end, the following simplified version of the mechanism is offered:—

$$\begin{cases} Sn^{++} + Pd^{++} & \rightarrow \quad Sn^{++++} + Pd^{\circ} \\ SnCl_2 + PdCl_2 & \rightarrow \quad SnCl_4 + Pd^{\circ} \end{cases} \dots\dots\dots\dots\dots(1)$$

$$\begin{cases} HCHO+OH^- \\ HCHO+NaOH \end{cases} \xrightarrow[\substack{\text{Catalyst}}]{\substack{Pd° \\ }} \begin{array}{l} H_2+HCOO^- \\ H_2+HCOONa \end{array} \quad \dots \dots \dots \dots (2)$$

$$\begin{cases} Cu^{++}+H_2+2OH^- \\ CuSO_4+H_2+2NaOH \end{cases} \rightarrow \begin{array}{l} Cu°+2H_2O \\ Cu°+Na_2SO_4+2H_2O \end{array} \quad \dots \dots \dots (3)$$

$$\begin{cases} HCHO+OH^- \\ HCHO+NaOH \end{cases} \xrightarrow[\substack{\text{Catalyst}}]{\substack{Cu° \\ }} \begin{array}{l} H_2+HCOO^- \\ H_2+HCOONa \end{array} \quad \dots \dots \dots \dots (4)$$

It may be seen that equation (4) is identical to equation (2) except that copper replaces palladium as the catalytic metal and the reaction will therefore proceed autocatalytically. (Copper for example is a known catalyst for the dehydrogenation of ethyl alcohol to acetaldehyde.) Equation (1) illustrates the general version of the role that stannous ions play in the reaction. However, the reaction can proceed in their absence, the formaldehyde in the alkaline electroless copper bath acting as the reducing agent according to the equation.

$$\begin{cases} Pd^{++}+HCHO+2OH^- \\ PdCl_2+HCHO+2NaOH \end{cases} \begin{array}{l} \rightarrow Pd°+HCOOH+H_2O \\ \rightarrow Pd°+HCOOH+2NaCl+H_2O \end{array} \quad \dots (5)$$

This may replace equation (1) in the above set of equations. It may be illustrated by using a glass slide which is first of all immersed in $PdCl_2$ and then transferred to the alkaline electroless bath. A black film is formed on the surface which is presumably palladium present in the colloidal (active) state, the initiation period until the onset of copper deposition decreasing with increasing pH. This, of course, is characteristic of formaldehyde's effectiveness increasing with increased pH.

pH	9	10	11	12	13	14
$E°$	+0·62	+0·71	+0·80	+0·89	+0·98	+1·07

On the whole, the reactions taking place are exceedingly complicated. For instance, the copper is present as a complex and therefore the value of $E°$ is different from that quoted in the simple ionic representation.

$$Cu^{++}+2\epsilon \rightarrow Cu° \qquad\qquad E°=+0·337V$$
$$Cu(NH_3)_4^{++}+2\epsilon \rightarrow Cu°+4NH_3 \qquad E°=-0·07V$$

Moreover, metals such as copper which can exist in two valency states, tend to react with each other resulting in the formation of the metal and the higher valency state.

$$2Cu^+ \rightarrow Cu° + Cu^{++}$$

Furthermore, side chain reactions take place. For example formaldehyde, which is typical of most aldehydes, undergoes a Cannizzaro reaction (disproportionation).

$$2HCHO + OH^- \rightarrow HCOO^- + CH_3OH$$
$$\text{or} \quad 2HCHO + NaOH \rightarrow HCOONa + CH_3OH$$

Outside of the complexing duties that tartrate performs, there is considerable speculation as to the other role it might play in the reaction. It may well function as a secondary reducing agent under favourable circumstances as shown in fig. 6.4 when the rate of deposition increases with increased tartrate concentration.

Hersch[22] prefers the hypothesis that the reaction mechanism centres around the hydride ion, H^-. He maintains that the oxidation of formaldehyde by alkaline cupric solutions, catalysed initially by palladium but autocatalytic in nature with the formation of hydrogen, represents an anodic process galvanically coupled with the reduction of Cu^{++} or H^+ as a cathodic process, the nucleus serving as anode and cathode simultaneously.

In a recent paper published by Lukes,[4] the conclusion reached is not unlike that of the hypothesis rendered by Hersch. He also favours the hydride ion transfer concept, dismissing the theory that hydrogen gas is the reductant for Cu^{++}. It was found that an alkaline formaldehyde solution under copper catalysis would not evolve hydrogen as had been proposed by Hartwagner.[23] The presence of the cupric ion is essential to obtain the evolution of hydrogen. From quantitative experiments involving OH^- and Cu^{++} consumption as a function of hydrogen evolution, the following data was obtained.

1   For each mole of copper deposited, at least two moles of formaldehyde and four moles of hydroxide ion are consumed.

2   For each mole of copper deposited, one mole of hydrogen gas is evolved.

Based on this information, Lukes proposes the following equation:—

$$Cu^{++} + 2HCHO + 4OH^- \rightarrow Cu^\circ + H_2 + 2H_2O + 2HCOO^-$$

The consumption of formaldehyde and hydroxide is always greater than that indicated by the above equation due to the side reactions taking place such as formaldehyde disproportionating into methanol and formate ion, and formic acid formed during the anodic oxidation of formaldehyde being neutralised by the sodium hydroxide present. This consumption is responsible, or partly responsible for the decrease in pH.

Based on the generally accepted hypothesis that formaldehyde exists in the following state of equilibrium:—

$$OH^- + H - \overset{\overset{\textstyle O}{\|}}{C} - H \rightleftarrows H - \overset{\overset{\textstyle O^-}{|}}{\underset{\underset{\textstyle OH}{|}}{C}} - H$$

Lukes postulates that a hydride ion is transferred from the alcoholate ion by means of an electron shift to the catalytic surface (anode).

$$
\begin{array}{c}
O^- \\
| \\
H - C - H \rightarrow HCOOH + H^- \\
| \\
OH
\end{array}
$$

He points out however, that the hydride ion is not free but probably linked momentarily to the catalytic surface. Two reaction mechanisms are offered to illustrate how the cupric ion may be reduced to metallic copper:—

$$Cu^{++} + 2H^- \rightarrow Cu^\circ + H_2$$
$$2Cu^{++} + 2H^- \rightarrow [2Cu^+ + H_2] \rightarrow Cu^\circ + Cu^{++} + H_2$$

Evidence in support of this concept is cited by the author in that Cannizzaro reactions are stated to proceed through an intermolecular transfer from an alcoholate system as illustrated above. Furthermore, it has been shown that metallic silver catalyses the hydride transfer in the disproportionation of benzaldehyde.

REFERENCES

1 Goldie W., *Plating*, **51**, 11, 1069 (1964).
2 Upton P. B., *J. Electrodep. tech. Soc.*, **32**, 45 (1947).
3 Chattaway F. D., *Proc. R. Soc.*, **80**, 88 (1947).
4 Lukes R. M., *Plating*, **51**, 11, 1066 (1964).
5 Saubestre E. B., *Proc. Am. Electropl. Soc.*, **46**, 264 (1959).
6 Packer J., Wark I. W., *J. chem. Soc.*, **119**, 1348 (1921).
7 Wark I. W., *J. chem. Soc.*, **123**, 1816 (1923).
8 Wark I. W., *J. chem. Soc.*, 1753 (1927).
9 Wark E. E., Wark I. W., *J. chem. Soc.*, 2474 (1930).
10 Wein S., " Copper Films," PB 111237, OTS, U.S. Dept. Commerce (1953).
11 Brookshire R. R., U.S. Pat., 3, 046, 159 (1962).
12 Wein S., private communication.
13 Bamberger C., Schweitzer R., *Chemikerzeitung*, **51**, 212 (1927).
14 Eyber G., *Chemikerzeitung*, **51**, 4 (1927).
15 French E. A., *Trans. opt. Soc.*, **25**, 229 (1923-24).
16 Volmer M., *Glastech. Ber.*, **9**, 133 (1931).
17 Agens M. C., U.S. Pat., 2, 938, 305 (1960).
18 Pearlstein F., Fujimoto K. T., Wick R., *Electron Inds.*, **21**, 117 (1962).
19 Cahill A. E., *Proc. Am. Electropl. Soc.*, **44**, 130 (1957).
20 Lukes R. M., U.S. Pat., 2, 996, 408 (1961).
21 *Electroplg Metal Finish.*, **19**, 6, 233 (1966).
22 Hersch P.
23 Hartwagner F., *Z. analyt. Chem.*, **52**, 17 (1913).

BIBLIOGRAPHY

1 " Copper Films," S. Wein, PB 111237, OTS, U.S. Dept. Commerce (1953).
2 " Electroless Copper Plating," S. Konishi, *J. Metal Finish. Soc.*, Japan, **16,** 11, 501 (1965).
3 " Electrochemical Studies on Chemical Copper Plating," Part I, S. Mamoru, *J. Metal Finish. Soc.*, Japan, **16,** 7, 300 (1965).
4 " Electrochemical Studies on Chemical Copper Plating," Parts II, III & IV, M. Saito, *J. Metal Finish Soc.*, Japan, **17,** 1, 14 (1966); **17,** 7, 258 (1966); **17,** 7, 264 (1966).
5 " Electroless Copper Plating," E.B. Saubestre, *Proc. Am. Electropl. Soc.*, **46,** 264 (1959).

CHAPTER 7

ELECTROLESS DEPOSITION OF NICKEL

Background

Following the discovery of this process by Wurtz,[1,2] the only other significant disclosure prior to the Brenner and Riddell[3] paper was in a patent granted to Roux[4] in 1916. The essence of this patent was that metallic nickel deposits were obtained from a solution containing a nickel salt (citrate), an alkaline hypophosphite and ammonia. It may be seen that this bath is qualitatively similar to the later Brenner bath. The principal difference is that the solution patented by Roux was one of spontaneous reduction, resulting in the object being plated and accompanied by general decomposition. The Brenner bath is catalytic and deposition occurs preferentially on the object.

As already mentioned, the process was put on a commercial basis in 1952 as the "Kanigen"[5,6] process and within the last few years commercial solutions have appeared which are reasonably stable for small scale operations, without the use of any elaborate equipment.

The original Brenner and Riddell[3] bath was an alkaline solution.

Nickel chloride	30 gm/l
Sodium citrate	100 gm/l
Ammonium chloride	50 gm/l
Sodium hypophosphite	10 gm/l
pH (adjusted with NH$_4$OH)	8 to 10
Temperature	98°C
Rate of deposition	0·3 mil/hr.

It was soon found that at this high operating temperature, ammonia volatilised rapidly and was extremely unpleasant. To overcome this difficulty they proposed an acid formulation which turned out to be easier to control and also exhibited faster plating rates.

Nickel chloride	30 gm/l
Sodium hydroxy acetate	50 gm/l
Sodium hypophosphite	10 gm/l
pH	4 to 6
Temperature	95 to 98°C
Rate of deposition	0·6 mil/hr.

The majority of commercial solutions operate in the acid range.

Reactions

Reactions occuring in the solution may be represented as follows:—

$$\begin{cases} Ni^{++}+(H_2PO_2)^-+HOH & \xrightarrow[\text{Surface}]{\text{Catalytic}} & Ni+2H^++H(HPO_3)^- \\ NiCl_2+Na(H_2PO_2)+HOH & \xrightarrow[\text{Surface}]{\text{Catalytic}} & Ni^\circ+2HCl+NaH(HPO_3) \end{cases}$$

$$\begin{cases} (H_2PO_2)^-+HOH & \xrightarrow[\text{Surface}]{\text{Catalytic}} & H(HPO_3)^-+H_2 \uparrow \\ Na(H_2PO_2)+HOH & \xrightarrow[\text{Surface}]{\text{Catalytic}} & NaH_2PO_3+H_2 \uparrow \end{cases}$$

It may be seen from the above equations that as nickel ions are reduced to the metallic state, hypophosphite is oxidised to phosphite. The reaction becomes acid and the pH of the bath decreases as plating proceeds. With increasing acidity of the solution, the reducing efficiency of the hypophosphite is lowered which slows the reaction down. Deposition will cease when the hydrogen ion concentration becomes high enough to start dissolving the metallic deposit

$$Ni+2HCl \rightarrow NiCl_2+H_2$$

To overcome this a buffer is added to the bath.

Gutzeit[7] considers that the catalytic surface (nickel) is responsible for the formation of the metaphosphite ion by catalytic dehydrogenation of the orthophosphite ion and the release of atomic hydrogen (equation 1). This atomic hydrogen is adsorbed on to the surface and being an extremely powerful reducing agent, reduces nickel ions to metallic nickel (equation 2). Simultaneously, the metaphosphite ion reacts with water to form the orthophosphite ion (equation 3).

$$(H_2PO_2)^-+Ni \text{ (catalyst)} \rightarrow (PO_2)^-+2H \text{ (catalyst)} \dots \dots \dots \dots \quad (1)$$
$$Ni^{++}+2H \text{ (catalyst)} \rightarrow Ni^\circ+2H^+$$
$$\text{or } NiCl_2+2H \text{ (catalyst)} \rightarrow Ni^\circ+2HCl \dots \dots \dots \dots \dots \quad (2)$$
$$(PO_2)^-+H_2O \rightarrow (HPO_3)^{--}+H^+ \dots \dots \dots \dots \dots \quad (3)$$

It may be seen that in equation 2, a fresh nickel surface is formed constantly which acts as a dehydrogenation catalyst in equation 1, so that the reaction proceeds autocatalytically. Since noble metals are well known as dehydrogenation catalysts, it is postulated that the mechanism is similar when plating plastics using the palladium chloride activator.

Brenner's[8] interpretation of the mechanism differs from Gutzeit's on one main point. He believes that the function of the hydrogen is to effect activation of the nickel, not chemical reduction of the nickel ion to metallic nickel. A two step reaction is suggested.

1 Catalytic decomposition of the hypophosphite ion resulting in the discharge of hydrogen.
2 Activation of the nickel ion due to the transfer of energy from the discharge of the hydrogen ion so that it can react with the hypophosphite ion.

It has been suggested by Hersch, as quoted by Gutzeit, that it is not atomic hydrogen supplied from the hypophosphite, but the more powerful hydride ion H^- that is responsible for the reduction of the nickel ion. He draws attention to the analogy exhibited by the two reducing agents.

1 Both liberate hydrogen on reaction with water.
2 When hypophosphites are used as reducing agents in electroless nickel solutions, nickel-phosphorus alloys are obtained whereas with borohydrides nickel-boron alloys are deposited.

Suggested reaction based on this hypothesis would be:—

$$(H_2PO_2)^- + O^{--} \rightarrow (HPO_3)^{--} + H^-$$
$$H^- + H^+ \rightarrow H_2$$
$$H^- + Ni^{++} \rightarrow H^+ + Ni^\circ$$

Developments

It was considered[8] that the following disadvantages existed with the Brenner baths and their industrial counterparts.

Lack of stability
Rough and dull deposits
Slow plating rate
Relatively high cost, because of instability of the bath
Non-homogeneous deposits in the vertical direction which led to the formation of stratified deposits.

With this in mind, the General Transportation Corporation of America instigated a research programme to overcome the difficulties encountered above. Many improvements have taken place by way of addition agents and operating conditions.

Addition Agents

Exaltant

This increased the rate of deposition and counteracted the slowing effect of the chelating agent and the stabiliser.

Stabiliser

This prevented decomposition of the solution by masking active nuclei.

Wetting agents were added. Alternative complexing agents and buffers were investigated and found to be suitable.

Operating Conditions

Phosphorus content is very dependent on pH and temperature. It is also dependent on ionic ratios. As plating proceeds, depletion occurs at the surface along with variations in pH and temperature. To overcome this stratification problem, continuous circulation and regeneration is necessary by adding the requisite amount of chemicals to keep the ionic concentration stable. Diagrammatic sketches of the plant used are shown in fig. 7.1 and 7.2.

Decomposition Potential

One serious factor which affects electroless baths in general is that of spontanteous decomposition. This must be avoided at all costs. When the solution is operating properly, evolution of hydrogen occurs only at the surface of the material being plated. If evolution of gas bubbles takes place throughout the solution, this is the first sign of decomposition. The reaction accelerates very quickly and within a short time vigorous gassing occurs accompanied by excessive foaming. A black precipitate also begins to form and float on top of the solution. The volume of solution increases considerably because of the amount of hydrogen evolved and it rapidly becomes uncontrollable.

Kreig[9] summarises the causes and remedies to this problem.
1 Local overheating.
2 Too rapid addition of hypophosphite.
3 Too much hypophosphite.
4 Adjusting the pH with caustic too suddenly.
5 Electroless nickel depositing on the sides of the tank acting as catalytic surfaces.
6 Drag out of catalysts such as noble metal activators in the plating of plastics.
7 Improper bath loading. V/A ratio should not exceed 10 to 1.
8 High phosphite content.
9 Adding the chemicals in concentrated form.
10 Solution should be at as low a temperature as possible when additions are made.

The following steps should be taken to overcome these problems:—
1 Avoid using direct immersion heaters.
2 Add chemicals to the bath slowly, in dilute form at low temperatures and with agitation.
3 Avoid any deposition on tank walls by keeping equipment clean.
4 When plating plastics, substrates should be thoroughly rinsed in water after noble metal activators have been used, to prevent drag out into the electroless bath.
5 Avoid excessive build up of phosphites. This may be achieved by cooling to room temperature and filtering occasionally which will remove the precipitate of nickel phosphite.

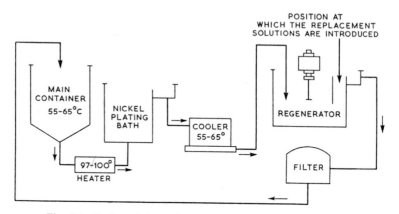

Fig. 7.1 Design of the equipment used for the Kanigen process.

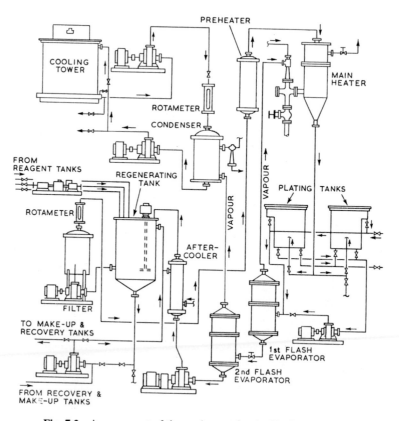

Fig. 7.2 Arrangement of the equipment for the Kanigen process.

6   Always use reagent grade sodium hydroxide.
7   The solution should not have prolonged periods of idleness. If so, the bath should be allowed to cool well below operating temperatures.

Parameters

Temperature

The rate of deposition increases with increasing temperature (it is an exponential function of temperature) hence baths should operate at the highest possible temperature below boiling point. Gutzeit and Kreig[10] found that a drop in temperature of 10°C from 100°C to 90°C causes a decrease of 52·5% in deposition rate (fig. 7.3). On the other hand, deposition did occur when the solution (pH4 to 5) operated below 70°C. The hypophosphite ion is oxidised in aqueous solution to phosphite, hydrogen being evolved, the rate being a function of temperature and hypophosphite ion concentration. It may be seen that although higher temperatures facilitate maximum deposition rates it is also responsible for the rapid build up of phosphite ion which is a prime factor in causing decomposition.

Control of temperature between narrow limits ($\pm$ 1°C) is essential because phosphorus content varies with temperature (although it is more interdependent on pH and hypophosphite concentration), this giving rise to a lamellar deposit.

An increase in temperature results in:—

(a)   a higher rate of deposition
(b)   an increase in phosphite ion
(c)   a greater possibility of decomposition (from b)
(d)   a decrease in solubility of phosphite
(e)   increased hydrogen evolution.

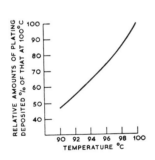

Fig. 7.3 Relative rate of deposition (in per cent of maximum) as a function of temperature. [Gutzeit]

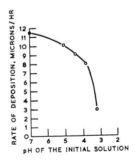

Fig. 7.4 Influence of the acidity of the solution on the rates of deposition. [Gorbunova and Nikiforova][36]

79

4

Hydrogen Ion Concentration

Hypophosphites are much more efficient reducing agents in acid than in alkaline media. Nickel reduction in this range is favoured at the upper limit, that is pH 5.5. However, maintaining a bath at this pH is not entirely satisfactory since the pH alters rapidly due to hydrogen ion formation during the course of the reaction (fig. 7.4). Furthermore, the organic compounds used for buffering the solution are not particularly effective in this range, exhibiting better characteristics at higher hydrogen ion concentrations. Alkali must therefore be added constantly to keep within the stipulated range. Because of variations in the pH, this results in variations in the phosphorus content of the deposit which leads to lamellar deposits being obtained. In addition to this, the solubility of nickel phosphite decreases with increasing pH (see table 7.1) and precipitation of this undesirable compound may initiate decomposition and lead to rough deposits. Again, at high pH values the reaction may change from catalytic to homogeneous.

Table 7.1
Solubility of Nickel Phosphite as a Function of pH

pH	Moles/litre Ni^{++}	Mole ratio of $(H_2PO_2)^-/H(H_2PO_2)^-$
3·0	0·160	0·329
4·0	0·141	0·280
5·0	0·089	0·203
6·0	0·0206	0·0274
7·0	0·0153	0·0163

For these very reasons, an acid bath is never operated above pH 5, in fact the optimum conditions are at a pH of 4·4 to 4·8. Below pH 4, deposition ceases; this is due to the attack of the metallic deposit by acid formed during the reaction. Agitation of the solution is therefore necessary since the solution at the substrate surface is at a much lower pH than the bulk of the solution.

In acid media, pH exerts the following influence on the process. Increasing the pH results in:—

    (a) Increased rate of deposition
    (b) A possible shift of hypophosphite from a catalytic to a homogeneous reaction which facilitates decomposition
    (c) Decrease in solubility of nickel phosphite
    (d) Decrease in phosphorus content.

Decreasing the pH :—

    (a) Prevents precipitation of basic salts or hydroxides.
    (b) Decreases the reducing property of the hypophosphite.
    (c) Below pH4, results in deposition ceasing due to metallic nickel being dissolved by acid present in the solution.
    (d) Makes buffers more effective.

Complexing Agents

The presence of a complexing agent in an acid electroless nickel is necessary to prevent precipitation of nickel phosphite. As the reaction proceeds, the amount of phosphite increases until its maximum solubility is reached, at which point precipitation occurs. This, however, can be retarded by employing a compound which will form a soluble complex with nickel (fig 7.5). The stability of the solution is therefore enhanced since there is a limited amount of free nickel ions available for reduction, preventing the formation of basic nickel salts.

The selection of a complexing agent is very important for it exerts a pronounced effect on the mechanism of the process. It might perform in a multiple role, invariably acting as a buffer as well. Occasionally it possesses the characteristics of an exaltant. Organic hydroxy carboxylic acids and their salts are generally used (fig. 7.6). Lactic acid[11] for example, combines all three functions whereas succinic acid[12] acts mainly as an exaltant and malic acid[3] as a complexing agent only. On the other hand, tartaric acid[3] forms a very stable complex which makes reduction difficult, leading to very low rates of deposition. The effects can be overcome to some extent because of the exaltant present in the bath. Citric acid and glycollic acid are the two most commonly used hydroxy carboxylic acids.

A characteristic of complexing agents is that they normally slow the rate of deposition somewhat, although lactic acid is an exception.

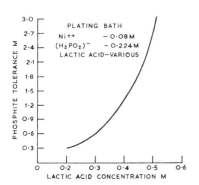

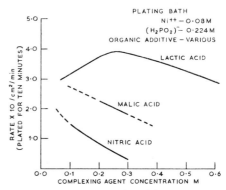

Fig. 7.5 Phosphite tolerance of plating bath as a function of lactate concentration. [Gutzeit]

Fig. 7.6 Rate of deposition as a function of chelating agent (hydroxy-carboxylic anions) concentration.
[Gutzeit]

Stabilisers

Even properly formulated solutions may tend to decompose at times because of the presence of foreign bodies in the bath. Solid nuclei act as catalytic centres which may be responsible for the occurrence of a self-accelerating chain reaction. The surface area increases considerably and ultimately ends with total decomposition. Gutzeit[7] postulates that this is initiated by a high hydroxyl concentration at the surface of the solid particles, causing localised reduction of nickel by a homogeneous reaction.

Among the principal offenders are dust particles, while another is the effect of the precipitation of basic salts, or hydroxides, even at the lowest normal operating pH.   In addition, the use of impure salts containing more than trace amounts of heavy metals capable of forming gelatinous precipitates at high hydrogen ion concentrations, may well be another cause.

To counteract this effect, stabilisers are added in trace amounts to render the suspended particles inactive.   They are essentially catalytic poisons, although it must be emphasised that all catalytic dehydrogenation poisons are not effective stabilisers since they may volatilise, or decompose, under the operating conditions of the bath.   The concentration of these stabilisers, or inhibitors as they are sometimes referred to, is extremely critical since plating may cease altogether if they are present in excess.   Some stabilisers when present at the optimum concentration, exhibit interesting characteristics inasmuch that they increase the rate of deposition and, furthermore, may also act as a brightener as well.

Basically, there are three types of compounds that can be employed in this context.   They may be classified in the following categories (see table 7.2).

1   Water soluble organic dipolar anions consisting of[13]:—

   (a)   long chain aliphatic compounds containing at least six carbon atoms in the chain.   Examples are sodium and potassium oleate.

   (b)   an acidic functional group like a carboxylic acid.

2   Cations of heavy metals capable of forming insoluble sulphides which are stable under the operating conditions of the electroless nickel solution. The cations must also conform to the following conditions[14]:—

   (a)   they must not be catalytic poisons

   (b)   they should not be catalysts for the oxidation of hypophosphite to phosphite like members of group VIII of the periodic table.

   Suitable metals are lead and tin.

3   Organic and inorganic thio compounds[14] that are water soluble and hydrolyse slowly in solution to supply a controlled concentration of sulphide ions to the bath.   Typical examples are thiourea and sodium ethylxanthate.

The concentration of the stabiliser is dependent on the nickel ion concentration but independent of any of the other constituents present in the solution.   The role that these compounds play may be either: (a) that they form a shell around the active catalytic nuclei rendering it hydrophobic and therefore inactive which prevents any further reaction, hence decomposition, taking place or (b) they are adsorbed on to the surface of the particle and, being a catalytic poison, prevent dehydrogenation of the hypophosphite taking place in the vicinity of the particle.

Table 7.2

Stabilising Effect of Trace Ions

Potassium oleate p.p.m.	None	10	25	50	75	
Rate of deposition	2·98	—	2·98	2·71	—	
Formation of black ppt (min)	10	10	15	15	stable	
Sample appearance (60 min)	BB—S	BB—S	BB—S	BB—S	BB—S	

Sn^{++} p.p.m.	None	0·1	0·5	2·0	10·0	50·0
Rate of deposition	4·59	5·32	5·36	5·68	4·99	4·56
Formation of black ppt (min)	16	40	40	stable	stable	stable
Sample appearance (60 min)	B—S	B—S	B—S	B—S	B—S	B—S

Potassium ethylxanthate p.p.m.	None	1·0	5·0	10·0	50·0	250
Rate of deposition	4·59	4·76	4·90	4·92	4·55	0·01
Formation of black ppt (min)	20	45	stable	stable	stable	stable
Sample appearance (60 min)	B—SR	B—S	B—S	B—S	D—S	D—R

Key: B—semi-bright, B-B—bright, V-B—very bright, S—smooth, S-R—slightly rough, R—rough, D—dull.

The solution used for the above experiments was a particularly unstable one in order to enable the effects of the stabilisers to be studied.

Nickel hypophosphite (recrystallised)	0·09 M Ni^{++}
Sodium hypophosphite (recrystallised)	0·045 M $(H_2PO_2)^-$
Sodium succinate (recrystallised)	0·060 M
Sodium chloride	0·18 M
pH adjusted to 4·6 with pure HCl	
Temperature 95°C	

Table 7.3

Comparison Between Deposition Rates in a Complexed Bath With and Without an Exaltant

Exaltant (succinate ion) M	Initial pH	Plating Rate $(R/10^4 gm/cm^2/min)$
—	5·03	0·06
0·03	5·01	2·53
0·06	5·00	4·02
0·06	5·51	4·86
0·09	5·03	5·16

Solution:—

Nickel chloride	0·0675M
Sodium hypophosphite	0·225M
Ammonium hydroxide	0·135M
Stabiliser (Pb^{++})	1·0 p.p.m.
pH (adjusted with HCl)	5·0 - 5·5

Sufficient ammonium ions were present to complex all the nickel ions present as the nickel diammine cation.

83

Exaltants

They are added specifically to increase the rate of plating and to counter-act the slowing down effect of the chelating agent (table 7.3). Normally, short chain aliphatic dicarboxylic acids are used for this purpose. So far, only one inorganic compound has been found which is suitable, this being a soluble fluoride.[15,16] As the effective range is very narrow, the concentration is extremely critical. The organic compounds used can be divided into three basic groups.

1 Short chain aliphatic monocarboxylic acids such as propionic, butyric, valeric and their alkali metal salts, the desired number of carbon atoms in the chain being between 3 and 6.[17] They are used in conjunction with particular chelating agents of the following type,

    (a) ammonium salts which form Werner co-ordination compounds

    (b) compounds of the general formula:—

where R = an aliphatic radical and X = a functional group containing a dissociable hydrogen atom and selected from the following category:—

$$-NH_2, =NH \text{ and } -OH$$

Y = a functional group containing a negative atom acting as a centre of co-ordination and selected from the following class of compounds containing OH, =O, $-NH_2$, =NH, $\equiv$N.

X and Y should be in the alpha and beta position. Typical examples are lactic acid, malic acid and amino acetic acid (glycine).

It may be seen that two compounds may perform the same function in electroless solutions as well as one compound acting in a dual role. Lactic acid, for example, acts as a complexing agent and exaltant, whereas in the case cited, both lactic and propionic acids are exaltants. The interchangeability of various compounds in this process make it rather unique.

Propionic acid is the best exaltant in this homologous series. It also has the advantage of being cheap and readily available commercially.

2 Aliphatic short chain saturated amino acids which are also exceptionally good chelating agents such as amino acetic acid.

3. Saturated, unsubstituted, short-chain aliphatic dicarboxylic anions, namely the homologous series consisting of malonic, succinic, glutaric and adipic acids.[12] The effectiveness decreases as we ascend the homologous series. Although the first shows the best exaltation properties, it is expensive and not easily obtainable. Consequently, succinic acid or succinates are used.

The concentration of exaltant present is dependent on the amount of nickel ions that can be reduced by the amount of hypophosphite present in the bath. A large excess of dicarboxylic ions however, may tie up the cations available for reduction as a complex resulting in deposition coming to a standstill. The correct molar ratio of exaltant to $Ni^{++}/(H_2PO_2)^-$ should therefore be used (fig. 7.7).

Nickel to Hypophosphite Ion Concentration

In the early stages of electroless nickel solutions, it soon became evident that the metal ion-hypophosphite ion ratio and absolute concentration were of importance in the catalytic reaction and in the prevention of bath decomposition. Brenner,[7] however, defined a rather broad spectrum of conditions which Gutzeit and Kreig[10] later reviewed, subsequently stipulating much narrower limits to obtain optimum conditions for deposition (fig. 7.8).

1   The absolute concentration of hypophosphite ion should be within the range 0·15 to 0·35M, the preferred concentration being 0·22 to 0·23M.

2   The optimum ratio of nickel ions to hypophosphite ions, $Ni^{++}/(H_2PO_2)^-$ expressed as a decimal fraction in terms of molar concentrations should be within the range 0·25 to 0·60M, the preferred figure being 0·3 to 0·45M.

3   The minimum absolute concentration of buffer anions (acetate) should be equivalent at least to two carboxyl groups per ion of nickel that can be deposited.

When the $Ni^{++}/(H_2PO_2)^-$ ratio falls below 0·25, a very dull deposit is obtained, whereas if in excess of 0·6, deposition is very slow. The higher the ratio the higher the phosphorus content. The higher the hypophosphite concentration the greater the decomposition potential.

The influence of the $Ni^{++}/(H_2PO_2)^-$ ratio and their absolute concentration may be summarised as follows:—

(a)   The higher the $(H_2PO_2)^-/Ni^{++}$ ratio, the higher the P content

(b)   The higher the $(H_2PO_2)^-$ concentration the greater the decomposition potential

(c)   The lower the $(H_2PO_2)^-$ concentration, the slower nickel is deposited

(d)   Nickel efficiency decreases with increased $Ni^{++}/(H_2PO_2)^-$ ratio

(e)   Deposition rate is independent of Ni^{++} content.

Properties of Electroless Nickel

Structure

The nickel deposit is an amorphous solid.[19] It has a lamellar structure that is due to variations in dissolved phosphorus; this reverts to a crystalline structure at low temperatures, being essentially a solid solution of nickel phosphide in a matrix of nickel (fig. 7.9).

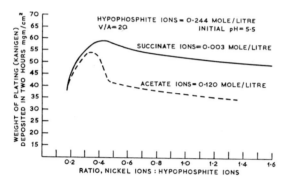

Fig. 7.7 Effect of Ni++/ (H₂PO₂)⁻ ratio and of "exalt-ant" addition (succinate ion) on rate of deposition. [Gutzeit]

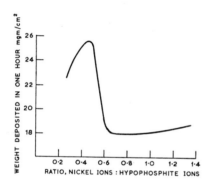

Fig. 7.8 Rate of deposition of electro-less nickel from an acetate bath as a function of the metal to hypophosphite ratio of the bath. NaH₂PO₂ = 0·224 M/l; acetate ion = 0·12 M/l; initial pH = 5·5. [Gutzeit and Krieg]

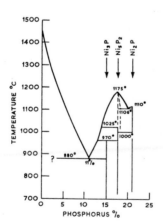

Fig. 7.9 Constitution of the Ni-P system. [Goldenstein et al]

Magnetic Properties

The phosphorus content influences magnetic properties considerably, greater than 8%P being non-magnetic whereas less than 8%P is markedly less magnetic than electrodeposited nickel. An improvement is obtained in magnetic properties when the deposit is annealed, normally in an inert atmosphere. This is brought about by the relief of internal stresses and a change in the atomic structure mentioned above.

It is reported that the magnetic permeability is lower than for pure nickel. Wesley[20] states that deposits greater than 11% are no longer ferromagnetic.

Alkaline Solutions

Interest has been revived in alkaline baths recently and this is due to the advent of special applications. Sullivan and Eigler[21] use a conventional alkaline electroless nickel for making ohmic contacts to silicon. One of the advantages claimed is that the hot alkaline solution with rapid evolution of hydrogen is an excellent cleaning medium for silicon.

Schwartz[22] recommends using pyrophosphates as complexing agents. He claims that a more stable solution is obtained and lower operating temperatures can be used (fig. 7.11). Furthermore, the rate of deposition is increased by using pyrophosphates and the deposit obtained is constant over a wide range of solution composition and operating conditions. The phosphorus content is around 5%.

Nickel sulphate, hexahydrate	25 gm/l
Sodium pyrophosphate	50 gm/l
Sodium hypophosphite	25 gm/l
pH	10-11
Temperature	68-74°C
Rate of deposition	0·6 mil/hr.

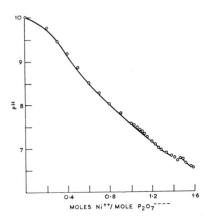

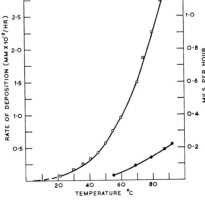

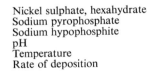

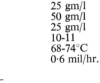

Fig. 7.10 Solubility relationship between nickel and pyrophosphate ions. [Schwartz]

Fig. 7.11 Effect of temperature on rate of deposition. ○ Pyrophosphate solution; ● Citrate solution. [Schwartz]

4A

Decomposition occurs rapidly if used above 85°C. Schwartz maintains that this is due to the increased activity of the pyrophosphate complex which, incidentally, is also responsible for deposition taking place at lower temperatures. A suggested structure for the complex by Schwartz based on a concept by Van Wazer and Campanella[23] on condensed phosphate chelate complexes involving metallic ions is:—

(a) Ni^{++} is attached to the same chain.

(b) Ni^{++} is attached to different chains.

Other pertinent points arising from this investigation are:—

1 Both reactants have a pronounced effect on the rate of deposition which is at variance with the findings of Brenner and Riddell[3] who found that only the hypophosphite content had any appreciable effect on the alkaline citrate bath.

2 Increasing the pyrophosphate content tends to make the complex more stable and depresses the plating rate.

3 Rate of deposition is increased when operating between 10 and 10·5 as opposed to a pH range of 9 to 9·5. Moreover, the deposition rate is more constant.

It has already been stated that the main disadvantage of alkaline electroless nickel baths is that of the presence of ammonia. In order to circumvent the use of this, Puls and Vincent[24] disclose the use of an alkyl or alkanolamine.

Nickel ion	0·005 - 0·2 M/l
Hypophosphite ion	0·01 - 0·4 M/l
Fluoride ion	0·2 - 1·0 M/l
Alkanolamine	N/Ni^{++} Mole ratio of 1:1 to 10:1
Carboxylic acid	$COOH:PO_2^-$ Mole ratio of 1:1 to 10:1
pH	7 - 11

Borohydrides

Alternatives to hypophosphites as reducing agents in electroless nickel solutions have been investigated by various workers in the field. Boro-hydrides are one of the few which have had any success. On examination one finds a distinct analogy between them and hypophosphites in that both react with water to produce hydrogen and that metallic nickel deposited by the borohydride $(BH_4)^-$ anion contains boron whereas nickel deposited by the hypophosphite anion $(H_2PO_2)^-$ contains phosphorus. Similarly, as nickel phosphide may be present in nickel produced from a hypophosphite solution, nickel boride may be present when borohydrides are employed.

An advantage is that the borohydride process may be operated at temperatures as low as 20°C, depending on the formulations used and is therefore suitable for plastic materials. Some critics believe that an economic advantage is obtained when using nickel instead of copper, for electrolytic copper can then be omitted, resulting in the following sequence being used:— electroless nickel → electrolytic nickel → chromium.

A recent patent[25] discloses the following information:—

Nickel chloride, hexahydrate	20 gm/l
Ethylenediamine (98%)	45 gm/l
Sodium hydroxide	40 gm/l
Sodium borohydride	0·67 gm/l
pH	>11
Temperature	97°C
Rate of deposition	7·8 - 9·2 mgm/cm²/hr.

Ammonium hydroxide may be used as the complexing agent and as the source of hydroxyl ions. The same patent cites the following bath:—

Nickel chloride	24 gm/l
Ammonium hydroxide	120 ml/l
Sodium borohydride	0·4 gm/l
Temperature	60°C
Rate of deposition	0·12 mgm/cm²/hr.

It may be seen when comparing the two baths that temperature is very important. In general the boron content of the alloy increases with increase of the $(BH_4)^-/Ni^{++}$ ratio, but the variations in boron content are small.

Deposits obtained from this bath contain 4% to 7% boron and it is an interstitial solid solution of boron in nickel. X-ray diffraction patterns fail to show boron and it is concluded that it is present in the atomic form and dispersed at random within the nickel framework. The hardness of the deposit is about 800 V.P.N. whereas the nickel-phosphorus alloy is only around 450 V.P.N.

It has been known for some time that alkali metal borohydrides MBH_4 react spontaneously with aqueous solutions of nickel salts to form a precipi-tate of black nickel boride, Ni_2B. In preparing solutions, nickel should be suitably complexed before addition of the borohydride. As the oxidation of borohydride ions by water is very rapid in acid and neutral solutions, the deposition of nickel must take place in the alkaline range. The sequestering agents used should form sufficiently strong complexes with nickel to prevent precipitation of nickel hydroxide or basic salts. Moreover, the complex metal ions must be soluble in the plating solution and sufficiently stable so that they will react with borohydride ions at a catalytic surface only and not in the bulk of the solution. Alkali metal borohydrides are generally used because of their availability. Choice of borohydride is important since many are unstable in solution and possess explosive tendencies. Others which can be used safely are tetramethylammonium salts and sodium trimethoxy borohydride $NaB(OCH_3)_3H$.

It has already been mentioned that the solution is pH dependent. In favourable conditions, pH 12 to 13, the following reaction occurs:—

$$2Ni^{++}+NaBH_4+2H_2O \rightarrow 2Ni^{\circ}+2H_2+4H^{+}+NaBO_2$$

In unfavourable conditions, less than 11 and greater than 13,

$$2Ni^{++}+NaBH_4 \rightarrow Ni_2B+\tfrac{1}{2}H_2+Na^{+}+3H^{+}$$

Under certain conditions both reactions occur yielding a nickel-boron alloy containing nickel boride.

The following bath has been patented by Sullivan[26]:—

Nickel sulphate	20 gm/l
Sodium potassium tartrate	40 gm/l
Sodium borohydride	23 gm/l
pH (adjusted with NaOH)	12·5
Temperature	41-99°C
Life	12 hours

It is stated that the parameters in this bath are critical, particularly pH. The alloy deposited from this solution contains less than 1% boron.

A number of solutions operating at room temperatures are disclosed in a recent patent.[27]

Solution		1	2	3	4
Nickel chloride	⎫	2·62	2·62	2·62	1·8
Sodium borohydride	⎪	0·45	0·45	0·45	0·22
Ammonium hydroxide	⎬ wt.%	17·20	17·20	13·90	3·32
Water	⎭	79·73	79·73	83·03	94·46
Temperature °C		22·5	40	40	40
Time (minutes)		213	213	52	108
Ave. plating rate (gm × 10³hr.)		0·0027	0·006	0·016	0·029

Solutions 1 and 2 illustrate increased plating rate with rise in temperature. The increase in plating rate with decrease in pH is shown in examples 2, 3 and 4. The preferred range is just below pH12. Spontaneous decomposition occurs at a pH of 10.

Farbenfabrieken Bayer, Germany, have employed borohydrides as reducing agents in the metallising of plastics. They claim[28] bright, smooth adherent deposits. Using sodium borohydride as a reducing agent, the efficiency of the solution is about 20% according to the equation:—

$$4Ni^{++} + BH_4^- + 2H_2O \rightarrow 4Ni^\circ + BO_2^- + 8H^+$$

compared to Brenner's estimate of 37% for the hypophosphite bath.

By adding a metal from group IIB, IIIB, IVB, VB or VIB of the periodic table, reduction yields are considerably improved, resulting in a higher rate of deposition (table 7.4). Moreover, they claim that the other advantages obtained are (a) improved utilisation of the reducing agent and therefore overall reduction in running costs, (b) increased plating rates, allowing a reduction in time of the substrates in the solution.

Nickel chloride, hexahydrate	30 gm/l
Ethylenediamine	50 gm/l
Sodium hydroxide	40 gm/l
Thallium nitrate	70 mgm/l
Sodium borohydride	0·6 gm/l
Temperature	90°C
Rate of deposition	1·5187 gm/4 sq. dec./20 min

The stabiliser from the groups mentioned may be present as the anion or cation.

Different stabilisers result in different efficiencies being obtained and concentration is critical.

Table 7.4

The Effect of Stabilisers on the Deposition Rate of Borohydride Electroless Nickel Solutions

Amount (mgm/l)	Reduction Yield %		
	$TlNO_3$	$Sn\,Cl_2.2H_2O$	As_2O_3
2	24·5	21·0	21·8
20	36·0	22·0	24·8
40	41·0	22·5	—
70	43·1	—	26·5
100	—	—	30·5
150	43·6	—	—
200	42·8	34·9	—
300	—	38·7	—

From the work carried out on borohydrides as a reducing agent for nickel, promising results may have been obtained but a considerable amount of work has still to be covered. It is interesting to note that the above firm is using a borohydride derivative and operating a bath at a temperature of 60°C, the resultant film being used as the initial conducting film on ABS, on a commercial basis.

Amine Boranes

Amine boranes have also been used as reducing agents for electroless nickel. Hoke[29] suggests the following bath which operates at room temperatures:—

N-dimethyl amine borane	37 gm/l
Nickel chloride	93 gm/l
Boric acid	25 gm/l
pH	4·3
Temperature	27°C
Rate of deposition	0·09 mil/hr.

A patent[30] filed by du Pont employs boranes of primary, secondary and tertiary amines as well as diborane diammoniate $(2NH_3:B_2H_6)$ and ammonia borane (NH_3BH_3). It is stated that the concentration of reducing agent affects the rate of deposition. The pH of the solution should be between 3·5 and 7·0. At lower pH values hydrolytic decomposition of the amine borane is favoured and by operating below pH7, the use of sequestering agents can be dispensed with. Since the reaction liberates acid, a buffer is used. A glycollate is effectively employed as a stabiliser and a small quantity of lead, present as lead acetate, is incorporated as an auxiliary stabiliser.

Nickel chloride gm/l	25	25	25
Sodium acetate gm/l	—	21	—
Sodium glycollate gm/l	15	—	15
Dimethylamine borane gm/l	1·0	1·0	1·0
Lead acetate p.p.m.	—	—	20
pH	5·0	5·0	5·0
Temperature °C	70	70	70
Decomposition time (minutes)	240	60	400

It may be seen above that by replacing the conventional buffer, sodium acetate, with sodium glycollate results in a marked improvement in bath life. Furthermore, the use of an auxiliary stabiliser, in this case lead, provides a still more stable solution. Mikulski[31] records the use of iso propylamine borane as a reducing agent.

There is, undoubtedly, a distinct similarity between hypophosphites and borohydrides (and derivatives) when used as reducing agents in electroless nickel solutions. This not only refers to the physical and metallurgical structures of the alloys formed, but in their reaction mechanisms as well. Finally, not only are the types of solution composition similar but the same types of addition agents are added to perform the same function.

Hydrazine

Only one paper of significance has been published[32] which deals with the electroless deposition of nickel using hydrazine as the reducing agent.

Hydrazine has previously been used in conjunction with hypophosphite in a synergistic reducing system, enabling a reaction which normally takes place at about 90°C to function at room temperature.[33] In this case an alloy containing phosphorus is deposited whereas in the system under review, relatively pure nickel is obtained.

The overall reaction may be represented by the following equation:—

$$2Ni^{++} + N_2H_4 + 4OH^- \xrightarrow[\text{Catalyst}]{\text{Ni}} 2Ni^\circ + N_2 + 4H_2O$$

A typical solution is:—

Nickel chloride	0·02M/l
Hydrazine	1·0M/l
Sodium tartrate	0·02M/l
pH	10·0
Temperature	95°C

The author of this paper concludes that the plating rate is a function of Ni^{++} activity, hydrazine activity, pH and temperature and that the thickness is linear with time, provided that these parameters remain constant. As nickel deposits spontaneously on a catalytic substrate, the solution can be used for plating non-conductors.

The illustration fig. 7.13 shows the effect of the hydrazine concentration on the deposition rate. It is suggested that as the hydrazine activity at the catalyst surface approaches saturation level, irrespective of further increases in concentration, this is indicative of the hydrazine molecule being adsorbed on the catalyst surface.

The equation indicates that pH will influence the rate of deposition. The plating rate actually increases exponentially with the pH of the solution (fig. 7.14). The plating rate also increases exponentially with temperature.

Effect of the complexing agent used and its concentration is illustrated in fig. 7.15. An increase in the concentration reduces the metal ion activity and hence the plating rate.

Malonates increase the rate of reaction while remaining relatively unaffected by increasing concentration. The rate of deposition remains at a high level (2000 Å/min) irrespective of the amount of malonate ion present between 0·02 and 0·12 m.p.l. This is attributed to the fact that they have a high proton affinity, removing protons from the vicinity of the catalyst surface, acting in the role of a catalyst promoter. The reaction rate is dependent on the nickel compound used.

Anion	Rate (Å/min)	Anion	Rate (Å/min)
Cl^-	1200	CH_3COO^-	1000
SO_4^{--}	1000	NO_3^-	420

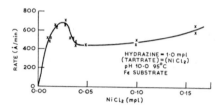

Fig. 7.12 Effect of nickel concentration on plating rate. Iron coupons were plated for 5 min at 95°C in a solution containing 1M hydrazine. Sodium tartrate equivalent to the molar nickel concentration was present; pH was adjusted to 10·0 with sodium hydroxide. [Levy]

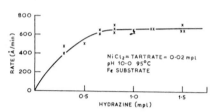

Fig. 7.13 Effect of hydrazine concentration on plating rate. Iron substrate, 5 min. 0·02M NiCl₂, 0·02M sodium tartrate, pH 10·0 (NaOH), 95°C. [Levy]

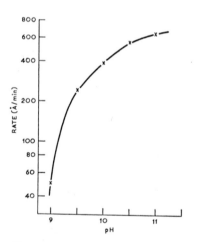

Fig. 7.14 Effect of solution pH on plating rate. Copper substrate, 0·1-1 hr, 0·02M NiCl₂, 0·02M sodium tartrate, 1·0M hydrazine, 95°C. [Levy]

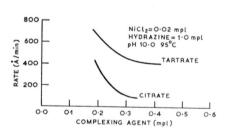

Fig. 7.15 Effect of ligand species on plating rate. Iron substrate, 5 min, 0·02M NiCl₂, 1·0M hydrazine, pH 10·0 (NaOH), 95°C. [Levy]

94

The magnetic properties of the film show that it is a reasonably square loop material having a B_r/B_s ratio of 0·9 (min). A coercivity of 14 to 22 oersteds is not unlike that obtained from evaporated and electroplated nickel films. Saturisation magnetisation is essentially the same as that of bulk nickel.

Pragst[34] has also investigated the use of hydrazine and its derivatives as reducing agents in electroless nickel solutions.

Hydrosulphites

Hydrosulphites have been used as reducing agents in electroless nickel solutions by Chakraborty and Banerjee.[35] A nickel-pyridine complex is utilised. The deposit contains an appreciable amount of sulphur.

Relative Merits of Electroless Copper and Nickel

Although the initial work on electroplated plastics utilised electroless copper to form the conducting film there has been a recent trend towards the use of nickel to fulfil this role. It is, therefore, worthwhile recapitulating on what has happened up to the present state of the art, and possibly predict what the future trend is likely to be.

As electroless nickel solutions were operated at very high temperatures (greater than 95°C), very few polymers could be treated, since this was beyond the distortion point of the majority. There was very little choice but to use copper, since this could be deposited at room temperature. However, the recent work carried out on borohydrides as the reducing agent in electroless nickel solutions commanded attention, for here nickel could be deposited at between 45 to 60°C which was well within the bounds of most polymers. Very quickly this was followed by the announcement that room temperature processes were obtainable. The argument put forward by the supporters of electroless nickel was that stability was much better than that obtained with electroless copper, hence it lended itself to production work and was more economic to run. This might have been the deciding factor in most cases except for the fact that running concurrently with these developments on low temperature electroless nickel, long life electroless copper solutions had been developed and marketed. The score at present would seem to be that there is not a great deal to choose from between the two, particularly when the price of nickel and copper are similar. The deciding factor could well be the application.

Electronics

For the majority of applications, copper is preferred because of its electrical conductivity. Exceptions to this are magnetic films and applications where high resistance tracks are required. The metal is therefore more or less pre-selected.

Engineering Industries

The choice here will be governed probably by two factors, (a) economics and (b) physical properties.

The attractive feature of using electroless nickel on articles which have subsequently to be plated with nickel and chromium, is that copper can be omitted entirely, thereby saving time and money. Corrosion resistance should be further improved. The main drawback is the poor ductility of nickel deposits which become suspect on thermal cycling. Work carried out at present suggests that an undercoat of electrolytic copper is essential to combat this problem. If this is the case, there is no advantage derived from using electroless nickel. This is a point which will have to be resolved in the future.

REFERENCES

1 Wurtz A., *Compt. rend. Acad. des. Sciences*, **18**, 702 (1844); **21**, 149 (1845).
2 Wurtz A., *Annls. Chim. Phys.*, **3**, 11, 250 (1844); **16**, 3, 198 (1846).
3 Brenner A., Riddell G. E., *J. Res. natn. Bur. Stand.*, **37**, 31 (1946); **39**, 385 (1947).
4 Roux F. A., U.S. Pat., 1, 207, 218 (1916).
5 Gutzeit G., *Metal Prog.*, **66**, 1, 113 (1954).
6 Gutzeit G., Mapp E. T., *Corros. Technol.*, **3**, 10, 331 (1956).
7 Gutzeit G., *Plating*, **46**, 10, 1158 (1959); **46**, 11, 1275 (1959); **46**, 12, 1377 (1959); **47**, 1, 63 (1960).
. 8 Serota L., *Metal Finish.*, **60**, 9, 73 (1962); **60**, 10, 74 (1962); **60**, 11, 76 (1962); **60**, 12, 58 (1962).
9 Kreig A., " Symposium on Electroless Nickel Plating," A.S.T.M. Special Tech. Publ. No. 265 (1959).
10 Gutzeit G., Kreig A., U.S. Pat., 2, 658, 841 (1953).
11 Gutzeit G., Talmey P., Lee W., U.S. Pat., 2, 822, 293 (1958).
12 Gutzeit G., Ramirez E., U.S. Pat., 2, 658, 842 (1953).
13 Talmey P., Gutzeit G., U.S. Pat., 2, 847, 327 (1958).
14 Talmey P., Gutzeit G., U.S. Pat., 2, 762, 723 (1956).
15 Gutzeit G., U.S. Pat., 2, 694, 019 (1954).
16 Reschan R., Kreig A., U.S. Pat., 2, 694, 017 (1954).
17 Gutzeit G., Talmey P., Lee W., U.S. Pat., 2, 822, 294 (1958).
18 Gutzeit G., U.S. Pat., 2, 999, 770 (1961).
19 Goldenstein A. W., Rostoker W., Schossberger F., Gutzeit G., *J. electrochem. Soc.*, **104**, 2, 104 (1957).
20 Wesley A. W., *Plating*, **37**, 7, 732 (1950).
21 Sullivan M. V., Eigler J. H., *J. electrochem Soc.*, **104**, 4, 226 (1957).
22 Schwartz M., *Proc. Am. Electropl. Soc.*, **47**, 176 (1960).
23 Van Wazer J. R., Campanella D. A., *J. Am. chem. Soc.*, **72**, 655, Part IV (1950).
24 Puls B., Vincent W. R., U.S. Pat. 2, 916, 401 (1959).
25 Brit. Pat., 836, 480 to Du Pont de Nemours (1960).
26 Sullivan E. A., U.S. Pat., 2, 942, 990 (1960).
27 Hoke R. M., U.S. Pat., 3, 150, 994 (1964).
28 Brit. Pat., 975, 964 to Farbenfabriken Bayer (1964).
29 Hoke R. M., U.S. Pat., 2, 990, 296 (1961).
30 Brit. Pat., 861, 703 to Du Pont de Nemours (1961).
31 Mikulski R. A., U.S. Pat., 3, 063, 850 (1962).
32 Levy D. J., *Electrochem. Technol.*, **1**, 1-2, 38 (1963).
33 Pessel L., U.S. Pat., 2, 430, 581 (1947).
34 Pragst W., Ger. Pat., 717, 547 (1952).
35 Chakraborty K., Banerjee T., *J. sci. industr. Res.*, **13B**, 433 (1954).
36 Gorbunova K. M., Nikiforova A. A., " Physiochemical Principles of Nickel Plating," 63—11003, OTS, U.S. Dept. Commerce (1963).

ELECTROLESS DEPOSITION OF NICKEL

BIBLIOGRAPHY

1 " Physiochemical Principles of Nickel Plating," K. M. Gorbunova and A. A. Nikiforova, 63—11003, O.T.S., U.S. Dept. Commerce (1963).
2 " Nickel Films," S. Wein, PB 111330, OTS, U.S. Dept. Commerce (1953).
3 " Symposium on Electroless Nickel Plating," A.S.T.M. Special Tech. Publ. No. 265 (1959).
4 " Electroless Plating Techniques," International Nickel Co. (1962).
5 P. Breteau, *Soc. Chim. Mem.*, No. 89, May 10th (1911).
6 " Reduction of Nickel and Cobalt Salts in Aqueous Solution," L. Friederici, Doctoral Thesis, University of Leipzig, Germany (1920).
7 C. Paal and L. Friederici, *Ber.*, **64**, 1766 (1931).
8 " Electroless Plating Comes of Age," A. Brenner, *Metal Finish.*, **52**, 11, 68 (1954), **52**, 12, 61 (1954).
9 " Studies on Electroless Nickel Plating," C. H. de Minjer and A. Brenner, *Plating*, **44**, 12, 1297 (1957).
10 " An Outline of the Chemistry Involved in the Process of Catalytic Nickel Deposition from Aqueous Solution," G. Gutzeit, *Plating*, **46**, 10, 1158 (1959); **46**, 11, 1275 (1959); **46**, 12, 1377 (1959); **47**, 1, 63 (1960).
11 " Science for Electroplaters—Electroless Nickel," L. Serota, *Metal Finish.*, **60**, 9, 73 (1962); **60**, 10, 74 (1962); **60**, 11, 76 (1962); **60**, 12, 58 (1962).
12 " The Mechanism for the Autocatalytic Reduction of Nickel by Hypophosphite Ion," R. M. Lukes, *Plating*, **51**, 10, 969 (1964).
13 " Chemical Nickel Plating with Sodium Borohydride or Amine Boranes: ' The Nibodur Process'," K. Lang, *Electroplg Metal Finish.*, **19**, 3, 86 (1966).
14 " Determination of Sodium Hypophosphite in Complex Electroless Nickel Plating Solutions," J. J. Surash and R. H. Lansing, *Plating*, **50**, 3, 221 (1963).
15 " Microcircuitry by Chemical Deposition," E. L. Hebb, *Electrochem. Technol.*, **1**, 7-8, 217 (1963).
16 " Electrical Conductivity of Electroless Nickel Coatings," A. Keil, *Mettalloberflache*, **10**, 12, 356 (1956).
17 " Volumetric Determination of Hypophosphite in Electroless Nickel Plating Solutions," J. P. McCloskey, *Plating*, **51**, 7, 689 (1964).
18 " Laboratory Studies on Electroless Nickel Deposits," J. Fléchon, *Rev. Nickel*, **27**, 123 (1961).
19 " Theoretical Considerations on Electroless Nickel Plating Process," S. Ishibashi, *Himeji Kogyo Daigaku Kenkyu Hokoku*, **13**, 68 (1961).
20 " Electrochemical Thermodynamics of Non-Electrolytic Metal Deposition," K. Muller, *Metalloberflache*, **14**, 65 (1960); **14**, 102 (1960).
21 " Industrial Nickel Coating by Chemical Catalytic Reduction," G. Gutzeit, *Trans. Inst. Metal Finish.*, **33**, 383 (1955-56).
22 " Influence of Heavy Metal Salts on the Brightness and Deposition Rate in Electroless Nickel Plating," W. Machu, and S. El-Gendi, *Metalloberflache*, **13**, 4, 97 (1959).
23 " On Simultaneous Determination of Hypophosphite and Nickel in Electroless Nickel Solution," S. Ishibashi, et al, *J. Metal Finish. Soc.*, Japan, pp 182 (May 1960).
24 " Relation Between Nickel Plating Speed and Concentration of Ammonia in Ammoniacal Electroless Nickel Plating Solution," S. Ishibashi, et al, *J. Metal Finish. Soc.*, Japan, pp 307 (July 1961).
25 " Studies on Alkaline Electroless Nickel Plating Solutions," S. Ishibashi, et al, *J. Metal Finish. Soc.*, Japan, pp 364 (1961).
26 " Radiochemical Studies of Thiourea in the Electroless Deposition Process," J. S. Sallo, J. Kivel and F. C. Alberts, *J. electrochem. Soc.*, **110**, 8, 890 (1963).
27 " Structure of Electroless Nickel," A. H. Graham, R. W. Lindsay and H. J. Read, *J. electrochem. Soc.*, **109**, 12, 1200 (1962).
28 " Investigation of Electroless Nickel Plating with an Ammonium Fluoride Buffer," N. A. Solove'ev, *Zh. prikl. Khim.*, **32**, 566 (1959).
29 " Regeneration and Analytical Control of Acetate Containing Solutions for Chemical Nickel Plating," K. Holocek, E. Souralová and J. Nassler, *Chemicky Prum.*, **15**, 6, 335 (1965).
30 " Electroless Nickel Plating from Alkaline Solutions," L. Domnikov, *Metal Finish.*, **64**, 3, 57 (1966).
31 " Chemical Nickel and Cobalt Plating," A. M. Kharitonyuk, *Metallov. term. Obrab. Metall*, **3**, 57 (1966).

32 " Effect of NH$_3$ on Deposition from Alkaline Electroless Nickel and Cobalt Plating Baths," G. S. Alberts. R. H. Wright and C. C. Parker, *J. electrochem. Soc.*, **113**, 7, 687 (1966).

33 " The Mechanism of the Catalytic Reduction of Metals with Hypophosphite," T. V. Ivanovskaya and K. M. Gorbunova, *Zaschita Metallov*, **4**, 477 (1966).

34 " Electroless Plating of Metals—1. Electroless Nickel Plating from Alkaline Sulphamate Solutions," L. Cadorna and P. Cavalotti, *Electrochimica Metallorum*, **1**, 1, 93 (1966).

35 " Electroless Plating—III. Electroless Nickel Plating," G. D. R. Jarrett, *Ind. Finish.*, Lond., **18**, 218, 41 (1966).

36 " Corrosion Resistance of Electroless Nickel Plating Film," S. Ishibashi, O. Takano and T. Shimizu, *J. Metal Finish. Soc.*, Japan, **16**, 6, 236 (1965).

37 " Phosphine, One of the Causes of the Instability of of Chemical Nickel Plating Baths," K. Schwitzgebel, *Metalloberflache*, **19**, 12, 390 (1965).

38 " The Effect of Thiourea on Alkaline Electroless Deposition," J. Kivel and J. S. Sallo, *J. electrochem. Soc,*, **112**, 12, 1201 (1965).

39 " Influence of Micro-Additives on the Chemical Nickel Plating Process," R. G. Rozenblyum and A. A. D'Yakov, *Zh. prikl. Khim*, **39**, 1987 (1966).

40 " An Automatic Analyser for Hypophosphite with Particular Reference to Electroless Plating Solutions," S. Greenfield and R. M. Cooper, *Talanta*, **9**, 483 (1962).

CHAPTER 8

PRECIOUS METALS

Electroless Gold

For many years processes have been known for the deposition of gold, but it is only within the last decade that the electronics industry has inspired further investigational work in this field. Although small pins, tabs and connectors have been plated by this method, the primary use has been in the manufacture of printed wiring, where interconnection between conductors proved difficult and could not be satisfactorily electroplated. As the properties of electroless gold, such as solderability, corrosion resistance and low contact resistance are extremely desirable, a fair amount of work has been carried out. A definite advantage that this process has over electroplated deposits is that the grain structure, being finer, considerably reduces porosity. Consequently, thinner deposits may be used to afford the same degree of protection along with a saving in cost.

By carrying out the normal sensitising and activation treatments, gold may be deposited directly on to plastic substrates.

The original approach to electroless gold was to use formaldehyde as the reducing agent. Wein[1] recommends the following solution:—

Solution "A"	Gold chloride	37·5 gm/l
Solution "B"	Sodium carbonate	100 gm/l
Solution "C"	Formaldehyde	65 ml/l

The final solution consists of equal volumes of the above three solutions. The process, operated at room temperature, is a batch type and is therefore non-regenerable. Any non-regenerable bath is uneconomic, particularly one so expensive as gold.

Interest has now been transferred to baths containing hypophosphite as the reducing agent. Brookshire[2] has patented the following solution:—

Gold cyanide	2 gm/l
Sodium hypophosphite, monohydrate	10 gm/l
Potassium cyanide	0·2 gm/l
pH	13·5
Temperature	96°C
Rate of deposition	9·85 mgm/cm²/hr.

Although the relationships between the various parameters have not been resolved, the rate of deposition appears to be independent of pH (7·5 to 13·5). This bath seems to function in a similar manner to the same author's hypophosphite copper and silver solutions.

Other methods using hypophosphites as the reducing agent incorporate citrates as the complexing agent and in fact, are similar to electroless nickel formulations. Citrates do not form such stable complexes as cyanides and, being more easily dissociated, are reduced to the metallic state under milder reducing conditions. The following bath was published by Swan and Gostin[3]:—

Potassium gold cyanide	2 gm/l
Ammonium chloride	75 gm/l
Sodium citrate	50 gm/l
Sodium hypophosphite	10 gm/l
pH	7 to 7·5
Temperature	92 to 95°C
Loading	72-107 cm²/l
Life	50 hours upwards

A stainless steel vessel with an external water jacket is preferred. Mild agitation is necessary and continuous filtration desirable. Control of the bath is fairly simple, the addition of chemicals to the solution being necessary to replace those that are consumed during the plating operation. Periodic additions of ammonia are necessary to control the pH. The deposition rate alters enormously with small increments of temperature.

Temperature °C	Average deposition (10^{-6} inches)	Temperature °C	Average deposition (10^{-6} inches)
91	10	93	92
91·5	17	93·5	121
92	37	94	161
92·5	62	94·5	188

Deposition rates fall off with time as follows:—

Period (hours)	Thickness (inches)	Total Thickness (inches)
5	0·0005	0·0005
10	0.0002	0·0007
15	0·0002	0·0009

The above rates are for plating on electroless nickel which is reported to yield the best results.

Properties

The deposit of gold is 99·34% pure and bright if the base metal is polished. Heavy deposits tend to become dull but, because of the softness of the metal, they are easily polished. Deposits are more dense than those of conventional electrodeposited gold.

The same two investigators[4] have also used hydrazine as a reducing agent for gold.

Potassium gold cyanide	3 gm/l
Ammonium citrate	90 gm/l
Hydrazine hydrate	0·0002 gm/l
pH	7 to 7·5
Temperature	92 to 95°C

An interesting approach has been made by Walton[5] to this subject. The particular formulations he discloses appear to have been investigated very thoroughly, nearly 100 solutions being examined. Apparently, the investigation was instigated after it was noticed, during the development of an acid bright gold solution using N, N-diethylglycine as a brightener, that gold was deposited on a steel Hull cell panel, although no current had been applied. The conclusion was reached that this organic compound was in fact the reducing agent.

Two basic types of solution have been investigated. They may be classified as (a) citric acid based and (b) tartaric acid based. Both are present to acidify the potassium gold cyanide. The optimum concentration of constituents and optimum operating conditions were determined from a series of statistically designed tests. As a result, the recommended formulation is:—

Potassium gold cyanide	28 gm/l
Citric acid (or tartaric acid)	60 gm/l
Tungstic acid	45 gm/l
Sodium hydroxide	16 gm/l
N, N-diethylglycine (sodium salt)	3·75 gm/l
Phthalic acid (monopotassium salt)	25 gm/l
pH	5 to 5·5
Temperature	87 to 94°C

Citric acid works best on ferrous materials like Kovar, whereas the equivalent solution containing tartaric acid is specified for non-ferrous materials like nickel. The process is said to be poor for copper. Tungstic acid is present as a grain refiner and phthalic acid acts as a buffer.

Parameters

Temperature

The rate of deposition increases with temperature as would be expected. However, operating the solution at boiling point should be avoided, particularly citric acid types, since a decrease in deposition rate may be obtained, caused by partial decomposition of organic constituents in the bath.

N, N-diethylglycine

This has a peculiar effect on the deposition of gold. A cyclic variation is in evidence and in citric acid solutions a maximum is obtained at 3·75 gm/l and 11·5 gm/l. In the tartaric acid solution only one maximum is recorded at 3·75 gm/l. Above this figure a gradual decrease in deposition rate is obtained. The effect is attributed to undesirable organic side chain reactions.

Agitation

Still solutions, mechanically agitated solutions using a magnetic stirrer and solutions agitated by ultrasonics have been examined. It was found that mechanical agitation is desirable and ultrasonics are to be avoided because of a decrease in plating rate.

The effect of the gold, citric (tartaric) acid and tungstic acid content on the solution is not illustrated. Their respective concentrations are selected from information derived from the following conditions (1) a correlation coefficient of 0·950 min., (2) quality of deposit and (3) maximum plating rate.

Preparation of Solution

Walton describes the preparation of the solution in the following manner.

1 A solution of acidified potassium gold cyanide is prepared by dissolving the salt in deionised water, dissolving the citric (tartaric) acid in deionised water, and combining the two solutions. The solution is mixed thoroughly, heated to about 60°C and allowed to cool to room temperature; this is solution "A". Adequate exhaust ventilation is required when performing the operation.

2 The tungstic acid is added to a solution of sodium hydroxide; this is solution "B".

3 Solution "C" is a buffer solution. It is prepared by adding the potassium acid phthalate to a solution of sodium hydroxide.

4 The sodium salt of N, N-diethylglycine is dissolved in deionised water; this is solution "D".

5 Solution "A" and "B" are combined together, the pH of the resultant being adjusted to between 5·0 and 6·0 with sodium hydroxide or citric (tartaric) acid. Solutions "A" and "B" should be combined as soon as possible to prevent decomposition of gold in solution "A"

6 The buffer solution "C" is added to the adjusted mixture of "A" and "B".

7 Solution "D" is finally added to the buffered mixture of "A", "B" and "C". The electroless solution is heated to a temperature of between 85 and 93°C and is ready for plating.

Mechanism

As the solution deposits gold at a constant rate with respect to time, it may be regarded as a true electroless solution, provided it will deposit on non-conductors. Extrapolation of all curves of immersion time versus gold deposited indicates the presence of gold at zero immersion time. This suggests that an immersion deposit of gold is first formed, which acts as a catalyst to break down the N, N-diethylglycine. One of the products of the reaction acts as a reducing agent, electrons being supplied to reduce the gold ions to the metallic state, very similar to a Wolff rearrangement.

A proposed mechanism is:—

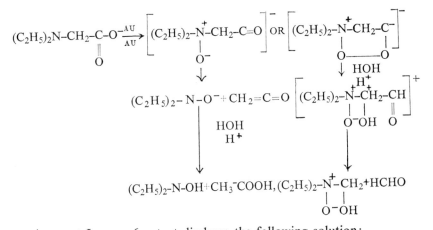

A recent Japanese[6] patent discloses the following solution:—

Potassium auric cyanide	1 to 3 gm/l
Potassium cyanide	1 to 17 gm/l
Sodium acetate	1 to 5 gm/l
Sodium hypophosphite	9 to 15 gm/l
Sulphuric acid	2 to 5 gm/l
pH	3 to 4
Temperature	70 to 80°C

Organo-gold Films

Certain organo-gold compounds when dissolved in a suitable solvent such as ethyl alcohol, to which alkali has been added, undergo decomposition and result in brilliant deposits of metallic gold. This can take place at ambient temperatures within a period of 7 to 9 minutes according to one author.[7] The compound used is diethylmonobromogold $[Au(C_2H_5)_2Br]_2$ but apparently others have also proved successful. No further information is offered in his paper.

A typical formula is:—

Diethylmonobromogold	0·8% by wt.
Sodium hydroxide	0·2% by wt.
Ethyl alcohol	99·0% by wt.

Electroless Palladium

This metal seems to have received less attention than any other metal which may be deposited by electroless methods. Palladium can easily be reduced from aqueous solution, using various reductants, precipitation of a black powder being obtained. The selection of a suitable stable palladium complex which has little tendency to deposit in the form of a black powder and an appropriate reducing agent, together with stringent operating conditions, are required to deposit metallic palladium. Although most of the work has been carried out using metallic substrates, it is reported[8] that this metal can be deposited on plastics by suitable pretreatment with sensitisers.

The general reaction may be illustrated by the following equation:—

$$2Pd(NH_3)_4^{++} + N_2H_4 + 4OH^- \rightarrow 2Pd^\circ + 8NH_3 + N_2 + 4H_2O$$

The following are typical solutions:—

Tetrammine palladium chloride	5·4 gm/l
EDTA (disodium salt)	33·6 gm/l
Ammonium hydroxide	350 gm/l
Hydrazine	0·3 gm/l
Temperature	80°C
Rate of deposition	1 mil/hr.

To decrease the possibility of decomposition taking place, stabilisers are added to the bath; EDTA is preferred in the range 0·01 to 0·10M/l. Others used include ammonium salts, ketones and 2-2 thiodiethanol. Although the latter compound is the best stabiliser, the deposit tends to be dull probably because of the sulphide group present in the compound; EDTA is therefore the most effective.

Ammonium hydroxide not only serves as a complexing agent for palladium, it acts as a solvent for the reaction. Substituted ammonias and their derivatives may also replace ammonium hydroxide as the solvent. Examples quoted are ethylamine and N aminoethyl ethanolamine.

A modification[9] of this bath is suitable for barrel plating.

Tetrammine palladium chloride	7·5 gm/l
EDTA (disodium salt)	8·0 gm/l
Ammonium hydroxide	280 gm/l
Hydrazine (1M solution)	8 ml/hr/1 solution
Temperature	35°C
Rate of deposition	0·035 mil/hr.

Parameters

The rate of deposition of palladium depends on several parameters. Primary factors which determine the rate of deposition are the concentration of palladium, hydrazine and the operating temperature. Secondary factors involved are those of the stabiliser and amine solvent used.

Temperature

A linear relationship is established between temperature and rate of deposition from 40°C upwards (fig. 8.1). However, baths have the tendency to decompose at temperatures above 70°C after periods of 15 to 20 minutes (not shown on graph).

Palladium concentration

A steady increase in deposition rate is obtained with increase in metal content. At concentrations of 0·04M/l and above, no further increase is obtained. Decomposition tends to occur with the higher palladium concentrations (fig. 8.2).

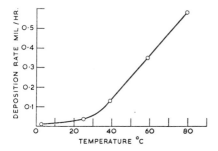

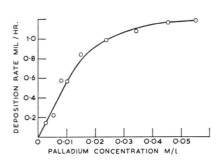

Fig. 8.1 Effect of temperature on the rate of palladium deposition. [Rhoda]

Fig. 8.2 Variation of the rate of palladium deposition with the palladium concentration. [Rhoda]

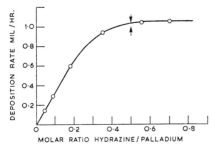

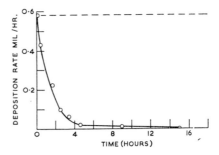

Fig. 8.3 Effect of the molar ratio of hydrazine to palladium on the rate of palladium deposition. [Rhoda]

Fig. 8.4 Rate of deposition during exhaustion of the bath. [Rhoda]

Hydrazine concentration

Rate of deposition varies with the hydrazine concentration in a similar manner to the palladium concentration. Figure 8.3 illustrates how the deposition rate is affected when the hydrazine-palladium concentration is considered on a molar ratio basis. According to Rhoda[8] a levelling off of deposition rate at a molar ratio of 0·5 is not unexpected in view of the general equation.

Ammonium hydroxide

Rate of deposition seems to remain constant when ammonium hydroxide content up to 5M/l is attained. A marked increase in deposition rate takes place above this figure.

The above factors illustrate the relationship existing between the parameters involved. By increasing both the concentration throughout and the temperature, the deposition rate increases greatly, but is accompanied by spontaneous decomposition. However, the addition of stabilisers tends to inhibit this.

It should be pointed out that the parameters of the solution were studied in the absence of a stabiliser. Although the above is an indication of the possible inter-relationship, the addition of a stabiliser may cause radical changes and more relevant information would be derived if it were repeated with the stabiliser present.

Preparation of Solutions

Palladium Complex

Palladium is present in the bath as a soluble amine complex and it is converted to this compound from a stock solution, before its addition to the bath. A stock solution containing about 50M/l palladium chloride in 2N hydrochloric acid may be converted to the tetrammine complex $Pd[(NH_3)_4]Cl_2$ by cautious addition of ammonium hydroxide and heating until the precipitate first formed dissolves.

Reducing Agent

Hydrazine may be obtained in a suitable form such as the hydrate. A 1M solution should be prepared and added to the bath just prior to the commencement of plating.

Stabiliser

The disodium salt of ethylenediaminetetra-acetic acid (EDTA) which appears to be the most effective stabiliser, readily dissolves in ammoniacal solutions.

Properties

Deposits are generally ductile although the operating conditions of the bath affect ductility and hardness. Higher rates of deposition tend to yield softer and more ductile deposits. The purity of the deposit is at least 99·4% and it is of a grey to white colour.

Purity	99·4%+
Lattice parameter	3·8865±0·0005Å
Density	11·96 gm/cm^3
Hardness	150 to 350 KHN$_{25g}$ (range)
	257 KHN$_{25g}$ (average)
Colour	Grey-White

Electroless Silver

The literature available on this subject is voluminous to put it mildly. The reason is undoubtedly due to the fact that it was the only metal which could be chemically deposited on a commercial basis for over a hundred years. Because the mirror industry is relatively large, a considerable amount of work has been carried out on these solutions in order to obtain more efficient processes. Unfortunately, an enormous amount of " cookery book recipes " have been published resulting in the process being commonly referred to as an "art." It is this image that the plating industry in general has found rather difficult to discard. Only the solutions of relative merit are therefore discussed here.

Silver may be reduced to the metallic state from aqueous solutions rather easily. Even mild reducing agents like sugars suffice. Wein,[10] in his reference bibliography, cites innumerable examples. Upton also cites many examples.[11] Formaldehyde, tartrates and sugars are the most commonly used. Silver nitrate is usually the source of silver ions because of its solubility, and ammonium hydroxide the complexing agent.

Narcus[12] recommends the following:—

Solution "A"	Silver nitrate	60 gm/l
	Ammonium hydroxide	60 ml/l
Solution "B"	Formaldehyde	65 ml/l

When preparing silver solutions, the silver nitrate should first he dissolved in distilled or deionised water prior to ammonium hydroxide being added. The precipitate formed on the addition of ammonium hydroxide will redissolve. The above solution is formulated to give the correct amount of excess alkali, this being important in the procurement of good quality films and in controlling the rate of reaction. Narcus continues by stating that too little excess ammonium hydroxide results in an exceedingly fast reaction, whereas too large an excess produces slow film formation. Inorganic addition agents such as lead acetate have been used to control the rate of reaction.

According to Heritage and Balmer[13] the best results are obtained using a combination of two well known methods, namely the formaldehyde and Rochelle salt methods. Following activation in stannous chloride and before reduction in the chemical silver bath, the polymer is immersed in the following solution for a period of 2 to 3 minutes:—

Formaldehyde (40% w/v)	70%	by vol.
Methyl alchohol	30%	by vol.

Although rinsing in running water is advocated by the authors it has been found to be beneficial to volatilise the solvents at a low temperature before transferring the material to the following bath:—

| Solution "A" | Silver nitrate | 30 gm |
| | Distilled water | 300 ml |

Ammonium hydroxide is added until the brown precipitate formed just dissolves. Make up to 600 ml with distilled water.

| Solution "B" | Sodium potassium tartrate | 30 gm |
| | Distilled water | 400 ml |

Solutions "A" and "B" are mixed in equal volumes prior to metallising. A sufficient thickness should be obtained for electroplating in about 30 to 60 minutes. Although the efficiency of this solution is low, the authors claim it is the best tested by them for plastics, since greater adhesion is obtained.

The well known Brashear[14] process, employing a sugar (sucrose) as a reducing agent and potassium hydroxide in addition to ammonium hydroxide, is used to a considerable extent. It has already been pointed out that this is not a true electroless solution since the thickness cannot be built up. In the solutions discussed a maximum limit is imposed which can only be increased by resensitising and immersion in a new silver solution. This is why the process is often referred to as "chemical silvering."

The reason for such a limitation in thickness is, according to Saubestre,[15] twofold. In the first instance it is difficult to obtain a reducing agent which will remain stable in the bulk of the solution for a reasonable period of time. Secondly, silver is not a catalyst for many reducing agents, hence the process is not autocatalytic.

In an attempt to overcome this problem, Brookshire[16] has approached it from a different angle. He offers the following solution:—

Silver cyanide	2·0 gm/l
Sodium hypophosphite, monohydrate	10·0 gm/l
Potassium cyanide	0·2 gm/l
pH	7·5 to 13·5
Temperature	96°C
Rate of deposition	5·26 mgm/cm²/hr.

The principle behind this is that the silver cyanide is virtually insoluble in aqueous solution (0·00023 gm/l at 20°C). It is, however, soluble in the presence of KCN, the soluble complex $KAg(CN)_2$ being formed. As this solution forms, reduction by hypophosphite ions to metallic silver occurs. The complexing agent is then released to dissolve a little more silver cyanide to form a fresh soluble complex. In this manner deposition is controlled since there is only a limited amount of reducible material present in the bath at any particular time.

Silver has rapidly lost popularity in recent years for metallising plastics. There are a number of reasons for this, namely:—

1   It is more expensive than copper
2   There are explosion hazards
3   There is a possibility of silver migration[17]
4   Copper solutions can now be maintained indefinitely, whereas silver baths, being non-regenerable, have to be discarded. Although silver can be reclaimed, the cost of reclamation must be taken into account.

Explosion Hazards

Compounds may be formed, such as silver azide and silver fulminate which are violently explosive and may detonate with the slightest mechanical disturbance. Precautions must therefore be taken to prevent this occuring. All residues from chemical silver solutions should be disposed of as soon as possible and not allowed to evaporate to dryness which favours explosive conditions. If the silver is to be recovered, the spent solution should be acidified with hydrochloric acid and the stable chloride formed, removing all possibility of an explosion.

As an alternative to ammonia, other complexing agents have been investigated[18] to lessen or remove the dangers of an explosive residue being obtained.

Silver Migration

The migration characteristic that silver exhibits has seriously affected its use for the metallising of dielectrics and probably this has been directly responsible for the amount of research and development work carried out on electroless copper within the past few years. It is this characteristic which has outlawed its use in the manufacture of electronic equipment, perhaps rather unjustly, since migration only occurs under particular conditions.

Conditions Favouring Migration

1   High humidity
2   High d.c. potential
3   Silver must be in intimate contact with the dielectric
4   Type of substrate used.
5   In sulphur containing atmospheres it is possible to "bridge over" because of the increased volume, enabling silver migration to continue, for example whisker formation.[19]

The rate of silver migration increases with increasing potential and relative humidity. It is also time and temperature dependent. The tendency of a dielectric to facilitate silver migration is characterised by its resistivity at high humidities, the lower the resistivity the greater the susceptibility. Another factor which aids migration is the use of fibrous materials, particularly glass filled substrates where migration can proceed along the fibres.

Instances have been reported,[20] however, where potentials as low as 2 volts d.c. and with humidities as low as 50% have affected migration, particularly on polar surfaces.

A means of predicting the extent of silver migration has been proposed[17] where it is expressed as a function of the relative humidity, temperature, time, voltage and substrate used.

Investigation of the migration tendencies of other metals show that copper, tin and gold, in decreasing order, also exhibit this characteristic but to a much lesser extent so that it can virtually be ignored. It has been reported[17] that the rate of silver migration is at least a thousand times more rapid than that of copper. Nickel, indium, tin, tin-lead and rhodium do not appear to possess migration tendencies.

Conditions Preventing Migration

1   Absence of d.c. potential
2   Relative humidity of less than 30%
3   Coating surface with a non-migratory metal
4   Hydrophobic surface
5   Avoid high sulphur containing atmospheres

Although government equipment has to withstand severe climatic conditions, not every piece of equipment is required to satisfy specifications of such severity. Neither does every polymer that is metallised always end up as a printed ₁wiring device, although this is a common application in the plating of plastics. Furthermore, only a few plastics are susceptible to migration, in various degrees, and a considerable number show no signs at all. However, the other disadvantages already mentioned, in addition to silver migration certainly justify the omission of silver in metallising.

Mechanism

Kohman, Hermance and Downes[21] offer the explanation that silver migration is due to silver ions leaving the anode in the adsorbed water film on the polymer. Silver hydroxide is precipitated in the alkaline region near the anode and immediately decomposes to silver oxide. This may be reduced to metallic silver by photocatalysis, or by reducing agents leaching out of the polymer. This is how bridging occurs in printed wiring, resulting in short-circuiting of the conductors and ultimate failure of the equipment.

Bell Telephone Laboratories[21] ascribe the unique position of silver in this migration problem as due to lack of a passivating oxide film around the metal. Saubestre[22] however maintains that the reaction involved $Ag \rightleftharpoons Ag^+ + \epsilon$ is essentially reversible, that is, there is virtually no activation overpotential involved. This is true of no other redox system.

REFERENCES

1 Wein S., *Metal Finish.*, **46**, 8, 58 (1948).
2 Brookshire R. R., U.S. Pat., 2, 976, 181 (1961).
3 Swan S. D., Gostin E. L., *Metal Finish.*, **59**, 4, 52 (1961).
4 Gostin E. L., Swan S. D., U.S. Pat., 3, 032, 436 (1962).
5 Walton R. F., *J. electrochem. Soc.*, **108**, 8, 767 (1961).
6 Jap. Pat., 1081/65/ to Shiboura Electric Co. (1965).
7 Gibson C., *Nature*, Lond., **140**, 3537, 279 (1937).
8 Rhoda R. N., *Trans. Inst. Metal Finish.*, **36**, 82 (1959).
9 Rhoda R. N., *J. electrochem. Soc.*, **108**, 7, 707 (1961).
10 Wein S., "Silver Films," PB 111236, OTS, U.S. Dept. Commerce (1953).
11 Upton P. B., *J. Electrodep. tech. Soc.*, **22**, 45 (1947).
12 Narcus H., "Metallising of Plastics," Reinhold, New York (1960).
13 Heritage R. J., Balmer J. R., *Metallurgia*, **47**, 281, 171 (1953).
14 Brashear H., *Eng. Mechanic*, **31**, 327 (1880).
15 Saubestre E. B., *Metal Finish.*, **60**, 6, 67 (1962).
16 Brookshire R. R., U.S. Pat., 2, 976, 180 (1961).
17 Chaiken S. W., Janney J., Church F. M., McClelland C. W., *Ind., Engng Chem.*, **51**, 3, 299 (1959).
18 Wein S., U.S. Pat., 2, 871, 139 (1959).
19 Jarrett G. D. R., private communication.
20 Short O. A., *Electron. Inds Tele-Tech*, **15**, 64 (1956).
21 Kohman G. T., Hermance H. W., Downes G. H., *Bell Syst. tech. J.*, **34**, 1115, 47 (1955).
22 Saubestre E. B., private communication.

BIBLIOGRAPHY

1 " The Metallising of Glass and Plastics by the Reduction of Aqueous Solutions," P. B. Upton, *J. Electrodep. tech. Soc.*, **22**, 45 (1947).
2 " Gold Films," S. Wein, PB 111332, OTS, U.S. Dept. Commerce (1953).
3 " Silver Films," S. Wein, PB 111236, OTS, U.S. Dept. Commerce (1953).

111

CHAPTER 9

FERROMAGNETIC MATERIALS

This chapter discusses the use of cobalt and alloys of cobalt, nickel and iron in various combinations. Nickel is excluded here because, although ferromagnetic, when codeposited with phosphorus it is virtually non-magnetic. Furthermore nickel, unalloyed, is very rarely used for its magnetic properties because of large hysteresis and eddy current losses, except in a few special applications. Consequently, it is normally used in conjunction with cobalt and/or iron. As the properties of ferromagnetic elements have their origin in uncompensated electron spins in one of the outer orbits of the atoms of such elements, the addition of valence electrons of phosphorus ($v=5$) has a compensating effect on nickel of Vu_B for each atom of phosphorus that is substituted for a nickel atom (u_B=Bohr magneton). A rough calculation indicates that Ni-P alloy of 89·2:10·8 atomic composition should exhibit no ferromagnetic properties; this is an agreement with Wesley's[1] findings. Ransom and Zentner[2] report the absence of hysteresis loops on electroless nickel deposits although they do not specify the phosphorus content. However, when phosphorus is codeposited with cobalt and/or iron, the resultant deposit is strongly ferromagnetic, although a decrease in magnetisation is apparent.

It is only within the last few years that an enormous amount of interest has developed in magnetic deposits. This is due to the large number of applications which have arisen in the electronics industry and the possible advantages envisaged by using magnetic films to replace conventional materials. The majority of these deposits are in the thin film category which in current nomenclature means up to 1μ or 10^4Å in thickness. A notable exception[3] to this is the use of nickel-iron deposits of high permeability for the magnetic shielding of devices from stray magnetic fields, where the thickness is of the order of 2·5 to 10 mils.

Quite early on it was recognised that the characteristics exhibited by thin ferromagnetic films would be of immense value in the computer field for the films were found to exist in two stable states, corresponding to positive and negative remanence, which could be switched by the application of a small magnetic field.

Present day computers using ferrite cores are extremely limited by their poor switching characteristics, since the process is one of domain wall motion which is inherently slow (microsecond). Furthermore, they do not lend themselves to miniaturising and are extremely costly to fabricate. Switching in thin films is a coherent rotation of the magnetisation in the plane of the film and is therefore possible at very high speeds (nanoseconds). In addition to this, thin films are ideal for miniaturising. Greater flexibility of design is also possible and standard techniques such as those employed in printed wiring may be adapted, dispensing with time consuming threading operations.

Although thin films find their greatest outlet in the field of information storage (from computers to tape recorders) there is no reason why they cannot be used as miniaturised counterparts to other magnetic devices such as transformers and permanent magnets. A possible future use is for non-linear devices, as required in parametric amplifiers.

To evaluate the properties of thin films, a hysteresis loop tester may be used. The resultant hysteresis loop, or B-H loop as it is sometimes referred to, yields the necessary information concerning the magnetic properties of the material.

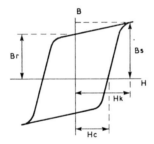

B — FLUX DENSITY	H — MAGNETIC FORCE (FIELD STRENGTH)
Br — REMANENCE	Hc — COERCIVE FORCE
Bs — SATURATION FLUX DENSITY	Hk — ANISOTROPIC FIELD

Originally, materials like copper-plated aluminium (for lightness) were used as substrates in drum recording systems but these have been superseded by plastic substrates. In tape recording mediums, plastics offer sufficient mechanical strength to support the film and besides they are cheap and more ideally suited for winding. In static memory devices, plastic substrates are also gaining wide popularity.

Generally, in digital magnetic recording systems high volume storage is a desirable feature. Because of the high packing density (2,000 pulses per inch of a half-inch wide tape) there is some danger of demagnetisation caused by the flux of one bit fringing over and affecting the adjacent bits. As the magnetic medium is usually in motion (drums, tapes, discs) the influence of one field (magnetised head) on another must be taken into account. It is therefore necessary to use a high coercive force (Hc) material so that stray magnetic fields will not cause a change in retentivity (Br) of the material and alter the stored information.

In a good recording system, the coercive force and remanence should both be as high as possible, since the former determines the permanency and resolution of the recorded information and the latter increases the signal strength of the output.

Requirements for High Density Storage

1 An Hc greater than 200 oersteds.
2 A relatively low remanence to coercive force ratio.
3 An almost rectangular B-H loop.
4 Consistent and reproducible magnetic characteristics.

In static memory systems the problem of isolation is not so acute and because the interrogating agent is an electric current, the problems encountered are very different from the previous applications cited.

A low coercive force material is used to make bistable storage elements for high speed computers or other high speed storage devices. The lower the Hc, the lower the power required and hence the lower the energy needed for switching. This provides a considerable saving in the power and a consequent reduction in the size of the equipment required to drive the memory unit.

By comparison, the ferrite core has serious drawbacks which have already been mentioned and although the cores themselves are 100% reliable, failure may still occur during manufacture; this is due to the wires being broken or damaged.

Requirements for High Speed Memory Elements

1 Since the store relies upon the switching characteristics of many bits, it is obvious that these must be reproducible to fairly close limits.
2 The cost of the present conventional elements, employing ferrite cores, is almost entirely a function of the fabrication where each element is individually tested and wired into an array. Therefore, the method of manufacture adopted must be cheap and suitable for production techniques.
3 High speed of switching from one remanent state to another should be possible with the current available from transistor circuit components. A low Hc is therefore essential.
4 So that maximum discrimination between the signal and the disturbance level can be obtained, the output should be as high as possible (high Br).
5 Square loop material is necessary. This is employed to facilitate fast complete switching from one state to another and must be above the noise level in the particular application.

Other desirable properties for storage elements are:—

(a) low crystallinity

(b) low magnetostriction

(c) chemical stability

Curie temperature is also of interest but considering the differential between this and the relatively low heat distortion points of polymers, it does not enter into the discussion.

In particular applications, an "easy" and "hard" direction of magnetisation is required, that is, the film must show anisotropic properties. (If no "easy" or "hard" direction exists, the film is isotropic.) The difference between the two hysteresis curves is that stronger fields are necessary to turn the magnetisation into the hard direction away from the easy axis it prefers. The excess of energy required to magnetise in a given direction over that required for the easy direction is called the crystalline anisotropy energy.

In some instances, it may be necessary to align the easy axis in a preferred direction. When metal substrates are used this may be induced by mechanical means, such as directional polishing of the material or by using hard drawn wire. The effect is probably due to slip bonds formed during working of the metal, the subsequent magnetic deposit aligning itself with the elongated grain structure already present. If plastics are used, anisotropy is induced by plating in a magnetic field, the easy axis aligning itself parallel to the applied field. The magnetic field strength should be greater than the coercivity of the resultant film deposited.

Methods of Producing Thin Films

The normal methods of producing thin films are as follows:—

(a) Electroless deposition

(b) Physical vapour deposition utilising
   (i) vacuum evaporation
   (ii) cathode sputtering

(c) Chemical vapour deposition

(d) Electroplating.

Electroless Cobalt

As the chemistry of cobalt is similar to that of nickel, it is not surprising that the conditions for producing deposits of both metals by electroless means are also similar. The recent requirement for films with particular magnetic properties has aroused a great deal of interest in this metal. Although it was originally codeposited with nickel, or with nickel and iron, the magnetic properties exhibited by cobalt alone are desirable for certain applications. However, the majority of deposits in this field are of the thin film category. There does not appear to be any demand for thick deposits, as in the case of nickel for corrosion and abrasion resistance. As the magnetic properties of thin films are now a separate technology, it is intended to deal with a few pertinent points only.

Like nickel, the most commonly used reducing agent for cobalt is sodium hypophosphite. A complexing agent-buffer system is also incorporated into the system. The bath is operated in the alkaline range near the boiling point. There does not appear to be any acid equivalent of electroless nickel, deposition ceasing at a pH of 7·0. The bath proposed by Brenner[5] may be regarded as a basic standard:—

Cobalt chloride, hexahydrate	30 gm/l
Sodium citrate, pentahydrate	35 gm/l
Ammonium chloride	50 gm/l
Sodium hypophosphite, monohydrate	20 gm/l
pH (adjusted with NH₄OH)	9 – 10
Temperature	91-96°C
Rate of deposition	0·6 mil/hour

Dull deposits are obtained from this bath. The solution produces films with a coercive force (Hc) of about 20 to 50 oersteds, depending on the operating conditions; this invalidates its use in high density storage applications since a high Hc is required. However, as Hc is dependent on the thickness of the film (fig. 9.1 & 9.2) increasing the thickness will result in a decrease in coercive force.

As such it is useful in current types of memory storage devices, particularly since it possesses other desirable magnetic characteristics which may be exploited in the production of bistable thin film memory elements.

The following bath, disclosed by Ransom and Zentner[2] is a modification of the Brenner bath:—

Cobalt sulphate, heptahydrate	24 gm/l
Ammonium sulphate	40 gm/l
Sodium hypophosphite, monohydrate	20 gm/l
Sodium citrate	80 gm/l
Sodium lauryl sulphate	0·1 gm/l
pH (adjusted with NH₄OH)	8·5
Temperature	92°C±1

An Hc of 1·01 is obtained at a thickness of 6,500Å with a relatively square hysteresis loop (Br/Bs 93%) and exhibiting uniaxial anisotropy. These films have potential applications as computer storage elements in high speed switching devices.

Further modifications to the Brenner bath have been used by investigators in the thin film field, particularly where applications involve the use of a high coercive force material. It has been reported[6] that the relatively high cobalt-hypophosphite concentration of the Brenner bath is responsible for the relatively low Hc (fig. 9.3). Dilute solutions have therefore been explored to obtain films with an Hc greater than 200 oersteds, which can be used as high density storage materials. Recording characteristics of the deposit are similar to those of commercial Fe_2O_3 recording tapes. Deposits have a packing density about twice that of conventional magnetic oxide.

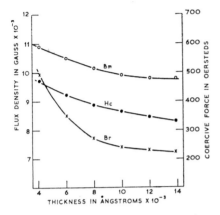

Fig. 9.1 Coercive force, remanent and maximum flux densities of cobalt deposits as a function of thickness. [Fisher and Chilton]

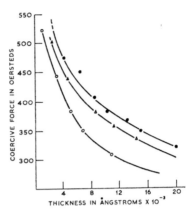

Fig. 9.2 Coercive force of chemically reduced cobalt as a function of thickness at various total concentrations of cobalt plus hypophosphite ion. ● Co^{++} plus $H_2PO_2^- = 7.3$ gm/l; △ Co^{++} plus $H_2PO_2^- = 4.0$ gm/l; ○ Co^{++} plus $H_2PO_2^- = 1.8$ gm/l; cobalt ion to hypophosphite ion ratio $= 0.86$. [Fisher and Chilton]

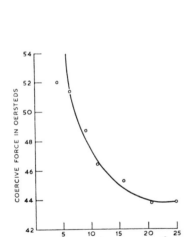

Fig. 9.3 Coercive force of chemically reduced cobalt as a function of thickness from a solution containing 14.5 gm/l of Co^{++} plus $H_2PO_2^-$ ion. Ratio of cobalt ion to hypophosphite ion $= 0.86$. This curve is typical of a bath based on the Brenner formula and illustrates the effect of a high Co^{++} and $H_2PO_2^-$ ion concentration on the coercivity of the deposit. [Fisher and Chilton]

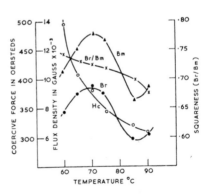

Fig. 9.4 Magnetic properties of chemically deposited cobalt at various temperatures but at constant time (60 min). ● Remanent flux density; △ maximum flux density; ○ coercive force; X squareness (Br/Bm). [Fisher and Chilton]

117

Fisher and Chilton[6] favour the following bath, typical deposits yielding a coercive force of 360 oersteds at a thickness of 13,000Å.

Cobalt chloride, hexahydrate	7·5 gm/l
Citric acid	17·9 gm/l
Ammonium chloride	12·5 gm/l
Sodium hypophosphite, monohydrate	3·52 gm/l
Sodium lauryl sulphate	0·0145 gm/l
pH (adjusted with NaOH)	8·2
Temperature	80°C±0.5°C

It may be seen from fig. 9.1 that the coercive force (Hc) remanence (Br) and maximum flux density (Bm) of deposits decreases with increasing thickness, within the range 4,000Å to 13,000Å. The squareness ($^{Br}/_{Bs}$) of the deposit decreases with increasing thickness from 90% at approximately 4,000Å to 74% at approximately 10,000Å. The average flux density of cobalt deposits (4,000 to 14,000Å) is 10,500 gauss in comparison to 18,000 gauss for pure cobalt. It is reported that the phosphorus content is 4% and it is this which is primarily responsible for the loss in maximum flux density of the deposited cobalt in comparison to pure cobalt.

Moradzadeh,[7] however, modifies the Brenner bath in the following manner:—

Cobalt chloride, hexahydrate	27·1 gm/l
Sodium citrate, dihydrate	90·0 gm/l
Ammonium chloride	45·3 gm/l
Sodium hypophosphite, monohydrate	9·0 gm/l
pH (adjusted with NH₄OH)	8·5±0·02
Temperature	75°C±0·5°C

In this investigation the author concludes that the four dominant factors in determining the resultant coercivity are deposition time, pH, temperature and hypophosphite concentration (fig. 9.5 to 9.8) which must be taken into consideration simultaneously. The thickness, which we have already seen influences the coercivity, is also dependent on these four factors (fig. 9.9 to 9.12). A wide range of coercivities are obtained and the higher ones, which are associated with a mirror like appearance, are suitable for conventional high density magnetic recordings.

Judge[8] and his collaborators, point out that for high density applications, the thinness of the recording surface is of prime importance, since this facilitates the writing of sharper transition regions by the recording transducer and is also more able to resist demagnetisation. One point which should be observed is that of the significant danger of atmospheric corrosion when there is a large surface-volume ratio in very thin films. The authors claim that film thicknesses of 600Å, which are considerably less than previously used, result in Hc's of about 1,000 oersteds.

Cobalt sulphate	0·11M
Sodium hypophosphite	0·19M
Ammonium sulphate	0·50M
Sodium citrate	0·12M
pH (adjusted with NH₄OH)	8·7
Temperature	80°C

From the above samples quoted, it may be seen that cobalt films may be used

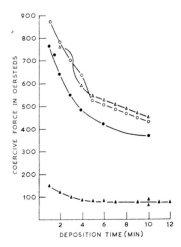

Fig. 9.5 Coercivity of cobalt-phosphorus films vs. deposition time at various pH. △ 8·70; ○ 8·42; ● 8·37; ▲ 7·66; bath temperature 75°C. [Moradzadeh]

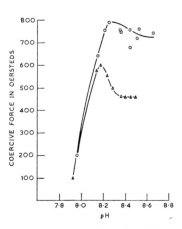

Fig. 9.6 Coercivity of cobalt-phosphorus films vs. bath pH for various deposition times. ○ 2 min; △ 10 min; bath temperature 75°C. [Moradzadeh]

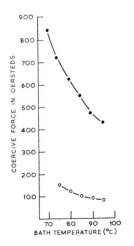

Fig. 9.7 Coercivity of cobalt-phosphorus deposition vs. bath temperature. Deposition time 5 min; ○ pH 7·45; ● pH 8·02. [Moradzadeh]

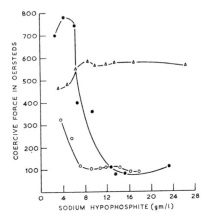

Fig. 9.8 Coercivity of cobalt-phosphorus films vs. sodium hypophosphite at various bath pH. △ 8·45; ● 8·13; ○ 7·78; bath temperature 75°C; deposition time 5 min. [Moradzadeh]

119

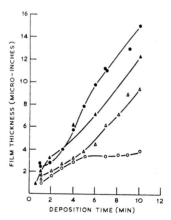

Fig. 9.9 Film thickness of co-balt-phosphorus vs. deposition time at various pH. ● 8·42; ▲ 8·37; △ 8·20; ○ 7·66; bath temperature 75°C. [Moradzadeh]

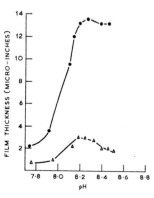

Fig. 9.10 Thickness of cobalt-phosphorus films vs. bath pH for various deposition times. ● 10 min; △ 2 min; bath temperature 75°C. [Moradzadeh]

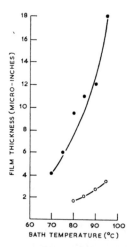

Fig. 9.11 Thickness of cobalt-phosphorus films vs. bath temperature. Deposition time 5 min; ○ pH 7·45; ● pH 8·02. [Moradzadeh]

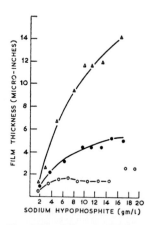

Fig. 9.12 Film thickness of cobalt-phosphorus vs. sodium hypophosphite at various pH. △ 8·5; ● 8·13; ○ 7·78; bath temperature 75°C; deposition time 5 min. [Moradzadeh]

120

as a soft magnetic material exhibiting a low coercive force for use in present high speed switching memory storage systems or as a hard magnetic material with a high coercive force for current high density storage applications. This can be accomplished by modifying electroless cobalt solutions and by simply altering operating conditions. Two of the most important parameters are pH and thickness of the film, the former influencing coercivity remarkably with slight variations. Ransom and Zentner[2] for example, state that Hc's of 1·01 oersteds were obtained at a pH of 8·5 whereas if the pH is increased to 9·5, an Hc of 350 oersteds is obtained for the same thickness. Moradzadeh also illustrates this in his investigation (see table 9.1). That is why such a finite control is kept on pH. Moradzadeh's investigation used a constant recorder controller to maintain the fine tolerance of ±0·02 pH units. As reproducibility is essential, especially with storage elements, probably more stringent control is necessary in magnetic film deposition than in any other field of metal deposition. There are other magnetic properties which are essential to specific applications such as flux density, remanence and so on. To satisfy these requirements, not only is tight control exercised over the solution (fig. 9.4, 9.13 & 9.14 show the influence of some parameters on the $^{Br}/_{Bs}$ squareness ratio) but, more often than not, the solution is tailor-made for the application.

Table 9.1
Effect of pH on Coercivity of Electroless Cobalt Films
At Various Constant Film Thicknesses (Moradzadeh)

Thickness	pH	Coercivity (oersteds)	Thickness	pH	Coercivity (oersteds)
2 μ in.	7·67	120	4 μ in.	7·67	75
	8·37	760		7·93	100
	8·41	800		8·37	450
	9·44	875		8·45	700

The last three papers cited, that is all those discussing high density storage applications, all used polyethylene terephthalate as the substrate. Fisher and Chilton[6] used an adhesive* as an intermediate organic coating to facilitate adhesion of the magnetic film to the base. Judge,[8] however, rendered the surface hydrophilic by employing a two-step process. This consisted of immersion in a hot chromic-sulphuric acid mixture followed by a hot sodium hydroxide solution.

Moradzadeh prefers to omit the chromic-sulphuric acid solution since he claims that it causes microscopic cracking of the surface and undue surface roughness. A 25% NaOH solution operating at a temperature of 95°C and containing a few drops of a surface active agent is suggested, the immersion time being five minutes. After the magnetic film is deposited, a few minutes heat treatment at a temperature of 110°C results in a large increase in the adhesion of cobalt to the polymer.

---

* Adhesive 200F. Shipley & Co., Wellesley, Mass., U.S.A.

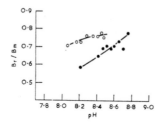

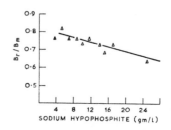

Fig. 9.13 Squareness ratio vs. bath pH for cobalt-phosphorus films. ● 5 min; ○ 10 min; bath temperature 75°C. [Moradzadeh]

Fig. 9.14 Squareness ratio of cobalt-phosphorus film vs. sodium hypophosphite content of the bath. pH 8·45; bath temperature 75°C; deposition time 5 min. [Moradzadeh]

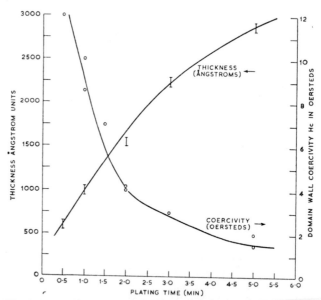

Fig. 9.15 Variation of coercivity and thickness with plating time for 50/50 Ni-Co layers. [Heritage and Walker]

Although much of the work initially performed on thin ferromagnetic films for bistable storage elements in high speed computers employed Ni-Fe alloys, Heritage and Walker[4] point out the possibilities of employing Ni-Co in this sphere. Comparing the output signals from electroless Ni-Co solutions and evaporated Ni-Fe, the evidence suggests that Ni-Co films have a smaller output for the same dimensions and switching speed, by a factor of between 2 and 3, which is consistent with the lower saturation magnetisation for these alloys compared with Ni-Fe.

The authors used the following solution in their investigation:—

Nickel sulphate	15 gm/l
Cobalt sulphate	10 gm/l
Ammonium sulphate	42 gm/l
Sodium citrate	84 gm/l
Hypophosphorous acid	8 ml/l
Ammonium hydroxide	13·2 ml/l
pH	8·5
Temperature	90°C±1°C
Rate of deposition	approx. 1,000Å/min.

The resultant film contains about equal amounts of Ni and Co with about 5%P. Domain wall coercivities of about 2 oersteds were obtained at a thickness of 3,000Å (fig. 9.15). The figures are reproducible to ± 10%.

Bagrowski and Lauriente[9] confirmed the above findings of Heritage and Walker, although a slightly modified version of the original solution was used. In this instance, the hypophosphorous acid was increased to 30 ml/l and the ammonium hydroxide content altered accordingly to obtain the same pH value initially used.

In a recent patent,[10] cobalt rich films have been proposed as information carriers, the claim being that greater resolution is achieved than with nickel rich alloys, both being superior to oxide coatings. (Resolution may be defined as the ratio of output at a double frequency as opposed to the fundamental frequency, the nearer this ratio approaches unity, the greater the resolution.) The higher the resolution, the more clearly one bit of magnetic information is distinguished from another. A higher packing density is therefore possible because of the greater discrimination obtained between bits. On a half-inch wide tape, up to 2,500 bits may be recorded per inch and recovered in clearly intelligible form. If maximum packing density is not an essential feature, the higher resolution characteristics may be utilised to produce a clearer output for a smaller number of bits.

The recommended solution is:—

Cobalt chloride, hexahydrate	60 gm/l
Nickel chloride, hexahydrate	2 gm/l
Sodium potassium tartrate, tetrahydrate	200 gm/l
Ammonium chloride	50 gm/l
Sodium hypophosphite, monohydrate	20 gm/l
pH	8·0 – 10·5
Temperature	77 – 82°C
Time	3 minutes

The composition of the alloy is about 90% Co, 7% Ni, 3%P. Compared to standard oxide coatings, a 60% resolution was obtained when tested at 600 pulses per inch over 300, as opposed to a 40% resolution with a standard oxide coating.

The substrate used in this application was polyethylene terephthalate. Prior to electroless deposition, the following sequence was used:—

1 Immersion in a solution of 100 gm/l NaOH at 77 to 82°C for 1 to 5 minutes
2 Sensitising in stannous chloride
3 Activation in palladium chloride.

Electroless Nickel-Iron

The principal use made of this alloy is solely for its magnetic properties. This time, however, they are not devoted entirely to thin films. Besides replacing ferrite cores as memory elements for high speed switching devices, they are used for their shielding properties. Nickel-iron alloys of high permeability have served as electromagnetic shields to protect delicate apparatus from stray magnetic fields. Such applications range from cathode tubes in radar equipment to potted circuits. The advantages obtained by replacing cumbersome Mumetal fabrications are:—

(a) saving in weight
(b) more economic
(c) not susceptible to shock
(d) ease of fabrication.

Permeability is dependent on alloy composition, the preferred composition being 80:20 nickel-iron.

Although a fair amount of work has been carried out on the electroplating of this alloy for computer storage elements, very little has been published on the electroless deposition of nickel-iron for this purpose.

Schmeckenbecker[11] has investigated this alloy because of its suitability for memory applications and because it exhibits a high creeping threshold and fast coherent rotational switching. He discusses the effect of certain parameters on the magnetic properties of the deposited film.

Electroless Iron

No commercial applications for iron deposits have appeared so far, hence very little work has been carried out on this metal except when in combination with nickel and/or cobalt.

Typical examples[12] of electroless iron solutions are:—

Ferrous sulphate, heptahydrate	30 gm/l
Sodium potassium tartrate, tetrahydrate	25–100 gm/l
Sodium hypophosphite	10 gm/l
pH	8–10
Temperature	75–90°C

Citrates[13] may be used as the complexing agent, similar to that used with nickel and cobalt.

Ferrous sulphate, heptahydrate	119 gm/l
Sodium citrate, dihydrate	170 gm/l
EDTA	50 gm/l
Sodium hypophosphite, monohydrate	100 gm/l
Formaldehyde	200 ml/l
pH (adjusted with NH_4OH)	10
Temperature	20°C

REFERENCES

1 Wesley W. A., *Plating*, **37**, 7, 732 (1950).
2 Ransom L. D., Zentner V., *J. electrochem. Soc.*, **111**, 12, 1423 (1964).
3 Wolf I. W., McConnell V. P., *Proc. Am. Electropl. Soc.*, **43**, 215 (1956).
4 Heritage R. J., Walker M. T., *J. Electron. Control*, **7**, 6, 542 (1959).
5 Brenner A., Riddell G. E., *J. Res. natn. Bur. Stand.*, **39**, 385 (1947).
6 Fisher R. D., Chilton W. H., *J. electrochem. Soc.*, **109**, 6, 485 (1962).
7 Moradzadeh Y., *J. electrochem. Soc.*, **112**, 9, 891 (1965).
8 Judge J. S., Morrison J. R., Speliotis D. E., Bate G., *J. electrochem. Soc.*, **112**, 7, 681 (1965).
9 Bagrowski J., Lauriente M. J., *J. electrochem. Soc.*, **109**, 10, 987 (1962).
10 Brit. Pat., 992, 660 to Sperry Rand Corp. (1962).
11 Schmeckenbecher A. F., *J. electrochem. Soc.*, **113**, 8, 778 (1966).
12 Eisenberg P. H., U.S. Pat., 2, 827, 398 (1958).
13 Cann L., U.S. Pat., 3, 178, 311 (1965).

BIBLIOGRAPHY

1 " Ferromagnetism," R. M. Bozorth, van Nostrand, New York (1951).
2 " Magnetic Materials," P. R. Bardell, McDonald, London (1960).
3 " Magnetic Thin Films," R. F. Soohoo, Harper and Row, New York (1965).
4 " Physics of Thin Films," E. W. Pugh (ed. J. Hass), Academic Press, New York (1963).
5 " Magnetism," Vol. III, I. S. Jacobs and C. P. Bean, Academic Press, New York (1963).
6 " The Effect of the Concentration of Hypophosphite Ion on the Magnetic Properties of Chemically Deposited Co-P Films," J. S. Judge, J. R. Morrison and D. E. Speliotis *J. electrochem. Soc.*, **113**, 6, 547 (1966).
7 " The Relationship Between Coercivity and the Structure and Composition of Electroless Cobalt-Phosphorus] Films," M. G. Miksic, R. Traveso, A. Arcus and R. H. Wright, *J. electrochem. Soc.*, **113**, 4, 360 (1966).
8 " Electroless Deposition of Iron Alloys," P. H. Eisenberg, U.S. Pat., 2, 827, 399 (1958).
9 " Electroless Deposition of High Coercive Magnetic Films," M. A. Foley, U.S. Pat., 3, 138, 479 (1961).
10 " Review of Deposited Metallic Films for Computer Application," J. S. Sallo, *Plating*, **54**, 3, (1967).

CHAPTER 10

MISCELLANEOUS METALS AND ALLOYS

Chromium

A very limited amount of work has been published on this subject. This may not be entirely due to lack of effort but through lack of any real success. Although laboratory scale solutions have been reported to work satisfactorily, no suitable industrial process has so far appeared. Since the throwing power of chromium electrolytes is very poor, a satisfactory method for depositing this metal by electroless means would be of great commercial value. Direct metallising of plastics using electroless chromium solutions has not yet been reported in any technical literature to date. It is believed that this is because of the difficulties encountered in catalysing the surface properly.

All of the solutions used in the past have employed hypophosphite as the reducing agent. Details of the first electroless chromium solution to appear in print were published by West[1] in 1955.

Chromic fluoride	15 gm/l
Chromic chloride	1 gm/l
Sodium citrate	7·5 gm/l
Sodium hypophosphite	7·5 gm/l
Temperature	71-88°C
Rate of deposition	0·1-0·14 mil/hour
Stability	About 1 week with filtration

The solution requires an initial deposit of copper, or copper alloy, such as brass, to initiate deposition.

Shortly afterwards Eisenberg and Raleigh[2] published details of a solution similar to that of West with one important difference. An addition agent is incorporated which reduces the dissolved chromic ions to the chromous state and also forms a readily reducible complex with the chromous ions, this complex being rapidly reduced to metallic chromium at the surface by the action of the hypophosphite ion. As a result, the rate of deposition is increased by a factor of between 2 and 3 because of the increased efficiency of the hypophosphite as a reducing agent. The addition agent must be capable of satisfying the following criteria (1) reducing chromium to the trivalent state, (2) forming a chromium complex that is soluble and (3) the resultant complex formed is capable of being reduced to metallic chromium. Typical compounds used are oxalic acid and alkali salts of oxalic acid.

Chromic bromide, nonohydrate	16 gm/l
Chromic chloride, hexahydrate	1 gm/l
Sodium acetate	10 gm/l
Sodium hypophosphite	10 gm/l
Potassium oxalate	4.5 gm/l
pH	4-6
Temperature	75-90°C
Rate of deposition	0·3 mil/hour

An alkaline bath is also disclosed in the same patent:—

Chromic bromide, nonohydrate	16 gm/l
Chromic iodide, nonohydrate	1 gm/l
Sodium citrate	10 gm/l
Sodium hypophosphite	10 gm/l
Sodium oxalate	9 gm/l
pH	8-10
Temperature	75-90°C
Rate of deposition	0·3 mil/hour

A nickel undercoat is necessary to initiate reaction in the chromium solution. Considering that these baths are similar to West's, an apparent peculiarity is that they require a nickel strike on copper, whereas in the former a copper strike on nickel is essential.

The most recent bath to make an appearance is again reported by West.[3]

Chromium acetate	30 gm/l
Sodium citrate	40 gm/l
Sodium glycollate	40 gm/l
Sodium hypophosphite	10-30 gm/l
Sodium acetate	20 gm/l
Nickel acetate	1 gm/l
pH	4-6
Temperature	100°C
Rate of deposition	1 mil/hour

This bath is basically similar to an electroless nickel bath, the deposit containing some phosphorus. A small amount of nickel is present in solution as an activator to initiate the reaction.

The general consensus of opinion about the chromium baths published to date is that they are not practicable. Some investigators claim that they cannot obtain any deposition whatsoever, whereas those who have been fortunate enough to achieve deposition appear to be very uncertain of what the deposit is.

Nickel-Chromium

The production of nickel-chromium alloy by electroless means has obvious advantages. Not only would the corrosion resistance of the deposit be excellent, but the high resistance obtainable from such a film

127

could be used in innumerable applications, one example being electrical heating elements. The literature makes only one reference[4] to this alloy, and then only a minor one. Although the inventor refers to an alloy of nickel-chromium being deposited, no results, that is no analysis of the deposit produced, are given to verify this supposition. Recommended formula is:—

Sodium citrate, dihydrate	142 gm/l
Chromic chloride	0·83 gm/l
Nickel chloride	4.2 gm/l
EDTA	41·7 gm/l
Sodium hypophosphite, monohydrate	83·4 gm/l
Formaldehyde	83·4 ml/l
pH (adjusted with NH₄OH)	10·0
Temperature	20-23°C

It is interesting to note that this is a room temperature process. Other unusual factors are the use of two reducing agents and three complexing agents, the latter providing a synergistic complexing action by reinforcing the complexing properties of each other.

Nickel-Tungsten

The following solution has been disclosed by Pearlstein[5] and collaborators:—

Nickel sulphate, hexahydrate	7 gm/l
Sodium citrate	10 gm/l
Sodium hypophosphite	10 gm/l
Sodium tungstate, dihydrate	35 gm/l
Temperature	B. pt.
Rate of deposition	0·3 mil/hour

The alloy deposited contains about 5·9% tungsten. Increasing the hypophosphite and tungsten concentration reduces the stability of the bath and spontaneous decomposition occurs. When the citric acid content is increased, the deposition rate decreases. The tungsten content increases up to a maximum of 18·7% at 40gm/l and tails off with further increases.

Table 10.1

Effect of Citrate Concentration on Electroless Nickel-Tungsten Deposition

Citrate Conc. gm/l	Deposit Wt mgm	Tungsten Content %
10	327	5·9
20	257	13·0
40	113	18·7
80	66	15·5
160	48	5·6

As this was an interim report, no further information is available regarding physical and chemical properties of the deposit.

Arsenic-Zinc

Very little commercial use seems to have been made of this bath. The method of operation is similar to electroless nickel. It does not appear to be possible to increase thicknesses above 0·0001 inch so one may regard it as chemical deposition as opposed to electroless deposition. The process seems to have been used on metal substrates only, principally aluminium, which obviates the well known zincate treatment. West[6] recommends the following:—

Sodium hypophosphite	50 gm/l
Sodium citrate	50 gm/l
Zinc sulphate	25 gm/l
Arsenic trioxide	25 gm/l
Sodium hydroxide	6·25 gm/l
Ammonium hydroxide	50 ml/l
Sodium cyanide	50 gm/l
Temperature	82-88°C
pH (adjusted with NH₄OH)	11·5
Rate of deposition	0·1 mil/hour (maximum obtainable)

Vanadium Alloys

Eisenberg and Raleigh[7, 8] report on the successful deposition of vanadium alloys, the alloying metal being a member of the group comprising Fe, Ni, Co and Cr. The intention, initially, was to deposit vanadium itself, but in this they were unsuccessful because of the high activity of the metal which resulted in the deposition of the oxide only. It is postulated that it may be successfully deposited from non-aqueous solutions.

When vanadium is co-deposited with Ni, Co or Cr an acidic or basic solution may be used, whereas when Fe is the alloying metal a basic solution must be used.

Typical examples:—

Chromic fluoride, nonohydrate	32 gm/l
Chromic chloride, hexahydrate	1 gm/l
Sodium acetate	10 gm/l
Sodium hypophosphite	10 gm/l
Potassium oxalate, monohydrate	50 gm/l
Sodium metavanadate	5 gm/l
pH	4-6
Temperature	75-90°C
Rate of deposition	0·3 mil/hour
Composition of alloy	Cr 80%, V 20%

Nickel sulphate, heptahydrate	30 gm/l
Sodium acetate	10 gm/l
Sodium hypophosphite	10 gm/l
Potassium oxalate, monohydrate	50 gm/l
Sodium metavanadate	5 gm/l
pH	4-6
Temperature	75-90°C
Composition of alloy	Ni 85%, V 15%

Cobalt chloride, dihydrate	45 gm/l
Sodium hypophosphite	20 gm/l
Sodium citrate	50 gm/l
Sodium metavanadate	5 gm/l
Sodium oxalate, monohydrate	20 gm/l
pH	4-6
Temperature	75-90°C
Composition of alloy	Co 90%, V 10%

In every case the substrate used was either steel or nickel.

REFERENCES

1 West H. J., *Metal Finish.*, **53**, 7, 62 (1955).
2 Eisenberg P. H., Raleigh D. O., U.S. Pat., 2, 829, 059 (1958).
3 West H. J., *Products Finish.*, **26**, 4, 58 (1962).
4 Cann L., U.S. Pat., 3, 178, 311 (1965).
5 Pearlstein F., Weightman R., Wick R., *Metal Finish.*, **61**, 11, 77 (1963).
6 West H. J., *Metal Finish.*, **55**, 1, 56 (1957).
7 Eisenberg P. H., Raleigh D. O., U.S. Pat., 2, 828, 227 (1958).
8 Eisenberg P. H., Raleigh D. O., U.S. Pat., 2, 827, 400 (1958).

CHAPTER 11

AEROSOL DEPOSITION

An alternative method to depositing metals by chemical reduction using immersion processes is to spray the reactants so that when the solutions impinge on the surface a metallic film is formed by their interaction. The reducing agent and the metal ions are kept separate until metallisation occurs so that decomposition is not possible when not in use. The apparatus normally used for carrying out this process consists of a gun, although air "brushes" have been employed and aerosol cans containing the fluoro-halogen refrigerants for small scale and laboratory work have been reported[1, 2] (plates 11.1, 11.2 and 11.3 illustrate the different types of equipment employed).

The conditions which favour spraying should, in effect, be the opposite of that required for immersion processes, that is instability. The more unstable the solutions are on interaction, the easier deposition should be. Weak complexing agents, powerful reducing agents and high absolute concentrations are advantageous. Other factors which facilitate high plating rates in immersion solutions and hence decomposition, such as increased temperatures, also favour spraying techniques. A compromise is normally made. The choice of specific reactants and concentrations is selected to obtain maximum efficiency and a deposit which is qualitatively sound.

Background

The first successful effort in this direction was accomplished by Barnes[3] as far back as 1898 when he devised a spraying technique for silvering incandescent lamps. In his patent he mentions that various attempts had previously been made along these lines by other investigators, but that they had proved unsuccessful for a number of reasons. Among the initial difficulties encountered was the blocking of the jets and nozzle by metallic silver, caused by the rapid reduction of silver to the metallic state. Although one claim in this patent refers to a " gravitational" method, a second method is disclosed wherein compressed air is used to effectively spray the reactants. This, in all probability, is the first use of compressed air to atomise the reactants in chemical deposition techniques.

131

Plate 11.1 Commercial double-head sprayer with siphon cups used to deposit gold on open-weave fabric for unfurlable spacecraft antenna. [Levy]

Plate 11.2 Air-brush type of sprayer depositing gold. [Levy]

Plate 11.3 Liquid propellant sprayers aspirate plating solutions for small experiments. [Levy]

Plate 11.4 Astronaut's visor exhibits specular reflectivity. [Levy]

In 1926[4] Bart disclosed a method for spray silvering on to glass moulds. Compressed air was used to atomise the solutions, tartaric acid being employed as the reductant in this instance.

Andres,[5] in 1934, described a method for applying gold by spraying techniques which was probably the first successful attempt to deposit gold by this means. This was followed shortly after by methods proposed by Schneider[6] for the deposition of gold, copper and lead. The deposition of a satisfactory metallic film of lead with the solutions he disclosed however, is extremely doubtful.

The first full scale commercial operation did not take place until 1940. This was developed by Peacock[7] and largely superseded the immersion techniques employed at the time in mirror manufacture.

Up until this time, the majority of the work involved the manufacture of mirrors, consequently silver was the metal predominantly investigated. Within recent years, the advantages offered by this technique have resulted in other metals being examined which can be deposited by chemical means. So far, chemically deposited gold,[2,8,9,10,11] has been successfully commercialised. A method published by the writer[12] for copper is currently being used on an industrial scale for depositing the initial conducting film in the production of "built up" printed circuits. In this case silver is unacceptable because of possible migratory effects. Nickel[12,13] has been reported in the literature but has not yet been used on any commercial scale. The successful deposition of platinum and palladium[14] has recently been announced.

Advantages and Disadvantages of Aerosol Deposition
Advantages
Speed

A conducting film may be formed much more rapidly by aerosol deposition. The time taken is dependent on the area to be metallised, whereas with immersion techniques it is independent of area. As a rough guide, using aerosol techniques, an average sized printed circuit board measuring 5in × 4in will take about 20 to 30 seconds to form a satisfactory conducting film, but will take anything from 4 to 30 minutes using the immersion processes currently available.

Efficiency

Under properly controlled conditions and choice of reactant concentrations, 100% efficiency can be obtained in specific cases resulting in no wastage of expensive metallic salts or an additional cost of reclamation. In order to achieve adequate deposition rates, some efficiency may have to be sacrificed.

Stability

Since the reducing solution is separated from the metal ions until metallisation occurs, there is no danger of decomposition taking place.

133

Although this was a valid point at one time and still is for silver, immersion solutions nowadays can be controlled to give a reasonably long life, so this point now assumes less importance.

Adaptability

The technique is portable, allowing for the metallising of very large objects such as reflectors which could not be carried out satisfactorily by other means.

Contamination

Since a number of plastics are susceptible to the ingress of moisture, the speedy deposition of a metallic film will act as a barrier to prevent this. As the substrate is only in contact with the solution for a short period, the risk of contamination is reduced. Furthermore, any leaching of impurities to the solution can be an embarrassment with immersion solutions.

Disadvantages

Economics

When aerosol deposition was introduced into the mirror industry, a significant reduction in processing costs was claimed.[1] This amounted to about 20%. As this estimate was compared against the "homogeneous" deposition of silver, the comparison is not valid when using autocatalytic plating techniques. In general, aerosol plating is more expensive than the equivalent electroless technique.

Configuration

Irregular shaped objects, particularly fine bore tubes, are much better processed by immersion techniques. Although the use of aerosol techniques is limited to geometric configurations which are not too complex, it is, nevertheless, a more versatile process than, for example, vacuum evaporation.

Atomisers

Atomisers are primarily designed to cause a liquid to accelerate and disintegrate as quickly as possible in a controlled manner and to direct the resultant particles in a preferred direction. They are normally classified according to the source of energy employed to effect atomisation. Various sub-headings within each classification exist but these are not discussed here since they are beyond the scope of the work.

1 Centrifugal
2 Pressure (otherwise known as hydraulic, airless, mechanical)
3 Gaseous (pneumatic, air, steam)

Fundamentally there is no difference in the basic mechanism of atomisation by the above methods. Pneumatic (compressed air) is the technique usually adopted because of its overall effectiveness, although liquid pressure (hydraulic) is employed in particular cases.

Hydraulic

The main disadvantage that this technique suffers from is that the flow rate is low since it varies with the square root of the pressure. Higher flow rates can be achieved by increasing the size of the orifice but this results in an increased droplet size as well. Droplet size is relatively large and as plating efficiency is improved by a decrease in the droplet size, the overall result is that plating efficiency is not particularly good. If a small droplet size is to be obtained by this process, very fine orifices are essential and there are innumerable complications in their production. A further disadvantage is that erosion of the orifices presents a severe engineering problem. This technique is therefore only resorted to when pneumatic means cannot be employed, such as the spraying of hot solutions which cannot be satisfactorily carried out due to the cooling effect of the compressed air, or reducing solutions are used which are very easily oxidised by the flow of air.

Pneumatic

This is the most satisfactory method in existence at present for producing fine sprays and is particularly attractive because fairly large orifices can be used. The mean diameter of the particles may be as small as 10 to 20 microns but they lack uniformity, a characteristic which is not so evident in the two techniques previously described. If uniformity could be improved, plating efficiency would increase. Although the overall plating efficiency is very high due to the relatively small droplet size, there is a finite optimum drop size for maximum efficiency. When this is reached, efficiency decreases with decreasing droplet size.

The guns used in pneumatic atomisation of liquids are available with various modifications. For example, mixing of the solutions may take place internally or externally. The former has certain disadvantages in that precipitation of the metal may occur inside the gun, since the reaction takes place on mixing. Consequently the orifices become blocked and have to be cleaned.

Single, double and treble nozzle guns may be used. When three solutions have to be sprayed, Y-tube connections may be utilised on single or dual nozzle guns and be reasonably effective in segregating solutions until commencement of spraying.

Stainless steel is normally used in the construction of the gun although plastic parts may be incorporated where necessary.

Liquified Propellents

An aerosol pack contains the solution together with a liquified propellent gas under pressure; the latter is normally of the fluorinated hydrocarbon family, such as Freon or Arcton. The free space is saturated with the vapour of the propellent, which on release of the valve ejects a stream of liquid from the orifice. On leaving the orifice, the reduction in pressure obtained on reaching the atmosphere causes the gas to vaporise. This is so rapid that the liquid stream is broken up, or atomised, resulting in fine droplets of solution being propelled towards the substrate in a stream of vapour.

When heated slightly, aerosols become more efficient since a rise in temperature increases the kinetic energy of the molecules in the enclosed space, which results in a greater pressure being exerted when equilibrium is attained between the vapour and liquid. Overheating should be avoided as the consequences could be dangerous.

Compatibility of the solution and propellent, and the solution and container should be investigated prior to their use.

Advantages and Disadvantages of Liquid Propellents

Advantages
1 Portability makes it extremely useful for small scale laboratory work.
2 Cleaning of equipment is unnecessary.

Disadvantages
1 The use of aerosols is not a cheap method of producing a metallic film.
2 Since a maximum flow rate of only about 30ml/min is obtainable, this imposes a restriction on the technique for production purposes.
3 Container is not refillable.
4 Mechanical failure can render the contents useless.
5 Intermittent spraying can only be carried out. Continuous use may result in a momentary reduction in pressure, since the gas inside the container must vaporise during spraying to replace the volume vacated by the liquid and so continue to exert a pressure on the surface of the remaining liquid.

Factors Influencing Atomisation
The general purpose of spraying is to increase the surface area of a mass of liquid and direct it towards the substrate and to speed up a chemical reaction. In order to design suitable equipment to administer this technique the fundamentals of fluid kinetics of rapidly moving liquid jets and their subsequent disintegration should be understood by the designer. They are discussed briefly in the following paragraphs.

Atomisers
The source of energy used for atomisation, which has already been discussed, and the design of the atomiser contribute directly to the efficiency of the process. As the droplet size decreases, the greater the area that the same volume of liquid will cover, hence the greater the efficiency because of the better chemical interaction of the particles. Smaller droplet size is not only accomplished by selecting the appropriate energy source but in the choice of orifice diameter, the smaller the diameter the smaller the droplet size.

Effect of Liquid Properties (Physical)
The properties which exert most influence in atomisation processes are (1) surface tension and (2) viscosity. Surface tension tends to resist the

formation of new surfaces as does viscosity. During the final stages of disintegration, viscosity will oppose surface tension unless the viscosity is very low. As aqueous solutions are normally used, this point is not pertinent. It is difficult to achieve a small droplet size with low viscosity liquids when hydraulic methods are employed.

Although low concentrations of surfactants usually improve the wetting of substrates, it is inadvisable to use excessive amounts of wetting agents to lower the surface tension of the liquid since the physical properties of the deposited film are frequently affected. Interference with the optical properties may also be encountered.

Effect of Flow Rate

Liquid flow rate affects the process of atomisation considerably. High flow rates increase the rate of deposition, but only at the expense of plating efficiency. This is due to the formation of a large droplet size, resulting in ineffective mixing and retardation of the chemical reaction.

In pneumatic atomisation the ratio of rate of air flow to rate of liquid flow is important and should be high to achieve a low particle size.

The principles of atomisation are exceedingly complex but the more pertinent points raised above will give the reader a general insight into what is involved.

Silver

More work has been carried out on the aerosol deposition of silver than on any other metal. This, of course, is understandable since in the past the incentive to deposit other metals was absent. Again, with silver, we come across the empirical approach to the subject, only one paper[15] of consequence appearing wherein the relevant parameters were studied. As the conclusions drawn in this paper have been verified by Levy in his intensive investigations into gold,[1,2] spray parameters are later discussed as a separate entity. As the choice of metal salt is limited to silver nitrate, most of the inventors have investigated reducing agents. Complexing agents have received scant attention, ammonia normally being used. Addition agents have been given some attention but this has mainly been pertinent to "mirror" manufacture.

Reducing Agents

A number of reducing agents have been used in aerosol deposition techniques such as aldehydes (formaldehyde,[6,15] glyoxal[16]), hydrazine,[17] its salts[18,19,20] and derivatives[21] (β hydroxy ethyl hydrazine),[22] triethanolamine and mixtures of reducing agents (glyoxal and triethanolamine).[23] Normally, fairly strong reducing agents are used to effect quick reduction. Hydrazine is sometimes preferred to formaldehyde because of the rather unpleasant odour of the latter. There is some support for using glyoxal, since a more stable solution is formed which lasts indefinitely. It is not particularly odorous and is less toxic than other reducing solutions which are sometimes employed.

Essentially pure silver is deposited by this technique and it is doubtful whether a great deal of difference is caused by the reductant used. Economics and reduction of the explosion hazard appear to be the main factors of concern, although the latter can be overcome by the correct choice of spraying equipment and the conditions adopted.

Typical Solutions

One of the original solutions used in aerosol deposition of silver was patented by Schneider.[6]

Solution "A"	Silver nitrate	3·6 gm/l
Solution "B"	Formaldehyde	61 ml/l

The Peacock formula,[17] which was to become accepted in the mirror industry, used a solution of ammoniacal silver nitrate and hydrazine as the reducing agent. It was a known fact at this time that the presence of an alkali hydroxide accelerated the reaction (Brashear 1890);[24] this was probably due to the reducing agent being more effective in a higher pH range. It was also known that this increased the possibility of explosion. Consequently, the alkali hydroxide used was always segregated from the ammoniacal silver nitrate until mixing took place on spraying. In some cases, the rate of deposition was fast enough to exclude the accelerator and hence reduce the danger of explosions taking place.

Solution "A"	Silver nitrate	10 gm/l
	Ammonium hydroxide	17·5 ml/l
Solution "B"	Hydrazine hydrate	20 gm/l
	5 gm/l of sodium hydroxide may be added to solution "B".	

Glyoxal as a reducing agent has been suggested by Peacock[16] as a more efficient reductant than hydrazine or hydroxylamine and their salts. As a result, accelerators can be omitted and a safer process is obtained. Furthermore, less reductant is required and being neutral, less ammonium hydroxide is required. A saving in material is therefore obtained.

Solution "A"	Silver nitrate	22·5 gm/l
	Ammonium hydroxide	16·8 ml/l
Solution "B"	Glyoxal	15 gm/l

Kantrowitz and collaborators,[23] recommend the use of a synergistic reducing solution utilising both glyoxal and triethanolamine. This is in considerable use today and is recommended by Narcus.[25]

Solution "A"	Silver nitrate	19 gm/l
	Ammonium hydroxide—to dissolve initial precipitate	
Solution "B"	Glyoxal	7·5 gm/l
	Triethanolamine	6 gm/l

Efforts have been made in other directions to eliminate the explosion hazards by modifying the gun. One such modification[26] was a plurality of nozzles. In each container which is attached independently to its nozzle, the following three solutions are used:—

Solution "A"	Ammoniacal silver nitrate	0·04 M
Solution "B"	Formaldehyde	0·02 M
Solution "C"	Sodium hydroxide	0·01 M

Table 11.1

Various Formulae used in Aerosol Deposition of Silver

Solution "A"		Solution "B"		Reference
$AgNO_3$	25 gm/l	$N_2H_4.H_2SO_4$	12 gm/l	Trevail & Gladney[18]
NH_4OH	20 ml/l	$MgSO_4$	3 gm/l	
$AgNO_3$ (ammon.)	12 gm/l	$N_2H_4.H_2SO_4$	7 gm/l	Milton et al[19]
Triton N-100	1 gm/l	NH_4OH	4 gm/l	
		Triton N-100	1 gm/l	
$AgNO_3$	10 gm/l	N_2H_4	20 gm/l	Peacock[17]
NH_4OH	17·5 ml/l			
$AgNO_3$	10 gm/l	$N_2H_4. H_2O$	20 gm/l	Peacock[17]
NH_4OH	17·5 ml/l	NaOH	5 gm/l	
$AgNO_3$ (ammon.)	7 gm/l	Monohydrazine tartrate	10 gm/l	Owen[27]
$AgNO_3$	25 gm/l	β Hydroxyethyl hydrazine	10 gm/l	Millard[22]
NH_4OH	63 ml/l			
$AgNO_3$	23 gm/l	$NH_2OH.H_2SO_4$	27 gm/l	Peacock[21]
NH_4OH	23 ml/l	NH_4OH	10 ml/l	
$AgNO_3$	3·6 gm/l	HCHO	61 ml/l	Schneider[6]
$AgNO_3$ (ammon.)	20 gm/l	HCHO	74 ml/l	Upton[15]
$AgNO_3$	22·5 gm/l	CHO·CHO	15 gm/l	Peacock[16]
NH_4OH	16·8 ml/l			
$AgNO_3$	25 gm/l	$N_2H_4.H_2SO_4$	12·5 gm/l	Petijean[20]
NH_4OH	56 ml/l	$MgSO_4$	3·1 gm/l	
$AgNO_3$ (ammon.)	19 gm/l	CHO·CHO	7·5 gm/l	Kantrowitz et al[23]
		$(HOCH_2CH_2)_3N$	6 gm/l	

Where "ammoniacal" (ammon.) is used this means that the original precipitate formed is just dissolved in ammonium hydroxide. In all cases, equal volumes of "A" and "B" are used with the exception of Owen where 4 parts of "A" to 1 part "B" is used.

Gold

Gold has many outstanding properties, the most important of which are its (1) high electrical conductivity, (2) high infra-red reflectance and ultra-violet absorption which make it useful for thermal control applications since it is classified as a solar absorber. It also finds use in optical control applications, particularly as visible light may be transmitted through thin transparent films. The remaining property (3) is that of its high degree of chemical inertness which supports the applications in which it is used.

Because of the characteristics exhibited by gold, it is a considerable asset in the field of space research. As many of the applications involved are large, it is more suitable to deposit the metal by spraying techniques rather than by immersion processes since objects up to 300 sq. ft. (assembled from panels of up to 50 sq. ft.) have been plated.[1,8]

A considerable amount of work has been carried out on the spray parameters of this process. As the variables recorded by Upton[15] have been verified by Levy[1,2] for gold, spray parameters are discussed separately.

Typical Solutions

Prior to the published work by Levy on aerosol gold solutions, only two references have been uncovered pertaining to the deposition of this metal. Andres[5] suggests the following formulation:—

Solution "A"	Gold chloride	25 gm/l
	Sodium carbonate	25 gm/l
Solution "B"	Formaldehyde	40 gm/l
	Sodium carbonate	40 gm/l

Later the following solutions were proposed by Schneider[6]:—

Solution "A"	Gold chloride	75 gm/l
Solution "B"	Glycerine	500 ml/l
	Sodium hydroxide	50 gm/l
	Mannitol	trace

Nothing further materialised for the next 25 years until the recently published work of Levy. As a result solutions are now available commercially under the trade name "Lockspray-Gold".* The deposited metal has a purity of 99·99% and a resistivity of 2·4μ ohm-cm, similar to that of bulk gold. Grain size is between 20 and 50Å. The process is carried out at room temperature and, as the efficiency is about 60%, it is desirable to collect and reclaim the gold from the spent solution.

A patent[28] recently assigned to Lockheed Aircraft Corporation describes the use of hydrazine as a reducing agent in aerosol gold plating. The source of metal ions is a soluble gold salt such as the chloride or bromide, and this is complexed with a suitable complexing agent like ammonium carbonate, ammonium hydroxide, or an aliphatic amine. Ethylenediamine is preferred.

---

* Lockspray-Gold distributors in U.S.A.—Enthone Inc., Newhaven, Mass.

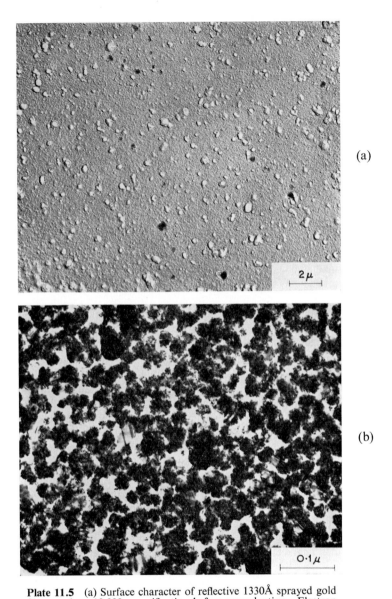

(a)

(b)

Plate 11.5 (a) Surface character of reflective 1330Å sprayed gold film on glass, 12,000 magnification before reproduction. Electron transmission micrograph of replica preshadowed in two stages with chromium and then carbon. Most of the surface is extremely smooth. Some nodules, about 2,000Å in diameter, are visible.

(b) Electron transmission micrograph of initial discontinuous gold deposit (about 200Å) on glass, 400,000 magnification before reproduction. Gold appears to be clusters of particles about 20-50Å in diameter, with occasional well developed crystals, some as large as 300Å. Newly formed particles adhere to one another. [Levy]

A typical solution is:—

Solution "A"	Gold chloride (0·2 M)	50 ml/l
	Ethylenediamine	1·5 ml/l
Solution "B"	Hydrazine (20 M)	100 ml/l
	Sodium hydroxide (1 M)	50 ml/l

The solutions are sprayed simultaneously at room temperature, the pH of the resultant solution being between 6 and 8.

Preparation of Solutions

Solution "A"

(1) 50 ml of 0·2 molar gold chloride are added to 700 ml of water and neutralised with a solution of sodium hydroxide.

(2) 1·5 ml of ethylenediamine are added to 50 ml of water and neutralised with hydrochloric acid.

Solution (1) is added to solution (2) and thoroughly mixed after dilution to 1 litre with water.

Solution "B"

The reducing solution is prepared by mixing 50 ml of 1 molar sodium hydroxide with 100 ml of 20 molar hydrazine and then diluting to 1 litre with water.

Applications

Optical Control

Thin gold films are used on "optical" plastics since they reflect eye damaging infra-red radiation, absorb ultra-violet and allow good transmission in the visible spectrum. A typical application (plate 11.4) is a sunshade visor worn by astronauts. By codepositing other metals with gold, transparent optical films may be selected on the basis of their transmission spectra. Applications envisaged[29] include eye protective filters with normal colour response and solar filters for optimising plant growth systems.

Thermal Control

One of the outstanding properties possessed by gold is that of its excellent heat reflecting power. Polished gold will reflect 97% of the incident infra-red radiation which is the highest reflecting surface of any metal. It is therefore used in thermal control applications. One such application is a thin gold film deposited on both sides of a lightweight plastic heat shield that insulates a subliming solid attitude control rocket motor in satellites.

Antennas

Synthetic fibres have been plated with thin gold films to make lightweight high reliability unfurlable antennas. (plate 11.1)

Factors Influencing Aerosol Deposition
Rate of Film Formation

Following an initial rapid rate of formation, it drops off somewhat and proceeds to increase linearly with time (fig. 11.1 & 11.2). This initial rapid reaction is attributed to the reducing action of the stannous ion prior to metallising.

Effect of Spraying Distance

Increasing the distance between the nozzle and substrate being metallised using a single nozzle gun, results in a decrease in deposition rate (fig. 11.3). A reduction in efficiency is also obtained (table 11.2). This is probably caused by a homogeneous action taking place before the metal reaches the substrate and is due to the design of the gun.

Table 11.2

The Effect of Spraying Distance on Efficiency

Spraying Distance inches	Efficiency %
3	32·8
6	30·7
12	28·7
15	27·7
18	23·6
21	19·7
24	18·3

Where dual nozzle spraying apparatus is used with intersecting sprays, the deposition rate and efficiency are at a maximum when the substrate is located in the zone of mixing of the two reactants. At greater distances efficiency decreases, homogeneous reaction taking place prior to the metal reaching the substrate. At shorter distances the two sprays do not mix before reaching the substrate, hence there is a sharp decrease in the amount of metal deposited.

Effect of Liquid Flow Rate

When the liquid flow rate increases, the plating rate increases. In fact it increases proportionately according to the square root of the liquid flow rate. Efficiency declines as flow rate is increased (fig. 11.4). This is because the liquid droplet size becomes larger and results in poorer mixing.

Effect of Concentration

As would be expected, the rate of deposition increases with increased concentrations. However, efficiency decreases (fig. 11.5 & 11.6). An interesting feature of fig. 11.6 is that 100% efficiency is almost obtained at low concentrations.

Air Pressure

An increase in the air pressure means that air velocity and air flow also increase which results in an improvement in the rate of deposition (fig.11.7), assuming liquid flow rate remaining constant. This is because

143

6

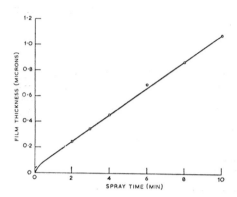

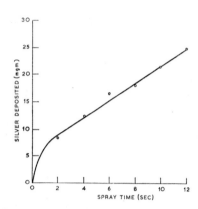

Fig. 11.1 Effect of plating time on deposition rate of gold. A glass plate, 5 cm² was sensitised in stannous chloride prior to spraying with a 0·0187 molar gold solution and a reducing agent using a dual nozzle sprayer. (Binks 181 SS) Liquid flow rate 22 ml/min; spraying distance 10 in. [Levy and Delgado]

Fig. 11.2 Effect of plating time on deposition rate of silver. Glass plates, 2 dm² were sensitised with stannous chloride prior to spraying with a 2% silver nitrate (ammoniacal) and 3% formaldehyde solution using a single nozzle sprayer (P.A.T.R.A. gun). Liquid flow rate 95 mil/min; pressure 24 p.s.i.; air flow 10 c.f.m.; spraying distance 20 in. [Upton et al]

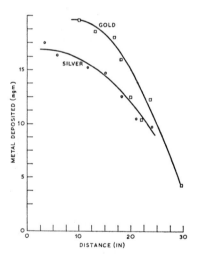

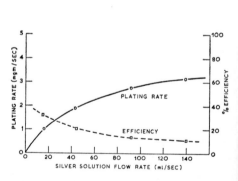

Fig. 11.3 Effect of substrate—nozzle distance on the amount of metal deposited. Silver solutions sprayed at 50 mil/min from a single nozzle gun for 5 sec. Conditions otherwise identical to fig. 11.2. Gold solutions sprayed at 50 mil/min from dual nozzle gun with sprays mixing at 10 in distance. [Silver—Upton et al; Gold—Levy]

Fig. 11.4 Effect of liquid flow rate on plating rate and efficiency. Spraying distance 24 in; spraying time 4 sec. Conditions otherwise the same as in fig. 11.2. [Upton et al]

144

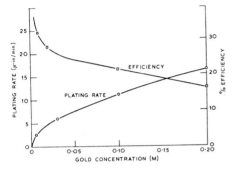

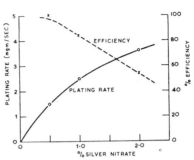

Fig. 11.5 Effect of gold ion concentration on plating rate. Conditions of spraying similar to that of fig. 11.1. The plating rate increases with the concentration of gold in the plating solution. Non-linearity indicates a decrease in plating efficiency which is highest in very low metal concentrations. [Levy and Delgado]

Fig. 11.6 Effect of silver salt concentration on plating rates and efficiency. Spraying distance 12 in.; spraying time 5 sec; liquid flow rate 28 ml/min. Other conditions as outlined in fig. 11.2. [Upton et al]

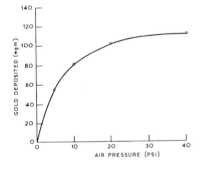

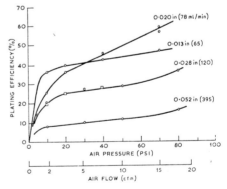

Fig. 11.7 Effect of air pressure on gold deposition. Increasing air pressure breaks the liquid stream into smaller droplets. The resultant improved mixing of reactants increases efficiency of deposition. Spraying conditions were 70 ml/min at 10 in distance using sensitised plates. Air flow is 9 s.c.f.m. at 50 p.s.i. [Levy]

Fig. 11.8 The highest plating efficiency is achieved with a high air flow rate and a small liquid orifice. Liquid flow rate and orifice diameter are indicated. [Levy and Delgado]

145

droplet size decreases and better mixing of the solutions takes place. The mass ratio, air flow/liquid flow, should be high, the higher the ratio the greater the efficiency, this being due to decreasing droplet size. Droplet size plays an important role in aerosol deposition. When hydraulic means are used, a smaller droplet size is obtained by using higher liquid pressures.

It has already been mentioned that orifice diameter influences atomisation considerably. The relationship between this and air pressure, flow and liquid flow is important.

In fig. 11.8, the effect of air pressure on plating efficiency is shown together with the effect of decreasing the orifice diameter. It can be seen that a minimum air pressure of about 20 p.s.i. is required to effect good atomisation with the type of nozzle employed.

Copper

The spraying of copper has not achieved any significant commercial success as yet. This may be due to a number of reasons, such as the limited amount of published literature on the subject and the fact that small intricate shapes are better accommodated using immersion techniques. As immersion processes become more and more stable, the cost differential will increasingly favour immersion techniques.

Hydrosulphites are used in one process[30] as the reducing solution, sodium nitrate being present as a stabiliser.

Solution "A"	Sodium cyanide	7·5 gm/l
	Cuprous cyanide	10·0 gm/l
	Sodium lauryl sulphate	0.86 gm/l
Solution "B"	Sodium hydroxide	6·7 gm/l
	Sodium hydrosulphite	25·0 gm/l
	Sodium nitrite	8·1 gm/l

The process may be carried out within a wide range of temperatures. At 20°C, the plastic should be sensitised previously with stannous chloride followed by activation with silver nitrate. Both solutions can be administered by spraying. Rinsing with water should be omitted between activation and metallising.

Sensitising solution	Stannous chloride	2-10 gm/l
	Sodium lauryl sulphate	0·5-2 gm/l
Activating solution	Silver nitrate	2-10 gm/l
	Sodium lauryl sulphate	0·5-2 gm/l

When the process is carried out with the temperature of the solutions at 60°C, the sensitiser may be omitted. Suggested pressure is 12 p.s.i. Equal volumes of solution should be used. No deposition rates are given.

Preparation of Solution

Solutions "A" and "B" may be made up as concentrates and diluted when they are to be used.

To prepare solution "A", dissolve the required amount of NaCN in water and heat to between 82 and 93°C. Slowly add the cuprous cyanide. Initially the solution is clear with a residue of undissolved Cu_2CN_2 lying at the bottom. On standing, the solution turns a clear blue but still has a residue. This colour is probably caused by the formation of the complex $Na[CuCN_2]$, the complexed state being the only one in which a soluble cuprous salt is stable. If an excess of NaCN is added, above the molar ratio 2.89:1, copper cannot be reduced because the complex is so stable. If a chelating agent from the diamine family is added, the residue dissolves and the solution forms a deep blue colour without losing its ability to be reduced.

Another method using hydrosulphite as the reducing agent is put forward by Swanson.[31] The compound used as the source of metal ions is cupric acetate. The reaction which takes place may be expressed as follows:—

$$Cu^{++} + S_2O_4^{--} + 2H_2O \rightarrow Cu^\circ + 2HSO_3^- + 2H^+$$

$$Cu(CH_3COO)_2 + Na_2S_2O_4 + 2H_2O \rightarrow Cu^\circ + 2NaHSO_3 + 2CH_3COOH$$

Solutions used in the process are:—

Solution "A"	Cupric acetate	20 gm/l
	Triton X-114	0·22 gm/l
Solution "B"	Sodium hydrosulphite	27·7 gm/l
	Sodium hydroxide	1·78 gm/l

As the hydrosulphite tends to be oxidised rather easily, certain precautions are taken. First of all hydraulic atomisation is preferred to pneumatic. In the latter case, an 18·7% loss of available hydrosulphite was encountered as opposed to a 4·7% loss in the former. However, this can be balanced by making an allowance loss, increasing the hydrosulphite concentration to 31·1 gm/l. Secondly, the surface of the reservoir containing the reducing agent should have a layer of toluene superimposed on it to prevent oxidation. If left unprotected, the available hydrosulphite is reduced to almost zero within a day, whereas only about a 5% reduction is obtained during this period when protected.

Parameters

Raising the pH above 11·4 results in increasing brightness of the deposit and in an increase in its conductivity until a pH of 11·65 is reached which corresponds to a concentration of 1·78 gm/l of NaOH. Any further increase beyond this figure results in a decrease in conductivity although the deposit continues to get brighter. The optimum pH to obtain a deposit of the lowest resistivity is 11·62 to 11·65 which is equivalent to a sodium hydroxide concentration of 1·55 to 1·78 gm/l. Although the film obtained under these conditions is suitable for subsequent electroplating, the resistance is of a fairly high order which suggests the presence of impurities and/or a granular structure.

Cupric Acetate

Increasing the concentration of cupric acetate improves the electrical conductivity considerably. Although the resistance decreases with increasing metal ion concentration, the law of diminishing returns appears.

Sodium Hydrosulphite

Increasing the concentration of hydrosulphite also improves the conductivity of the film. The concentration like the cupric acetate is not critical.

A further method[32] is based on the theory that aqueous solutions of cuprous salts are stable only when suitably complexed and if the complex cuprous salt is rendered acidic, metallic copper is deposited and a soluble cupric salt formed by disproportionation.

$$Cu_2O + 2NH_4^+ + 2NH_3 \rightarrow 2[Cu(NH_3)_2]^+ + H_2O$$

$$[Cu(NH_3)_2]^+ + 2H^+ \rightarrow Cu^+ + 2NH_4^+$$

$$2\,Cu^+ \rightarrow Cu^{++} + Cu^\circ$$

Solution "A"	Cuprous oxide	10 gm/l
	Ammonium sulphate	30 gm/l
	Ammonium hydroxide	25 ml/l
Solution "B"	Sulphuric acid	5 gm/l

The solution of the complex "A" should flow at a rate of 160 ml/min/ft^2 to be processed and "B" at the rate of 200 ml/min/ft^2 to be processed.

About the earliest attempt to deposit copper by spraying techniques is attributed to Schneider.[6] In his patent covering the deposition of silver, he briefly refers to the successful deposition of copper using 20 to 50% hydrazine hydrate as the reductant and a diluted solution of copper sulphate. No further details are given.

The use of hydrazine as a reducing agent for aerosol copper deposition has been reported by Momyer and Levy.[33] The effect of reactant species and concentrations on reaction kinetics and film resistivity have been examined. The overall reaction may be represented as:—

$$2Cu^{++} + N_2H_4 + 4OH^- \rightarrow 2Cu + N_2 + 4H_2O \tag{1}$$

As the reaction has been observed to proceed through a soluble cuprous state, it is somewhat more complex than that illustrated above. The suggested mechanism is therefore better represented by the following sequence of equations:—

$$2Cu^{++} + xN_2H_4 \rightarrow 2Cu(N_2H_4)_x^{++} \tag{2}$$

$$2Cu(N_2H_4)_x^{++} + \tfrac{1}{2}N_2H_4 + 2OH^- \rightarrow 2Cu(N_2H_4)_x^+ + \tfrac{1}{2}N_2 + 2H_2O \tag{3}$$

$$2Cu(N_2H_4)_x^+ + \tfrac{1}{2}N_2H_4 + 2OH^- \rightarrow 2Cu + xN_2H_4 + \tfrac{1}{2}N_2 + 2H_2O \tag{4}$$

It may be seen that the plating rate is not only dependent on the activity of the hydrazine, hydroxyl ion and cupric ion as suggested by equation (1), but also on the rate of formation and reduction of the cupric and cuprous hydrazine complexes. In addition to this, the normal factors influencing atomisation also affect the rate of copper deposition.

Recommended solution is:—

Solution "A"	Cuprous acetate	0·17 M
Solution "B"	Hydrazine	15 M (in 0·35 M NaOH)

The solutions are sprayed simultaneously at room temperature (22°C) from a dual nozzle, atomising sprayer. Sensitising with stannous chloride and activation with silver nitrate is carried out prior to spraying. Although activation is not mandatory it reduces the initial time lag before the onset of constant plating rate from 15 to 10 seconds.

Relatively pure copper is deposited by this process, the film exhibiting a resistivity ($2 \cdot 0$ μ ohm-cm) of a little higher than that of bulk copper ($1 \cdot 7$ μ ohm-cm). Average plating rate is about $1 \cdot 25$ microns/min/4in^2 and deposits up to 6 microns have been produced.

Owen[27] uses monohydrazine tartrate as the reducing agent, as he does for the reduction of silver.

Solution "A"	Copper sulphate	10 gm/l
	Sodium potassium tartrate	45 gm/l
	Sodium hydroxide	17 gm/l
Solution "B"	Monohydrazine tartrate	5 gm/l

The solutions are heated to 40°C and applied for 1 to 2 minutes.

Three solutions for the deposition of copper have been suggested by Saubestre[34] and are listed below in order of preference. In each instance the solution is heated to 80°C.

Formula 1

Solution "A"	Copper sulphate, pentahydrate	35 gm/l
	Sulphuric acid (S.G. 1.84)	50 ml/l
Solution "B"	Sodium hypophosphite	500 gm/l
	Ratio of A:B used for spraying 2:1	

Formula 2

Solution "A"	Copper sulphate, pentahydrate	35 gm/l
	Sulphuric acid (S.G. 1.84)	50 ml/l
Solution "B"	Sodium hydrosulphite	100 gm/l
	Ratio of A:B used for spraying 2:1	

Formula 3

Solution "A"	Sodium potassium tartrate, tetrahydrate	170 gm/l
	Sodium hydroxide	50 gm/l
	Copper sulphate	35 gm/l
Solution "B"	Hydrazine sulphate	20 gm/l
	Ratio of A:B used for spraying 10:1	

It will be seen that in formula 1, hypophosphite is used in acid solution to make the most of its reducing power. In the second formulation, hydrosulphites are again used. In both cases it may be seen that the copper is present in the free state. All three solutions are powerful reducing agents, all having high concentrations.

A technique evolved by the writer[12] employs a catalyst. The principle of this method is identical to that used in immersion processes, where drag-out of the catalyst (activator) into the electroless solution initiates decomposition. As spray solutions are based on instability, a catalyst is sprayed simultaneously with the metal and reducing solution, resulting in the deposition of metallic copper on the surface. Ideally, the use of a three orifice gun connected to three separate containers would be desirable. However, the catalyst may be incorporated in the reducing solution if a one or two orifice gun is used.

Solution "A"	Copper sulphate, pentahydrate	80 gm/l
	Sodium potassium tartrate, tetrahydrate	80 gm/l
	Sodium hydroxide	80 gm/l
Solution "B"	Formaldehyde (37-41% w/v)	80 ml/l
	Palladium chloride 1% aq.	4 ml/l
	Hydrochloric acid conc.	2 ml/l.

The solution "B" is rendered acidic by adding a small amount of a mineral acid, preventing palladium chloride from being reduced slowly by the formaldehyde. Other noble metals may be used as a catalyst, success being obtained with platinic chloride and auric chloride. Formaldehyde may be replaced by other reducing agents such as hydrazine hydrate but in this case the catalyst is incorporated in the copper solution because of the rapid reduction of $PdCl_2 \rightarrow Pd°$ with hydrazine. In solution "A" complexing agents like ammonia can replace sodium potassium tartrate with hydrazine hydrate as the reducing agent. In this case sodium hydroxide can be omitted. The technique having proved to be successful on small production runs is now being used on a commercial scale for depositing the initial conducting film in "built-up" printed wiring techniques. Deposition rates are high, being about 0·03 mil/194 cm^2/20 sec.

It is felt that the incorporation of a catalyst is basically a good step. Nevertheless, there is room for considerable improvement. Factors which may be advantageous in improving the process are high temperatures, a stronger reducing agent and weaker complexes (preferably used in the acid range in the free state).

Another process using formaldehyde as the reducing agent is attributed to Maho.[35]

Solution "A"	Cuprous nitrate	60 gm/l
	Ammonium hydroxide (28%)	60 ml/l
Solution "B"	Formaldehyde (40% w/v)	65 ml/l

The same author uses a modification of this formula to deposit what is presumably an alloy of copper and silver. No details are given apart from the formula.

Solution "A"	Cuprous nitrate	20 gm/l
	Silver nitrate	40 gm/l
	Ammonium hydroxide	80 ml/l
Solution "B"	Formaldehyde (40% w/v)	65 ml/l

Nickel

A process for depositing nickel by a spraying technique has been disclosed by Carlson and Prymula.[13] This resembles very closely their process for depositing copper. Sodium hydrosulphite is again used as the reducing agent, but on this occasion it is supplemented by the presence of the hypophosphite ion.

Solution "A"	Nickel sulphate, hexahydrate	20 gm/l
	Citric acid	10 gm/l
Solution "B"	Sodium hydroxide	8 gm/l
	Sodium hydrosulphite	70 gm/l
	Sodium hypophosphite	10 gm/l

The solutions may be sprayed hot or cold. When used cold to spray plastics (15 to 38°C), the material is first sensitised in stannous chloride and activated in silver nitrate. The former may be omitted when used at higher temperatures. Since the reducing solution "B" decomposes at higher temperatures, a limiting temperature of 60°C is imposed. Solution "A" may be taken up to 80°C.

In an investigation by the present writer,[12] the following solutions were used:—

Solution "A"	Nickel sulphate
	Sodium citrate
	Ammonium hydroxide
Solution "B"	Sodium hypophosphite

In the experimental work carried out with this system, a phenolic substrate was heated to a temperature of 95°C before commencement of spraying. Although hot solutions were used, the effect of atomisation using compressed air resulted in a solution being sprayed which was only at room temperature. Initially a vigorous reaction took place as nickel was deposited on the substrate but due to the cooling effect of the sprayed solutions, the temperature of the phenolic dropped rapidly and deposition ceased at 65°C. The results exhibited during this short period were very encouraging, a deposition rate of 0·03 mil/194 cm^2/30 sec. being obtained. When the process was repeated, the thickness increased to 0·06 mil. The process was repeated four times in all, giving a final thickness of 0·12 mil/194 cm^2/2 min. This would indicate that if solution temperatures could be maintained, a continuous process with a high deposition rate would be developed.

REFERENCES

1   Levy D. J., *Proc. Am. Electropl. Soc.*, **51**, 139 (1964).
2   Levy D. J., Delgado E. F., *Plating*, **52**, 11, 1127 (1965).
3   Barnes A., Brit. Pat., 9, 977 (1899).
4   Bart B., U.S. Pat., 1, 583, 268 (1926).
5   Andres F. O., U.S. Pat., 1, 953, 330 (1934).
6   Schneider H., U.S. Pat., 2, 136, 024 (1938).
7   Peacock W., U.S. Pat., 2, 214, 476 (1940).
8   Lockspray-Gold Process, Technical Data Bulletin 6-76-66-9, Lockheed Missiles & Space Co., Palo Alto, California (1966).
9   Gomes G. S., Levy D. J., *Products Finish.*, **27**, 10, 36 (1963).
10 Levy D. J., " Materials for Space Vehicle Use," Vol. III, Soc. of Materials & Process Engineers Symposium, Seattle (1963).

11 Levy D. J., *Metal Finish J.*, **10**, 115, 157 (1964).
12 Goldie W., *Plating*, **51**, 11, 1069 (1964).
13 Carlson A. M., Prymula C. E., U.S. Pat., 2, 956, 900 (1960).
14 Levy D. J., private communication.
15 Upton P. B., Soundy G. W., Busby G. E., *J. Electrodep. tech. Soc.*, **28**, 103 (1952).
16 Peacock W., Brit. Pat., 538, 026 (1941).
17 Peacock W., U.S. Pat., 2, 214, 476 (1940).
18 Trevail C., Gladney K. P., U.S. Pat., 2, 367, 903 (1945).
19 Milton et al (Wein S., " Silver Films," PB 111236, OTS, U.S. Dept. Commerce, 1953).
20 Petijean T., Brit. Pat., 1, 681 (1855).
21 Peacock W., Brit. Pat., 537, 987 (1941).
22 Millard E. H., U.S. Pat., 2, 822, 289 (1958).
23 Kantrowitz M. S., Gosnell E. J., General B., U.S. Pat., 2, 602, 757 (1952).
24 Brashear H., *Eng. Mechanic*, **31**, 327 (1880).
25 Narcus H., " Metallising of Plastics," Reinhold, New York (1960).
26 New F. M., U.S. Pat., 3, 178, 118 (1965).
27 Owen J. T., U.S. Pat., 2, 801, 935 (1957).
28 Brit. Pat., 1, 027, 652 to Lockheed Aircraft Corp. (1966).
29 Levy D. J., Shellito K. K., " Gold Spray Process Solves Spacecraft Thermal Control Problems " (unpublished work).
30 Carlson A. M., Prymula C. E., U.S. Pat., 2, 936, 901 (1960).
31 Swanson D. W., U.S. Pat., 3, 122, 449 (1964).
32 Kay S. E., Ball R. J., Brit. Pat., 859, 448 (1961).
33 Momyer W. R., Levy D. J. (to be published).
34 Saubestre E. B., *Sylvania Technol.*, **12**, 1, 6 (1959).
35 Maho C. W., Brit. Pat., 861, 710 (1961).

PART III

OTHER METHODS OF PRODUCING THE METALLIC DEPOSIT

CHAPTER 12

VACUUM EVAPORATION

The mechanism of vacuum evaporation is simpler than that of cathode sputtering. It is essentially a system of evaporation and condensation. A metal is heated in a high vacuum (0·5 microns), at an applied temperature which exceeds the melting point of the metal being deposited until the vapour pressure is 10^{-2} mm Hg, or greater, whereupon it vaporises emitting molecular rays in all directions (see table 12.1).[1-5] The vacuum should be such that the mean free path of the molecules is larger than the diameter of the vacuum container. As a result, molecular rays propagate from their source until they impinge on the walls of the vessel and objects within it, condensing on their surfaces and resulting in the formation of a metallic film.

Table 12.1

Evaporation Temperature of Different Metals

Material	Evaporation Temperature $T°$ Absolute	Material	Evaporation Temperature $T°$ Absolute
Hg	320	Pb	1000
Cs	433	Sn	1148
Rb	450	Cr	1190
K	480	Ag	1319
Cd	541	Au	1445
Na	565	Al	1461
Zn	623	Cu	1542
Mg	712	Fe	1694
Sr	811	Ni	1717
Li	821	Pt	2332
Ca	878	Mo	2755
Ba	905	C	2795
Bi	913	W	3505
Sb	973		

The atoms direct themselves in a linear fashion similar to light waves, obeying the Lambert cosine law. When the vacuum pressure is insufficient, distribution depends on the diffusion laws.

The process is very rapid although it suffers from the disadvantage of deposition taking place in all directions, necessitating the use of screening devices. No electron beam effect is produced on the substrate and it remains relatively cool provided that the substrate to source distance is not close enough to facilitate damage of the polymer by radiation and heat of condensation.

Whether or not a particular metal is suitable for evaporation is determined by the thermal stability and vapour pressure of the material and the practicability of bringing the material to the evaporation temperature in a vacuum without excessive heating to withstand radiation.

Background

Although some attribute the discovery of vacuum deposition to Edison (1890) it is generally credited to Pringsheim and Pohl[6] (1912). Inasmuch that Faraday[7] had previously succeeded in preparing deposits by evaporating metals in inert atmospheres and Conn[8] had volatilised gold, silver and aluminium in inert gases at reduced pressure, Pringsheim and Pohl were the first to achieve controlled deposition. The reason why this process arrived on the scene many years after cathode sputtering, was because of the lack of an efficient pumping system to obtain the necessarily high vacuum required.

In 1915 Gaede[9] discovered the principle of the diffusion pump. Langmuir,[10] in 1916, presented the mercury diffusion pump which was a practical adaptation of Gaede's discovery.

Around 1928,[11] the oil diffusion pump arrived on the scene, replacing the existing mercury diffusion pump which is now only used for a few special applications, so simplifying vacuum techniques enormously. Together with the introduction of refractory metal filaments in 1931,[12] this constituted a tremendous advance towards the industrialisation of the process.

The use of lacquer coatings in Germany in the early 1940's and the subsequent impetus supplied by America shortly afterwards helped to popularise the technique and today the metallising of plastics by vacuum evaporation is big business.

Vacuum Equipment

Vacuum Chambers

Although the size and shape of vacuum chambers vary, there are two types in general use today: (1) the cylindrical chamber with dish ends, one of which opens, and (2) the hemispherical chamber or bell jar. The first type is normally used for industrial purposes, whereas the second type finds application in both laboratory and small scale production work.

Laboratory units normally measure about 18 inches in diameter and about 24 inches in height, whereas the commercial units may measure up to 72 inches in diameter and 98 inches in length. Vacuum chambers are normally constructed from stainless steel. Glass may be used for the smaller laboratory models.

Filaments and Foil Vapour Sources

Filament heaters are normally constructed from one of the refractory metals. Originally tungsten was nearly always used until Countryman[13] found that for some metals (Ag, Cu) other filament materials (Ta, Mo) were preferable.

Refractory metals are easy to construct and evaporation temperatures are easily obtained with a large number of metals. They may be constructed in one of two main forms.

(a) Filaments made from wire in the form of helices or conical baskets (fig. 12.1a, 12.1b & 12.1c). Multi-strand filaments are generally preferred since they promote uniform wetting.

(b) Boats and troughs constructed from foil where, through lack of adhesion, filaments are unsatisfactory (fig. 12.1d & 12.1e).

The metals used are those which exhibit high melting points combined with low volatility. Tungsten, tantalum, molybdenum and columbium can be used although tungsten, followed by molybdenum are the two most commonly employed. Other metals that can be used in the manufacture of filaments are platinum, iron, nickel, chromel, and silver. According to Caldwell,[14] there are three factors to be considered when selecting a filament material.

1 The metal must adhere to the filament.

2 The metal to be evaporated must have sufficient vapour pressure to evaporate while still at a temperature below the melting point of the filament material.

3 It should not form an alloy with the filament.

There are exceptions to this rule; silver for example, does not wet tungsten but may be evaporated from a tungsten helical basket. Nevertheless the rule provides a very useful guide. A reasonably comprehensive list outlining suitable filament materials and forms for the evaporation of the more common metals is given in tables 12.2, 12.3 and 12.4.[14,15,13]

Holland[16] has elaborated somewhat on this theme and incorporated the results of Countryman,[13] Caldwell,[14] Cartwright and Strong,[17] and Holland[18] in a comprehensive table.

The filament should have a low tension power supply of between 6 and 24 volts and 20 and 600 amperes, depending on the number and size of the filaments. Filaments should be cleaned prior to use either by etching or by heating in vacuo.

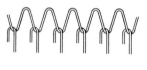

(a)   Sinusoidal filament.   Sometimes used for evaporating aluminium for front surface mirrors but is considered to be of poor design since the accumulation of evaporant facilitates alloying. A further limitation is that it can only be used for metals which wet the surface.

(b)   Multi-strand helical filament. This is the most common technique for evaporating aluminium on a batch type process. The multi-strand core results in a large surface area being obtained for evaporation.

(c)   Conical basket filament.   This is normally used for metals which do not normally wet refractory metals such as silver, and is used for metals which are in pellet form.

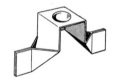

(d) Dimple type molybdenum strip for powders and metallic flakes and pellets.

(e)   Boat sources may be used when evaporating metals in large quantities.

Fig. 12.1   Typical Filament and Foil Vapour Sources.

Table 12.2
Suitable Filament Materials for the Evaporation of a Variety of Metals

The table below lists filament materials (rows) against metals to be evaporated (columns, arranged alphabetically). Each cell contains the wetting (W), evaporation (E) and reaction (R) codes defined in the legend.

Metal (evaporated)	Tungsten 3370–5900°C	Tantalum 2850–4100°C	Molybdenum 2620–3700°C	Columbium 1950–2900°C	Platinum 1773–4300°C	Iron 1535–3000°C	Nickel 1452–2900°C	Chromel 1350°C	Silver 960–1950°C
Aluminium 659–1800°C	$W_1\,E_1\,R_2$	$W_2\,E_3\,R_3$	$W_1\,E_3\,R_3$	$W_3\,E_3\,R_1$	$W_2\,E_3\,R_2$	$W_1\,E_3\,R_1$	$W_1\,E_3\,R_1$	$W_1\,E_3\,R_3$	$W_1\,E_3\,R_1$
Antimony 630–1380°C	$W_1\,E_1\,R_1$	$E_1\,R_1$	$W_1\,E_1\,R_1$	$W_1\,E_1\,R_1$	$W_1\,E_1\,R_1$	$W_1\,E_1\,R_1$	$W_1\,E_1\,R_1$	$W_1\,E_1\,R_1$	$W_1\,E_1\,R_1$
Barium 850–1140°C	$W_1\,E_1\,R_1$	$W_1\,E_1\,R_1$	$W_1\,E_1\,R_1$	$W_1\,E_1\,R_1$	$E_3\,R_1$	$W_1\,E_1\,R_1$	$W_1\,E_1\,R_1$	$W_1\,E_1\,R_1$	$W_1\,E_1\,R_1$
Beryllium 1350–1530°C	$W_1\,E_1\,R_1$	$E_1\,R_1$	$W_1\,E_1\,R_1$	$E_3\,M_3\,R_1$	$W_1\,E_2\,R_2$	$M_3\,E_3\,R_1$	$E_3\,R_1$	$E_3\,R_1$	$E_3\,R_1$
Bismuth 271–1470°C	$W_2\,E_1\,R_1$	$W_2\,E_1\,R_1$	$W_2\,E_1\,R_1$	$W\,E_1\,R_1$	$W_1\,E_1\,R_1$	$W_1\,E_1\,R_1$	$W_1\,E_1\,R_1$	$W_1\,E_1\,R_1$	$W_3\,E_1\,R_1$
Cadmium 320–767°C	$W_2\,E_3\,W_3$	$W_3\,E_3\,R_1$	$W_3\,E_1\,L$	$W_2\,E_1\,R_1$	$E_1\,R_1$	$W_3\,E_3\,R_1$	$W_1\,E_3\,W_3$	$W_1\,E_1\,R_1$	$W_3\,E_1\,R_1$
Cobalt 1960–2900°C	$M_2\,E_3\,W_3$	$W_2\,E_3\,R_3$	$M_3\,E_3\,W_2$	$E_2\,R_2\,W_1$		$E_2\,R_2$	$W_1\,E_3\,R_3$		
Copper 1083–2310°C	$W_1\,E_3\,W_3$	$E_2\,R_3\,W_3$	$W_1\,E_3\,W_3$	$E_3\,R_1\,W_1$	$E_2\,R_1$	$W_1\,E_2\,R_1$	$W_1\,E_1\,R_1$	$W_3\,E_2\,R_1$	$R_3\,E_2\,R_1$
Germanium 959–2700°C	$W_1\,E_1\,R_1$	$E_1\,R_1$	$W_1\,E_1\,R_1$						
Gold 1063–2600°C	$W_3\,E_1\,W_3$	$E_1\,R_1\,L$	$W_3\,E_1\,W_2$	$L\,R_1\,W_3$	$W_1\,E_1\,R_2$	$W_1\,E_1\,R_1$	$W_1\,E_1\,R_1$	$W_1\,E_1\,R_1$	$E_3\,R_3$
Iron 1535–3000°C	$W_1\,E_3\,R_3$								
Lead 327–1613°C	$W_3\,E_1\,W_3$	$E_3\,R_1\,W_3$	$W_3\,E_1\,W_3$	$L\,R_1\,W_3$	$E_1\,R_1$	$W_1\,E_1\,R_1$	$W_1\,E_1\,R_1$	$W_1\,E_1\,R_1$	$W_1\,E_1\,R_3$
Magnesium 651–1110°C	$M_3\,E_1\,R_1$	$M_3\,E_1\,R_1$	$M_3\,E_1\,R_1$	$M_3\,E_1\,R_1$	$M_3\,E_1\,R_1$	$M_3\,E_1\,R_1$	$M_3\,E_3\,R_1$		
Manganese 1260–1900°C	$W_1\,E_1\,R_1$	$E_1\,R_1$	$W_1\,E_1\,R_1$	$E_1\,R_1\,B$	$E_3\,R_3$	$M_3\,E_3\,B$	$M_3\,E_3\,W_1$		
Nickel 1452–2900°C	$W_1\,E_3\,W_3$	$E_3\,R_3\,W_1$	$W_1\,E_3\,W_3$	$R_3\,R_3\,E_3$	$E_3\,R_3$	$W_1\,E_3\,R_3$	$E_3\,R_3$	$R_3\,E_3\,R_3$	$R_3\,E_3\,R_3$
Platinum 1777–4300°C	$W_1\,E_1\,R_3$	$4\,R_2\,W_1$	$W_1\,E_3\,R_3$	$E_3\,R_3\,W_1$		$E_3\,R_3\,W_1$	$E_3\,R_3$	$E_3\,R_3$	$E_3\,R_3$
Selenium 200–688°C	$W_1\,E_1\,R_1$	$L\,R_2\,W_3$	$W_3\,E_1\,R_1$	$E_1\,R_1\,W_1$	$E_1\,R_1\,W_2$	$W_1\,E_1\,R_1$	$W_1\,E_1\,R_1$	$W_1\,E_1\,R_1$	$E_3\,R_1$
Silver 960–1950°C	$W_2\,E_1\,R_1$	$E_1\,R_1\,W_1$	$W_2\,E_1\,R_1$	$E_2\,R_1\,W_1$	$E_3\,R_3$	$W_1\,E_1\,R_1$	$W_1\,E_1\,R_1$	$W_1\,E_1\,R_1$	
Strontium 762–1150°C	$W_1\,E_1\,R_1$	$E_1\,R_5$	$W_1\,E_1\,R_1$	$R_1\,W_1$	$E_2\,R_1$	$W_1\,E_1\,R_1$	$E_1\,R_5$	$E_1\,R_1$	$M_3\,E_3\,R_1$
Tellurium 452–1390°C	$W_1\,E_1\,R_1$	$E_1\,R_1\,W_1$	$W_1\,E_1\,R_1$	$E_1\,R_1\,W_2$	$E_1\,R_1\,W_3$	$W_1\,E_1\,R_1$	$W_1\,E_1\,R_1$	$W_1\,E_1\,R_1$	$E_2\,R_3$
Thallium 303–1650°C	$W_2\,E_1\,R_1$	$E_1\,R_2\,L$	$W_2\,E_1\,R_1$	$R_1\,W_2$	$E_1\,R_1$	$W_1\,E_1\,R_1$	$W_1\,E_1\,R_1$	$W_1\,E_1\,R_1$	$E_3\,R_3$
Thorium 1845–3000°C	$W_3\,E_1\,W_3$	$E_2\,R_2\,W_1$	$M_3\,E_3\,R_1$	$R_3\,R_1$					
Tin 231–2270°C	$W_3\,E_3\,W_3$	$E_3\,R_1$	$W_2\,E_1\,R_1$	$R_1\,R_2$	$W_2\,E_1\,R_1$	$W_1\,E_1\,R_1$	$W_3\,E_1\,R_1$	$L\,R_1$	$W_3\,R_3$
Titanium 1800–3000°C	$W_2\,E_1\,R_1$	$E_1\,R_3$	$W_3\,E_1\,R_2$	$R_1\,W_4$	$E_2\,R_3$	$W_1\,E_2\,R_3$	$W_1\,E_2\,R_1$		
Vanadium 1715–3000°C	$W_1\,E_1\,R_2$	$E_1\,R_1$	$W_2\,E_1\,R_2$	$R_3\,W_1$	$E_1\,R_1$	$W_1\,E_1\,R_1$	$W_1\,E_1\,R_1$	$E_2\,R_1$	$E_3\,R_2$
Zinc 419–907°C	$W_1\,E_1\,R_1$	$E_1\,R_2\,W_1$	$W_1\,E_1\,R_1$	$W_3\,E_3\,R_1$	$E_1\,R_1\,W_1$	$W_1\,E_1\,R_1$	$W_1\,E_1\,R_1$	$W_1\,E_1\,R_1$	$E_3\,R_1$

Legend

W_1—The metal wets the filament well.
W_2—The forces of wetting are not large. Drops of the metal may occasionally fall from the filament.
W_3—The metal will not adhere to the filament.
M_3—The metal is not melted.
E_1—Evaporation of the metal takes place readily.
E_2—Evaporation of the metal proceeds slowly.
E_3—No evaporation of the metal takes place.
R_1—No reaction of the metal with the filament.
R_2—Reaction of the metal with the filament proceeds slowly usually without much effect on evaporation.
R_3—Reaction of the metal with the filament results in burning out the filament.
B—The filament burns out due to heating the metal to nearly the melting point of the filament.

filament. Although evaporation occurs, the occasional dropping of molten metal from the filament is an undesirable characteristic.

2. In an attempt to evaporate columbium, wire with a diameter of 0.03 in was used. Apparently the heat transfer from filament to the columbium was not efficient enough to melt the columbium, but the columbium wire wrapped tightly about the filament should melt quite easily.

3. Iron is difficult to evaporate because it forms low melting point alloys. However, if several turns of tungsten are wrapped tightly about a short length of iron wire, the iron can be evaporated successfully. An iron-tungsten alloy is formed along the whole length of the helix, but a core of tungsten is left unaffected so that the iron tungsten-iron alloy probably takes place. Nickel can be evaporated by this same procedure.

4. Due to its low vapour pressure, platinum evaporates very slowly. If very fine platinum wire is wrapped tightly around a tungsten filament, the efficiency of heating is adequate to melt and to evaporate the platinum.

5. A shell of some refractory compound of strontium separated the molten strontium from the filament so that the wetting properties could not be examined. (Caldwell)

NOTES:
1. In some cases where the metal does not wet the filament, the surface tension is such that the globule of molten metal is supported mechanically by the spiral

159

Table 12.3

Suggested Methods for Evaporation of Various Metals
[Olsen, Smith and Crittenden]

Metal	Method for Small Quantities	Method for Large Quantities
Aluminium	Helical coil of W	Helical coil of W
Antimony	Conical baskets of W, Ni, or Chromel	Alundum crucible
Arsenic	Alundum crucible	Alundum crucible
Barium	Conical baskets of W, Ni, Fe, or Chromel	Conical baskets of W, Ni, Fe, or Chromel
Beryllium	Conical basket of W	
Bismuth	Conical baskets of W, Fe, Ni, or Chromel	Alundum crucible
Calcium	Conical basket of W	Alundum crucible
Cadmium	Conical baskets of W, Ni, Fe, or Chromel	Alundum crucible
Carbon	Unsuccessful	Unsuccessful
Chromium	Conical basket of W	
Cobalt	Helical coil of W	Alundum or BeO crucible
Columbium	Helical coil of W	
Copper	Helical coil of W or conical basket of W	Alundum crucible
Germanium	Conical basket of W	Alundum crucible
Indium	Conical baskets of W or Fe	Alundum crucible
Iron	Helical coil of W	Alundum or BeO crucible
Lead	Conical basket of Fe	Alundum crucible
Magnesium	Conical baskets of W, Ni, Fe, or Chromel	Alundum crucible
Manganese	Conical basket of W	Conical basket of W or Alundum crucible
Molybdenum	Melting of Mo filament	
Nickel	Helical coil of W	Alundum or BeO crucible
Palladium	Helical coil of W	
Phosphorus (red)	Unsuccessful	Unsuccessful
Platinum	Helical coil of W	
Selenium	Conical baskets of W, Ni, Fe, or Chromel	Alundum crucible
Silicon	BeO crucible	BeO crucible
Silver	Helical coil or conical basket of W	Alundum crucible
Strontium	Conical basket of W	Large conical basket of W
Tellurium	Conical baskets of W, Ni, Fe, or Cromel	Alundum crucible
Thorium	Conical basket of W	Conical basket of W
Tin	Conical basket of W	Alundum crucible
Uranium	Conical basket of W	
Vanadium	Conical basket of W	Conical basket of W
Zinc	Conical baskets of W, Ni, Fe, or Chromel	Alundum crucible
Zirconium	Conical basket of W	

Table 12.4

Satisfactory Filament Materials for the Evaporation of Various Metals
(listed in order of merit). [Countryman]

Metal	Filaments
Aluminium	Tungsten, tantalum, molybdenum, columbium
Antimony	Chromel, tantalum, tungsten
Barium	Tungsten, tantalum, molybdenum, columbium
Beryllium	Tantalum, tungsten, molybdenum
Bismuth	Chromel, tantalum, tungsten
Cadmium	Chromel, columbium, tantalum
Cobalt	Columbium
Copper	Columbium, molybdenum, tantalum
Germanium	Tantalum, molybdenum (other filaments not tried)
Gold	Tungsten, molybdenum
Iron	Tungsten
Lead	Iron, nickel, chromel
Magnesium	Tungsten, tantalum, molybdenum, columbium
Manganese	Tungsten, tantalum, molybdenum, columbium
Nickel	Tungsten
Platinum	Tungsten
Selenium	Chromel, iron, molybdenum
Silver	Tantalum, molybdenum, columbium, iron
Strontium	Tungsten, tantalum, molybdenum, columbium
Tellurium	Tungsten, tantalum, molybdenum, columbium
Thallium	Nickel, iron, columbium, tantalum
Thorium	Molybdenum
Tin	Chromel
Titanium	Tungsten, tantalum
Vanadium	Tungsten, molybdenum
Zinc	Tungsten, tantalum, molybdenum, columbium

Pumping Systems

The exceptionally high vacuum required to carry out the evaporation may be obtained with a combination of mechanical and diffusion pumps. It is the oil diffusion pump which has made vacuum deposition a commercial proposition. Formerly, pumps capable of producing such a vacuum had low capacities and the evacuation of all but the smallest volume demanded painstaking care and considerable time. Today, diffusion pumps can evacuate within minutes chambers large enough to hold many thousands of articles (fig. 12.2).[16,19]

Mechanical Rotary Pumps

The mechanical pump is used to lower the pressure in the chamber below the normal atmospheric pressure. However, mechanical pumps lose pumping speed rapidly as the pressure falls and will not reduce the pressure much below 200 microns. It is at this point that their efficiency falls off. This initial stage of evacuation is sometimes referred to as the "roughing stage."

When outgassing materials containing large quantities of condensable vapour, for example moisture, acetone, plasticisers and so on, the oil in the

161

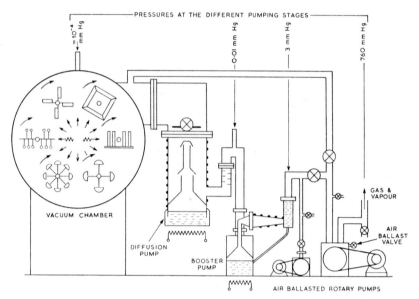

Fig. 12.2 Pumping system of modern design (Holland). A schematic end view of the open vacuum chamber showing racks with various spoke designs for a variety of plastic parts is also illustrated. In this instance the racks do not revolve around the filament but on their own axis only to expose all surfaces of the part to the metallic radiation from the filament. [Shaw]

rotary pump will soon become saturated and the pumping efficiency drop rapidly. To prevent this happening, gas ballasted mechanical pumps are used where a small quantity of air is introduced into the pump during the compression cycle, diluting the vapour and preventing it from condensing. This slightly increases the ultimate pressure obtained by the mechanical pump, but does not impair its performance if it is used with a diffusion pump.

Heavy gas ballasting is required when exhausting systems containing plastics such as Cellophane, which have large quantities of absorbed moisture.

Diffusion Pumps

Diffusion pumps can attain the necessarily high vacuum within a few minutes because of their tremendous pumping speeds. They are therefore used in the final stages of evacuation to bring the pressure down to 0·5 microns, the level required by the process for successful evaporation.

Diffusion pumps cannot operate at atmospheric pressure and begin pumping only when the pressure is down to about 200 microns. They also require their exhaust to be expelled from the system being evacuated. Valves controlling both the mechanical and diffusion pumps are operated sequentially to effect the necessary degree of evacuation. The mechanical pump backs-up the diffusion pump by removing the exhaust delivered by the diffusion pump, so expelling it from the system.

An oil diffusion pump or mercury diffusion pump may be used, although the former is preferred in most cases since its pumping speed exceeds by many times that of the latter. Mercury diffusion pumps operate at slightly higher back pressures and often one pump will suffice where two oil diffusion pumps in series are normally used.

Another disadvantage associated with the use of mercury diffusion pumps is that because the vapour pressure of mercury is so high, traps are necessary to prevent it from diffusing into the vacuum system and destroying the vacuum. Unfortunately, the traps have a high resistance to the flow of gas and may choke the pump. They do, however, find use in certain applications where possible contamination by hydrocarbons from the oil diffusion pumps must be avoided. Two such applications are those used in the manufacture of rhodium mirrors and the manufacture of silver mirrors for interferometry purposes.

Booster Pumps

These pumps are used because of their high pumping speeds at inter-mediate pressures. They may operate against back pressures of up to 3,000 microns and give a satisfactory pumping performance in reducing the pressure to about 10 microns. Booster pumps are therefore used over the range where the mechanical rotary pump loses its pumping efficiency and the diffusion pump reaches its maximum efficiency.

It is within this range that a large percentage of volatiles are evolved from plastics when they are in vacuo. Because the evacuation of the chamber may be prolonged over this stage, unless an expensive, large capacity rotary pump is used, a booster pump is employed since it fulfils this function admirably. It can be backed by a reasonably small rotary pump.

Such a combination is designed to operate in sequence, that is rotary → booster → diffusion, and will reduce the pressure to less than 0·4 microns. The diffusion pump is backed by the booster, which in turn is backed by the rotary pump.

For evacuating large capacity chambers, the most economic and efficient method is to support a diffusion pump with a booster and mechanical rotary pump. For smaller capacity vacuum chambers (less than 100 litres), the use of a booster pump may be omitted. The final choice of pump combination is dependent on a number of factors, such as the capacity of the chamber and the amount of outgassing likely to be encountered. In any sequence of pumps used, more than one of each type may be employed.

Degassing of Plastics in Vacuo

Polymeric materials may contain volatile constituents in the form of solvents, moisture, or plasticisers; these may be liberated in vacuo and possibly prevent the obtaining of a vacuum pressure which is sufficiently low enough for evaporation purposes. The vapours add to the amount of gas which the pumping system must handle and tend to lengthen the time required for successful coating[16] (fig. 12.3). If the metal is evaporated before the plastic is sufficiently outgassed, a metal coating of burned appearance may result.

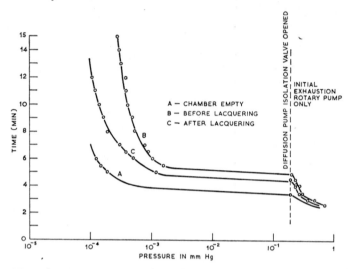

Fig. 12.3   Effect of plastic materials on exhaustion time of an evaporation plant.   The 4 ft³ vacuum chamber is pumped by a 1500 litres/second oil diffusion pump; (a) empty chamber; (b) with 144 small cellulose acetate mouldings in the chamber; the increase in exhaustion time at 0·5 mm Hg is due to liberation of moisture, and the increase in ultimate pressure due to plasticiser and solvent; (c) pump performance improves when mouldings are dipped and sealed by melamine primary lacquer. [Holland]

Plasticisers which may be incorporated into plastics normally have, for various reasons, a low vapour pressure, otherwise evaporation losses during life would result in a decrease in their concentration. Nevertheless, in a high vacuum they may evaporate sufficiently to cause a considerable rise in the chamber pressure.

Solvents (from the base lacquer) and plasticisers may cause four kinds of trouble:—

1 Failure of the evaporant to adhere to the film
2 Contamination and hence erroneous reading of gauges
3 Contamination of pump oils
4 Inhibition of the deposition of high quality coatings

Moisture is objectionable because of its effect in prolonging the exhaustion time but even so it is not so troublesome as volatile plasticisers. Moisture can be liberated by raising the temperature of the plastic, but plasticisers cannot be so removed without changing the properties of the material.

Fortunately these problems have been overcome by various means. For example, the surface of polymeric materials can be lacquered to considerably reduce outgassing in vacuo. Low gas pressures can be obtained with most materials by exceptionally high pumping speeds. On the other hand, polymers like polyesters and fluoroplastics do not require outgassing since they contain no additives and their moisture absorption rate is negligible. Polymers with substantial amounts of volatile constituents should be avoided wherever possible in order to simplify the base coating operation and avoid extended pumpdown cycles.

Continuous Metallising

Rapid developments and new applications for metallised films have warranted the investigation and production of new techniques for polyethylene terephthalate and polystyrene on a continuous or semi-continuous basis. As a result, the price of metallised film capacitors is now comparable with that of capacitors constructed by other means, this being but one example where a large economic saving has been obtained.

Because a number of plastics contain a relatively high content of volatile matter, degassing of the film must take place prior to metallising. This of course is essential, for the operation is likely to be prolonged and contamination of the coating chamber may result from the volatile constituents evolved. Although desorption of the material may be accelerated by increasing the temperature, some degree of caution should be exercised since the plasticiser may evaporate at elevated temperatures and result in a brittle material with different properties from the original.

The degassing process may be carried out in a separate chamber and the film then transferred to the metallising unit. The technique employed necessitates the film being wound backwards and forwards over a series of rollers to expose all of the surface in vacuo until sufficient volatile constituents have been removed to allow a rapid pumpdown in the vacuum chamber. This may be accomplished with a photo-electric reversing device attached to the rolling mechanism.

Following the degassing operation the material is transferred to the vacuum chamber, the plastic absorbing no appreciable amount of moisture during its brief exposure to the atmosphere provided that it is kept in its rolled state. Metallising can now be carried out satisfactorily since a sufficiently high vacuum can be obtained without contamination.

Tremendous strides forward have been witnessed in the manufacture of equipment for metallising film over the past few years, widths of up to 60 inches and lengths of several thousand feet being processed at speeds reported to be in the region of 1,500 feet per minute. For example, polyester film, 12 inches wide, 1 mil thick may be processed in lengths of 6,000 yards at speeds of 250 feet per minute. Truly continuous metallising has also been achieved by using air-to-vacuum-to-air locks.

Some films have the metal deposited on one side only (tinsel foil). Base coats may or may not be used, the same conditions applying to top coats. Polyester film has proved to be one of the most successful materials since it absorbs little moisture and contains no additives. A degassing operation is therefore unnecessary.

As the process is continuous, the metal being deposited must also be fed in a continuous fashion. This may be accomplished by feeding it automatically in wire form from a reel. Tungsten heating elements are unsuitable since they cannot withstand sustained evaporation of the metal for extended periods. Instead induction heated crucibles are used and techniques have been developed where aluminium can be evaporated continuously for periods in excess of 8 hours.[21] Further refinements permit changing of the evaporation sources without interruption of the process.

Ionic Bombardment

Ionic bombardment of glass substrates is often used as a method of cleaning since it removes adsorbed films and facilitates adhesion of the subsequently deposited film. The effect on polymers, however, is not quite the same.

The bombardment of polymers raises the temperature of the substrate and accelerates the degassing stage by removing moisture, solvents and plasticisers, producing a contaminant free surface to aid adhesion of the metallic film. Although plastics which contain no volatile matter generally show little improvement, Holland[16] claims that if PTFE is bombarded almost to its softening point, the adhesion of aluminium deposits shows considerable improvement.

Bombardment should not be too intense otherwise the polymers may be degraded. Materials which are hydrophobic may develop hydrophilic surfaces as has been observed with polystyrene. Optical polymers tend to become discoloured with a resulting increase in their light absorption (fig. 12.4).[16] Electron bombardment of most polymers results in damage to the polymer.

Adhesion

The adhesion of evaporated metal films to plastics is much less than that to glass or metals. There is, however, some correlation between the two.

The tenacity with which aluminium adheres to glass suggests that chemical action between the film and the glass surface takes place. Bateson[22] suggests that the bonding of the metallic layer to the glass is accomplished by chemical reaction with a neutral layer of OH groups present on the freshly formed glass surface. Metals which tend to form oxides easily, such as Al, Mg and Cr, adhere to glass, whereas the non-oxide formers, or noble metals like gold and silver, exhibit poor adhesion qualities. A further point is that evaporated platinum will not adhere well to glass, but platinum sputtered in an oxygen atmosphere and contaminated with PtO_2 exhibits improved bonding characteristics to glass.

Bateson maintains that adhesion is greater for cations of lower ionic radius and for those with co-ordination numbers similar to Si^{++++} (see table 12.5).[22]

Table 12.5

Relationship Between Ionic Radius, Co-ordination Number and Adhesion [Bateson]

Ion	Crystal Radius (Cation)	Radius Ratio (Cation/Anion)	Co-ordination Number	Electro Negativity
Si^{4+}	0·65	0·37	4	1·8
Al^{3+}	0·72	0·41	4 or 6	1·5
Cr^{6+}	0·81	0·46	4 or 6	—
Ag^+	1·26	0·72	8	—
Au^+	1·37	0·78	9	—
O^-	1·76	—	—	3·5

With plastics a similar pattern is obtained, oxygen active metals exhibiting better adhesion to polymers. Holland[16] reports that an initial layer of nichrome deposited on to phenolics gives rise to good bonding properties between the substrate and the subsequent electroplated copper deposit. Work is now progressing along the lines of chemically conditioning the polymer surface to provide receptive groups prior to evaporating an oxygen active metal; this should give rise to stronger chemical bonds.

Such conditioning is ideal for polymers having no plasticiser present or containing no moisture, that is, polymers requiring no degassing. If a material does require degassing, the presence of exuded plasticiser will prevent bonding. As surface lacquering is essential, surface treatment of the polymer is therefore pointless.

One patent[23] claims adherent deposits of copper to untreated PTFE. Although there is considerable conjecture about the mechanism of adhesion of metals to plastics, it is extremely unlikely that good adhesion could be obtained by the method outlined without preconditioning of the polymer.

Thickness of Evaporated Deposit

If the pressure in the system is sufficiently low for the mean free path of the evaporating atoms to be comparable with or greater than the evaporating distance, then the source material will propagate outwards from the source in straight lines.

The following assumptions are made:—

(a) The physical size of the source is small compared with the evaporating distance and substrate size, it being a point source.

(b) The source material evaporates equally in all directions through 4π solid angles.

(c) All evaporating material condenses on the surround and does not re-evaporate.

(d) The plane substrate is normal to the source.

If these are accepted then the mass/unit area on a substrate at distance h from source produced by evaporating m gm of material is:—

$$\frac{m}{4\pi h^2}$$

For example, if 1 gm of aluminium is evaporated on to a plane substrate over a distance of 30 cm,

$$\text{mass/cm}^2 \;=\; \frac{1\cdot 0}{4\pi \times 30^2}\ \text{gm/cm}^2$$

Assuming film has bulk density of $2\cdot 7$ gm/cc

$$\text{thickness } t \;=\; \frac{1\cdot 0}{4\pi \times 30^2 \times 2\cdot 7}\ \text{cm}$$

$$\simeq 3{,}300\ \text{Å}$$

If the substrate is inclined at an angle to the source then thickness $t = t_o \times [\cos (\text{angle to the normal})]$
t_o = thickness for zero inclination.

For practical cases where the dimensions of the substrate are comparable to the evaporation distance, then the thickness distribution is given by fig. 12.5.[16]

If a long helicoil is used as the source and its length is comparable with the evaporating distance, then the thickness distribution is given by fig. 12.6.[16]

Structure of Deposit

The structure of thin films is normally that of an agglomerate of atoms formed by the migration of the atoms on the substrate. Although it was thought at one time that vacuum evaporated deposits were amorphous, they are in fact crystalline in nature. The size and orientation of the crystals in the deposits may be related to their melting points. High melting point metals (Ni, Cr, Pt) consist of small crystals, whereas low melting point metals (Zn, Sn) produce a large grain size. If the substrate temperature is increased, the grain size is increased. As the deposition rate is increased, the tendency to form agglomerates decreases and a finer grain structure is obtained. A highly agglomerated film, one that is discontinuous, would result in characteristics of reduced electrical conductivity and increased optical absorption.

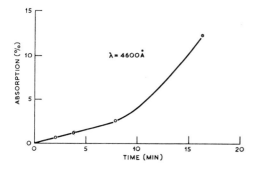

Fig. 12.4 Rise in the absorption A = 100 — R — T, where R and T are the reflectivity and transmissivity respectively, of 1·5 mm thick acrylic sheet as a result of ionic bombardment cleaning at an applied voltage of 4 kV and 100 mA in an 18 in diameter bell. [Holland]

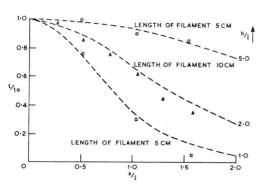

Fig. 12.5 Distribution of plating from a cylindrical source deposited on a plane surface, parallel and in the same plane as the source. The source was a helix with a diameter of 0·4 cm made of three strands of 0·5 mm diameter tungsten wire. The pitch of the helix was five turns per centimetre length of filament. Dotted lines show the theoretical distribution assuming a thin wire source. Points indicate the values obtained experimentally. [Holland]

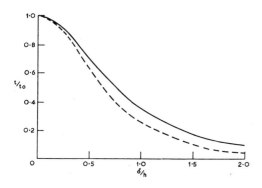

Fig. 12.6 Distribution of deposit on a plane surface for (a) evaporation from a small directed surface source (dotted line), (b) evaporation from a point source (full line). [Holland]

169

Stresses, normally tensile, may be present in deposits. These may be correlated to their melting points, for as the melting point decreases, so is the stress reduced (see table 12.6).[24]   A reduction in stress is also obtained when the temperature is raised.   A relationship exists between the stress and the temperature of formation of the deposit and consequently the atomic mobility in the deposit.

Table 12.6

Observed Stresses in the Metal Deposits Condensed from the Vapour " in vacuo " and some Associated Properties [Murbach and Wilman]

Metal	M.Pt. (°C)	Recryst. temp. (°C)	Coefficient linear expansion $10^6 \propto$	$\triangle T(°C)$†	$10^{-11}E$ (dyne cm^{-2})	Mean stress $S(Kg\ cm^{-2})$ Observed	Calculated
Fe	1539	350—450	12	200—300	21	3100	~3000*
Ni	1455	530—660	14	380—500	21	3500	~3000*
Pd	1555	450	11	300	11	7400	~1500*
Cu	1083	200—230	17	80—110	12	900	~1000*
Au	1063	200	14	80	8	850	900
Ag	960	200	19	80	8	750	1200
Sb	630	—	11	—	8	250	—
Al	659	150	24	30	7	100	500
Mg	651	150—200	27	30	4	0	300
Bi	271	—	13	0?	9	0	0?
Zn	419	<20	26	0	9	0	0

* Above the elastic limit.
† Approximate temperature range in which stress is developed.

Structure of the deposit is dependent on the prevailing conditions at the time of formation, such as rate of condensation, pressure, substrate temperature and so on.   Contamination of the deposit from the source material also exhibits a considerable effect on the structure.

Operating Conditions

To ensure maximum efficiency in vacuum metallising, certain working conditions must be observed.   Humidity should be controlled to prevent the appearance of those difficulties normally associated with lacquering at high humidities, such as lacquer blush, contamination with moisture, or the need for excessive drying times.   Increasing the humidity results in a decrease in pumping speeds and can result in contamination of the oil.

A dust free atmosphere is advisable to prevent pick up of dust particles by the lacquer which would detract from the appearance of the film.   Air filters and a room which is slightly pressurised are desirable. Establishments fitted with air conditioning plant and humidity control claim that exhaustion times remain constant and that the properties of the films are improved.

In depositing aluminium for optical applications it has been found that the number of rejects due to poor adhesion has decreased.

The pumping system should be in a separate room from the vacuum chamber, since its presence in the clean area will result in contamination of the atmosphere.

Surface Lacquering

Base Coat

To overcome the difficulties encountered with the degassing of plastics in vacuo, the majority of plastics can be satisfactorily metallised by the simple expedient of applying a suitable lacquer to act as a sealant, preventing the liberation of occluded gases and volatile matter. Obviously the more impervious the lacquer is, the more effective it will be.

Base coats fulfil a number of other functions. In general, the following characteristics are desirable in a base coat formulation. It should:—

1 Adhere well to the surface

2 Not attack or craze the polymer surface in any way which would adversely affect the optical properties of reflecting films

3 Cover mould marks and other minor surface imperfections

4 Provide a barrier to prevent outgassing during vacuum processing and to permit rapid pump down times

5 Provide a hard, smooth, glossy surface for subsequent metallising and a satisfactory base to which the metallic film will adhere well

6 Be balanced so that it will dry smoothly and quickly without showing sags, craters or drops.

Other necessary factors involved are as follows.

7 Although quick air drying is desirable to avoid attracting dust particles which will result in faulty films, it is not essential and may need to be sacrificed to obtain other essential properties. Anyway, for good class work a clean atmosphere is essential.

8 The volatile content of the base coat must be strictly controlled to prevent the migration of plasticisers to the surface where they may cause trouble by out-gassing at a later date.

9 The base coat should not yield volatile matter which will affect the passage of metal vapour during evaporation and contaminate the pumping system. The partial pressure of any volatile constituent must be less than 10^{-3} torr to allow for satisfactory metallising.

10 The base coat should be compatible with the top coat. When the latter is applied there should be no attack by the solvents through the porous metal film since this will lead to distortion of the metal film.

171

Base coats normally used may be divided into three categories, namely:—

(a)   Air drying (solvent evaporation)

(b)   Stoving (cured through crosslinking with or without the aid of catalysts)

(c)   Air curing (catalysts required)

Thermosetting lacquers are normally preferred since they can be cured to a hard glossy mass and they are unaffected by solvents. With base coatings, stoving is recommended because thorough curing is essential to ensure that all remaining solvents are driven off. (This is not so critical with top coats and air drying lacquers may be used. On the other hand the same lacquer is sometimes used for top and base coats.) Catalysed thermosetting pairs are often used although a top coat of air drying lacquer may replace the thermoset when durability is not a criterion. Air drying pairs are seldom employed since they are unsatisfactory because of solvent action. Among the thermosets used are phenolics and alkyds. For example, a melamine-alkyd resin combination has been used successfully on cellulose acetate and cellulose acetate butyrate. As an aid to selecting base coats and top coats which are compatible with polymer surfaces and with each other, Bateson[22] has compiled a useful chart providing the user with all the necessary properties.

Top Coat

Since the metallic film deposited by vacuum techniques is very thin and possesses no resistance to abrasion, a top coat of lacquer is necessary to protect the rather delicate film. Where a durable surface is required, lacquers which can be stoved are preferred. In cases where durability is of secondary importance, air drying lacquers can be used, obviating the need to oven cure the top coat.

Properties required for general acceptance of the top coat are given below. It should:—

1   Not tarnish or affect the brilliance of the aluminium

2   Adhere satisfactorily without distorting the optical properties of the metal film

3   Be water white, transparent and have a high gloss

4   Remain water white even under adverse weather conditions

5   Possess good mar resistance

6   Protect the system against attack by moisture or any solvent or chemical to which it will be exposed in service

7   Be stable and not undergo dimensional changes in service which would cause undue stress in the metallic film

8   Be unaffected by ultra-violet radiation.

Frequently when colour is desired, the top coat may be dyed to produce certain visual effects. The colour range obtainable through lacquering and dyeing covers the entire visible spectrum.

Lacquer Application

The principal methods of applying lacquers are by spraying, dipping, spinning and flowing. Selection is somewhat dependent on the geometry of the article and whether subsequent dyeing of the top coat is required.

Spraying

This is the best method for intricate shapes, although more than one coat may be necessary. A uniform coating is obtained and dyes may be incorporated into the system.

Dipping

Lacquer films of the highest specular reflectivity are achieved by this method. Because of irregularities in film thickness (it tends to build up at the edges) dyeing must be carried out separately otherwise it produces differences in intensity of shade. In this instance after the lacquer film is dry, it is immersed in the dye bath, rinsed in clean water and finally dried. To obtain coatings free from flow marks and tears, dipping should be carried out under controlled conditions of extraction angle and withdrawal rate.

Flow Coating

The parts are rotated in a closed chamber and the lacquer is sprayed on them through nozzles under pressure. It may also be allowed simply to flow over them. The coating material must have a sufficiently low viscosity to atomise at practical pressures. Control of the rotating speeds until the parts are touch dry is necessary to avoid tears and sags.

This technique has become quite popular for items which are difficult to coat by spraying because of their geometry. It is commonly used for small toys and novelties, since it is a very economical method on long runs.

In all cases the lacquer itself should be filtered regularly and the viscosity controlled. If thermosetting lacquers are used as top coats, strong dye solutions should be employed for deep tinting, because thermosetting lacquers resist spirit penetration.

Designing for Metallising

The designer should give ample consideration to the design of the part and in the selection of material, together with the metal to be deposited. A discussion between the designer, moulder and metalliser is obviously advantageous. Shaw[19] lists a number of points which the designer should take into account prior to embarking on any project.

Part Design

1 When selecting a polymer, the designer should remember that it will be subjected to the solvents used in base and top coat lacquers, and to the elevated temperatures involved in stoving these lacquers.

173

2 Large flat unbroken surfaces should be avoided. Anything over 2×2 inches is considered to be a large area. As none of these surfaces can usually be moulded optically flat, there is always some unevenness or distortion on the surface. When metallised, the surface distortion is magnified and becomes plainly visible. The flat surface also interferes with base coat run-off and may result in visible flow lines and drips.

3 Generous use should be made of rounded surfaces, such as ribs and flutes. The smaller the radius of curvature, the better. Broken surfaces display brilliant highlights and promote better base coat run-off.

4 Avoid specifying the metallising of those surfaces of the plastic which would be prone to moulding sink, marks due to studs, plugs or walls butting into the underside of the metallised surface.

5 Try to incorporate as much three-dimensional detail as possible, keeping in mind the idea that startling and smart effects are always produced by contrasting highly polished and dull surfaces.

6 Avail yourself of the moulding finishing techniques of engine turning, stippling, hammer tone, embellished design, vapour blasting, and etched and cut patterns on the flat portions, leaving rounded surfaces clear and smooth.

7 Stay away from the use of fine or feather edges. It is difficult to get a good base coat on such edges and adhesion of the finish will suffer.

8 Do not use deep, narrow depressions or slots in the design since it may not be possible to get enough metal down in between the slot walls. If the slots are too narrow they may also become clogged with lacquer during base coating. A simple rule is to maintain a 1:1 ratio between the width and the depth of the slots.

9 Do not design configurations with long unbroken surfaces or very thin wall sections. Because the parts may have as much as three hours of total baking at elevated temperatures for base coating and top coating, warping may result.

10 The design should not require the utilisation of a mould cavity with so little side wall draft that a lubricant will be necessary to eject it from the mould. Mould design must be such that no lubricants will be required.

Moulding Techniques

Shaw[19] continues with the following points:—

1 Obviously the mould must be designed to incorporate the design features mentioned in the preceding section. In addition, the mould designer should be careful to locate knockout pins, parting lines, and mould section demarcations which will appear on the part so that, if possible, they will not appear on the decorative metallised surface. Any such mark from the mould surface will be transferred to the finished object and although it may not be objectionable on an un-metallised surface, the metallic coating will serve to magnify the marks and make them plainly noticeable.

2 Care should also be taken to lay out the parts and runner system so that flow line and weld marks will be minimised, since these will also show up clearly on a metallised surface.

3 Most important, the moulder should keep in mind that the parts will be placed on racks for handling during the process. Sometimes significant savings can be made if the runner system is designed to facilitate racking. A tab on the runner system may be provided for clamping the parts cluster in the rack. Double gates may also be provided so that the individual parts will not fall off the runner and parts cluster when handled.

4 Mould layout can also be used to advantage to facilitate the process and reduce operating costs. One part may be located within another so that both can be loaded into the rack simultaneously, saving both space in the vacuum chamber and the time taken in racking. The metallising of mating parts at the same time is also advisable, since there is some variation in colour of the finish from load to load, and mating parts processed at different times may not match exactly.

5 When moulding mating parts in family moulds containing both items to be metallised and others which will not, the mould maker should provide sufficient cavities so that enough extra items can be produced. They are required to replace losses caused by rejects detected during the metallising process. Rejects in the process generally run to between 3 and 5 per cent.

6 If moulded parts need quenching in water then clean water, free from impurities such as oil and grease, should be used. After quenching, rinsing in clean water with a suitable detergent incorporated in it will facilitate the removal of any mineral residue spots left by the water on evaporation.

The following points may also be observed.

7 A highly polished surface must be maintained in the mould to ensure high quality mouldings that are free from blemishes and defects.

8 Mould release agents should be avoided wherever possible. If used, they should be chosen judiciously since some are removed with comparative ease; the only disadvantage obtained is an extra operation. Silicone release agents should be avoided because of the difficulties encountered with their removal.

Problems Encountered in Metallising

Many problems arise in metallising systems, but in the majority of cases they concern the lacquer system and not the metallising operation. Some of the more typical problems are discussed below.

General Defects

One of the many functions which a base coat has to perform, is that of covering imperfections on the substrate, for metallising will magnify any defects present. It is also imperative that an optically smooth surface

175

7

should be provided by the base coat. If the base coat is too thin, the defects are not completely obliterated and the subsequent metallic film will lack brilliance.

In order to achieve the right thickness, the correct viscosity and solids content, together with the proper solvent system, should be used. If the viscosity is too high, this may give rise to poor levelling characteristics and orange peel effects, whereas if the viscosity is too low, due to the presence of excess solvents, this may result in craters and a film which is too thin to cover up the surface defects. In the former case it is necessary to add more medium or slow drying solvents to induce better levelling power, while in the latter, the removal of solvents is necessary to inhibit mobility during drying.

It may be seen that these cures are diametrically opposed. To obtain a fine balance of properties, a compromise is often made.

Iridescence

This is a term used to describe distortion of the film, caused by movement or swelling of the base coat. A loss of brilliance occurs. The defect may be due to the following factors.

1 Alternate swelling and contraction of the base coat. Films which absorb substantial amounts of moisture are the worst offenders. A loss of adhesion may also be encountered.

2 By heat distribution, as is experienced when baking the top coat at temperatures above the softening point of the base coat thereby causing movement. This can be overcome by baking at lower temperatures.

Loss of Adhesion

This may occur on ageing if catalysed air-dry or low temperature cure systems have been used. It may also happen when using baking systems as well. The defect is caused by further curing taking place over a period of time. It is attributed to the fact that although the polymer exists at one stage of cure which provides good adhesion, further reaction in the course of time may alter the active groups originally present to promote adhesion.

Inconsistent adhesion may also be caused by the base coat being over sensitive to the presence of foreign matter on the substrate. Anti-static treatments are recommended to avoid this situation.

Effects of the Base Coat on the Plastic

Some base coats are formulated to slightly etch the plastic surface, the result being to promote good adhesion between them. In first surface metallising, the metallic film may cover this up, but in second surface metallising the etched surface is directly viewed through the plastic. The metallic film exaggerates this defect which shows up as blemishes. Reformulation is therefore necessary to overcome the effect, while still maintaining adhesion.

Outgassing

One of the prime functions of a base coat is to prevent outgassing of moisture and plasticiser from the plastic during metallising. It is therefore important that the constituent parts of the base coat itself are not overlooked in this connection and the necessary steps are taken to ensure that all volatile matter (solvents) is removed, otherwise voids and blisters will appear on the metal film accompanied by dark patches.

All residual solvents should be removed by first drying the base coat, even though the application of heat serves no purpose other than the removal of solvents. In most cases a temperature of 50 to 65°C for a period of about 30 minutes is quite adequate.

Effect of the Top Coat on the Base Coat

This must be avoided otherwise the metallic film will show the blemishes on both first and second surface decorating. Solvents in the top coat must not attack the base coat since distortion may occur due to swelling and flowing of the base coat.

Discoloration of Top Coat

This is probably due to overheating and therefore over curing of the top coat. A uniform temperature should be used in the curing oven and proper heat circulation control exercised to prevent any local hot spots.

Humidity Blush and Fogging

Generally, this is due to the metallising operation being performed in a too humid atmosphere. If the incorrect coating is used, or the application faulty, fogging may result. Both the base and top coats must be good if the article is expected to withstand prolonged exposure to humid conditions.

Curing Ovens

It is necessary to use ovens providing a uniform temperature and having accurate control, since local hot spots may cause a great deal of trouble when curing base and top coats. They should be equipped with exhaust fans to remove solvent vapours and other by-products of the curing cycle, otherwise they present a personnel hazard and retard the effective baking cycle. In addition to this, re-circulation fans are essential to maintain an even distribution of heat.

A number of different types of oven are available; these are heated by various means. Infra-red heating is acceptable for curing base coats, since the coating is penetrated by radiation and the surface beneath is heated which results in curing of the film from the inside out. However, difficulties are encountered with the top coat, for the radiant energy is reflected back by the metallic film, through the top coat, often resulting in undercuring.

Convection type ovens are preferred, the two most commonly used being electric and indirect gas fired, since these have proved to be the most satisfactory. The subject of ovens, their function and use, has been described by Nixon.[25]

Metallising Characteristics of Individual Polymers

Vacuum metallised plastics may be used for either functional or decorative purposes, the number of decorative applications by far outnumbering the functional ones. Frequently, for applications which are functional, the metal is deposited direct on to the material. Of course there are exceptions, one example being in the manufacture of reflectors. In the electronics field, this rule generally holds good, since the polymer is normally chosen for its dielectric properties which would of course be changed if an intermediate base coat was used.

For decorative use, the reverse generally holds true and lacquer systems are employed in the form of base and top coats. The exception is where second surface metallising is carried out, here the base coat is often dispensed with. As already pointed out, the proper selection of lacquer systems is of the utmost importance, and where a base coat is used, it is probably the most critical part of the system. Not only is the application a directive towards whether lacquer systems are necessary but the polymer itself is also a deciding factor.

Acetals

The surface of this material must be treated to provide adhesion of the base coat to the substrate. This may be carried out using a mixture of chromic-sulphuric acid or by using an etch primer. Typical systems are discussed under polyacetals in volume 2 and as such (excluding the etch primer) are fairly representative of the other materials reviewed in this section.

Applications are found mainly in the automotive and appliance industries.

Acrylonitrile Butadiene Styrene

This polymer is fairly easy to metallise. Recently it has become a very popular choice and no doubt this is partly due to the success that the polymer has enjoyed when electroplated. A large number of applications exist, such as automotive trim, radio and television parts, household appliances and business machines.

ABS is solvent sensitive and care should be taken in selecting the right base coat, since degradation of the polymer, such as stress cracking and impact resistance, has been experienced and attributed to this factor. Acrylics and modified acrylics have been reported as the worst offenders, causing reductions of up to 50% in impact resistance. It is suggested that the best approach is to use low bake lacquers other than acrylics. The application of heat is recommended in order to evaporate quickly any solvents before they have a chance to be absorbed by the polymer.

Acrylics

Acrylics were among the first polymers to be vacuum metallised. As these are optical polymers, both first and second surface coatings are in current use, the latter lending itself to producing three-dimensional effects. Originally only second surface coatings were used so that they were not subjected to any form of abrasion. Nowadays, with lacquer formulations constantly improving, the top coats available are sufficiently abrasion resistant to withstand fairly rough handling.

Moulded acrylics are very susceptible to stressing so careful consideration should be given to base coat formulations and in the solvents used in order to minimise this defect. Even so, annealing is sometimes necessary.

Applications include signs and displays, automotive instrument panels, horn buttons, tail light rings and housings, and appliance parts. Acrylics have also been used for lenses and mirrors. However, they do not possess very good dimensional stability; this is due to water absorption which precludes their use as back-reflecting mirrors where dimensional stability is a criterion. Other uses include heating mats for the de-icing and de-fogging of aircraft windows.

Cellulosics

Cellulose acetate and cellulose acetate butyrate are the two polymers in this family of materials which are used. The main disadvantage with these materials is that of the high plasticiser content present. Of course this presents problems of outgassing under high vacuum and in the selection of a suitable compatible base coat. Although both incorporate plasticisers in their make up, the problem associated with acetates is worse than that experienced with butyrates because, in the former, plasticisers are less compatible with acetate resins. Addition agents which may increase outgassing considerably, such as ultra-violet inhibitors, can be omitted from butyrates, allowing for some improvement in metallising conditions. Baking temperatures of about 60°C are normally used.

Applications for cellulosics include household and automotive decorative fabrics, catering for the spangle and sequin industry and in fabrics for clothing to impart a glistening effect. Originally most of the metallic yarn produced was based on cellulose materials, now these have been largely replaced by others such as polyesters and polyamides. In the photographic industry, metallised cellulose acetate butyrate is used for flash reflectors. In the record industry, the acetate is employed in the manufacture of master discs.

Phenolics

Phenolics are the most widely used of the thermosetting materials. Trouble may arise because the outgassing of phenolics results in the liberation of amines and these interfere with the base coats since they are baked at a high temperature and are frequently acid catalysed. Consequently low temperature curing is carried out to reduce the outgassing tendency, temperatures of about 150°C rarely being exceeded. Applications include the manufacture of appliance and automotive parts and bottle caps.

Polyamides

The ease with which polyamides may be metallised is dependent on the moisture content of the polymer. Small articles such as knobs are not affected by this problem but large parts, where there is a large dimension to thin wall ratio, are subject to warpage and shrinkage. This can result in iridescence when baking the top coat. The moisture may be removed by pre-baking which will help to stabilise the part. Another solution to overcome the iridescence problem is to bake the top coat at the lowest practical temperature that is compatible with the system being used.

Applications for polyamides are found mainly in the manufacture of automotive parts.

Polycarbonates

Although this material is suitable, instances have been reported where inconsistent adhesion has been obtained. This is probably due to inherent problems in the resin-solvent system. Careful selection is therefore necessary when considering the solvent sensitivity of the polymer. If crazing should occur, even with the careful choice of solvents, an annealing stage should be included. A temperature of 120° C is recommended.

It has been suggested that it is inadvisable to use base coats that cure at temperatures exceeding 120°C, consequently low bake varnishes are available (about 60°C) which can be used for less stringent applications. Nevertheless, to obtain high quality coatings possessing excellent hardness, stain and solvent resistance, light stability and good adhesion characteristics, a high temperature (125-135°C) curing system is necessary.

The polymer is being considered for first surface metallising in the automotive and appliance industry for such items as knobs, air conditioners, louvres, push-buttons and a number of other uses.

Polycarbonate film is also used for the manufacture of capacitors. There the metal is deposited directly on to the polymer, no base coat being used since this would interfere with the electrical characteristics of the metal-dielectric system.

Polyethylene Terephthalate

This polymer is metallised direct, without the use of base lacquers. Although chemical treatments such as oxidation with chromic-sulphuric acid or treatment with trichloroacetic acid, have been proposed for the material prior to metallising to improve bonding properties, they are rarely used in this context.

The one exception is in the manufacture of hot leaf stamping foils where the polyester contains a release agent on the surface to facilitate separation when heat is applied during the stamping operation.

As the material is only obtainable in film (or fibre) form, continuous metallising is carried out, as opposed to the batch type process with which most of the other materials in this section are generally associated.

Innumerable manufacturing outlets for metallised polyethylene terephthalate exist, both functional and decorative. They range from capacitors, magnetic tapes and lightweight mirrors to stamping foils, decorative trim, non-tarnishing textile yarns and labels.

Polyethylene and Polypropylene

Since these polymers are among the cheapest available, there are obvious advantages to be obtained by using them. As a result many suppliers are trying to interest the automotive and other markets.

Metallising of polyolefines has posed many problems in the past and still leaves much to be desired. In order to increase their impact resistance, fillers have been added but problems have arisen here because of soak-in which has resulted in a roughened, dull finish.

Because of their inert, non-polar structure, pretreatment of the surface is essential before application of the base coat. Flame treatment, corona discharge or oxidation with chromic-sulphuric acid may be used for polyethylene. Flame treatment appears to be the popular choice here, but information dealing with the relative economics has not been published. On the other hand, polypropylene is best treated by aromatic solvents, or in the vapour phase of boiling solvents. These additional steps have, of course, added to the cost of the metallised article and are a reason for the lack of manufacture of sizeable quantities. Applications at present are therefore somewhat restricted to the manufacture of toys and novelty items.

4-Methyl-Pentene-I

This material requires a suitable surface treatment before metallising can be carried out. Corona discharge is the preferred method.

As it has excellent optical properties combined with high heat stability, it is intended to utilise these advantages in the manufacture of vehicle head and tail lamp reflectors allowing high intensity light sources to be employed.

Polyphenylene Oxide

Because of its heat resisting characteristics it is anticipated that PPO will appear on ranges and stoves where full use can be made of this valuable property. Knobs, handles and controls are the suggested parts.

Base coats similar to those used for polycarbonates may be employed. An added advantage is that higher stoving temperatures may be used, somewhere in the region of 175°C.

Some stress crazing may occur, but dry annealing is not the answer. To obtain the best results the crazed parts should be annealed in nitrogen gas at a temperature of 180°C for 1 hour for every inch of cross section. Care must be taken, since any oxygen present will cause reduction in impact resistance and elongation.

Polystyrene

Polystyrene was not only one of the first polymers to be metallised along with acrylics, but it is also one of the easiest. Difficulties may occur however with special formulations such as high impact polystyrenes. Generally, varnish type coatings adhere better than lacquers.

Very often polystyrene mouldings have inherent stresses built into them and this may be further aggravated by the solvents used in the lacquer system. According to Bateson,[22] stresses can be removed by annealing for about two hours at a temperature of 70 to 80°C. Immersion in a petroleum solvent for about five minutes, following baking, should determine whether the annealing time has been sufficient.

Applications have been found in surface replicas and on back surface mirrors. Use has been made of the material in the liquor industry but it cannot be used in the cosmetic field since it is not resistant to the esesential oils present in perfumes.

Polysulphones

It has been suggested that a possible market exists for this material in the automotive industry (hub caps and fender extensions) and in the electronics field.

Base coats made of acrylic cause deterioration in impact resistance particularly when treated on the reverse or unpainted side. Although crazing and etching of the surface is not considered a serious problem, ketones are to be avoided. There is some evidence of solvent absorption into the plastic which might contribute to the reduction in impact resistance.

Since a high stoving temperature is possible with this polymer, a base coat of the thermosetting category may be used, with anticipated baking temperatures of about 175°C.

Sequence of Operations

The sequence of operations carried out is dependent on the nature of the plastic itself. Allowances have to be made for volatile constituents which may be present in the polymer, whether or not the surface has non-polar characteristics and the intended application.

The following list represents the possible stages (excluding drying stages) which the polymer may have to undergo.
1 Cleaning
2 Conditioning (chemical, electrical, flame treatment)
3 Destaticising
4 Primer coat
5 Base coat
6 Metallising
7 Top coat
8 Miscellaneous finishes (e.g. paint overlay)

A few typical examples are listed below of the steps involved when metallising certain polymers for particular applications, namely:—

(a) Polyethylene terephthalate (capacitor manufacture); stage 6
(b) ABS (decorative; automotive trim); stages 3, 5, 6, 7, 8
(c) Polyacetals (decorative; automotive trim); stages 1, 2 or 4, 5, 6, 7
(d) Polyethylene (decorative; toys); stages 1, 2, 5, 6, 7

Production Metallising

The production rate is dependent upon a number of factors such as the capacity of the vacuum chamber, number in operation, pump-down cycle, whether base and/or top coats are used and their curing times and method of application, not to mention other finishes like paint overlay. In order to familiarise the reader with the possible times involved in performing each operation, two examples are cited below.

Procedure A[25] (stage)	Operation	Duration (minutes)
1	Racking of plastics in jigs	30
2	Base coat in time-draw dip	10
3	Bake at 60°C	60
4	Metallising in coating chamber	30
5	Top coat of lacquer in time-draw dip	10
6	Hardening of lacquer coat	30
7	Dye dip and rinse	5
8	Dry after rinsing	25
	Total	200

Efficient vacuum metallising units are capable of working 15 minute cycles. Stoving times may be as low as 30 minutes. On the other hand, they may be higher, as illustrated in the second example (procedure B).

Procedure B (stage)	Operation	Duration (minutes)
1	Destaticising and racking	45
2	Base coat application by spraying (90/hour)	53
3	Bake at 77°C	90
4	Metallising in coating chamber	20
5	Top coat application by spraying (90/hour)	53
6	Partial curing	30
7	Paint overlay —inner rings (35/hour)	138
	—main area (30/hour)	160
8	Final curing	60
9	Remove from jigs, insert jewels, individual packaging (22/hour)	216
	Total	865

(a) Fascia panels are each wrapped in brown paper and transferred to the metallising shop where they are de-staticised with ionised air. Mouldings are then fastened to the formers (as illustrated) and are not touched by hand for the remainder of the process.

(b) Here the operator is seen applying the base coat of lacquer by spraying.

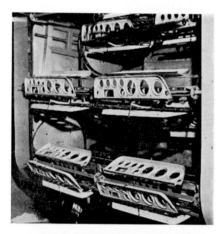

(c) The mouldings are transferred to a curing oven for 90 minutes at a temperature of 77° C. During this period the mouldings continually rotate to permit uniform heating of the base coat.

(d) Following baking, the mouldings are transferred to the vacuum chamber. During the evaporation period (about 20 sec), the planetary jig revolves around its own axis allowing uniform distribution of the aluminium.

Plate 12.1 Production of Vacuum Metallised ABS Fascia Panels
[Courtesy National Plastics Ltd.]

(e) A close-up showing the tungsten helical coil and the aluminium wire used for evaporation.

(f) Following the application of the top coat of lacquer the mouldings are replaced in the oven for partial curing.

(g) Application of paint overlay to the fascia panels.

(h) Final assembly and insertion of jewels.

Plate 12.1 (continued)

In the sequence described in procedure B,[28] the material being metallised is ABS and the application is that for the production of automobile dashboards. A load comprises 80 such items (this sequence is illustrated in plates 12.1a-h).

It can be seen that two painting operations add considerably to the total time taken per load. The times quoted are for individual personnel at each station. It can also be seen that production could be stepped up, since the vacuum chamber is idle for very long periods. This can be accomplished by increasing the personnel at stages 1, 2, 5, 7 and 9.

Advantages and Disadvantages of Vacuum Metallising

Advantages

1 The process is a "dry" one and is not susceptible to contamination by the ingress of moisture or chemicals which may have a derogatory effect on the polymer.

2 Thin film deposition is easier to control, particularly for applications of an optical nature.

3 Optical properties of the films are much superior to those deposited by other means except cathode sputtering.

4 Metals may be deposited which cannot be deposited by electroless techniques or satisfactorily by any other means.

5 The substrate may remain relatively cool throughout the process.

6 Because of the fine grain structure of the films normally deposited, they will follow the contours of a substrate much more faithfully and ensure more accurate reproduction.

7 Brilliant film deposits require no buffiing or polishing.

8 Thickness of films can be more accurately controlled by vacuum techniques.

9 Exceptionally pure metal films are obtained.

10 The process is much more amenable to the production of metallised film in bulk (for example metallised foils, capacitors and similar items and materials).

11 The deposit is unlikely to contain occluded gases.

12 Aluminium mirrors are superior to silver mirrors. (Aluminium cannot be deposited by electroless means.) The latter tend to deteriorate rapidly when exposed to sulphur containing atmospheres, whereas the protective oxide film which forms on the surface of the former affords a considerable degree of protection.

Disadvantages

1 Initial cost of equipment is expensive.

2 The durability of the film is entirely dependent on the durability of the top coat of lacquer, if a first surface coating is used. An exception to this rule is when the conducting film is subsequently electroplated,

but here again satisfactory adhesion has not yet been obtained between the metal and polymer to dispense with the technique of enveloping.

3 Thick films, in general, are not normally evaporated due to it being uneconomical and the resultant deposit obtained is extremely brittle. (Thick, ductile deposits have been reported which are reputed to be as cheap to deposit as conventional electrodeposited coatings.)

4 Adhesion of metal to polymer is not particularly high at present, although improvements in this field should become apparent in the near future.

5 Parts with deep recesses cannot be metallised satisfactorily; this applies to articles which do not have a plane geometric configuration.

6 If a base lacquer must be employed, the electrical properties are altered.

7 With very thin films, agglomeration may result, leading to high resistance and areas of unprotected polymer.

8 It is virtually impossible to produce an evaporated coating free from pin holes.

Applications

Electronics

Evaluation of Electrical Characteristics of Polymers

The preparation of test specimens[29] for evaluation of the electrical properties of polymers, such as dielectric constant, dielectric strength, dissipation factor and insulation resistance. Excellent electrical contact is obtained because the deposited film is in intimate contact with the surface of the dielectric. By masking the surface, the area of the metal electrodes can be controlled.

Capacitors

At the beginning of the century, Mansbridge[30] first pointed out the advantages of manufacturing capacitors from metallised paper. Not only was there a large reduction in volume and weight of the component, which, at a later date was to prove advantageous with the need for miniaturisation in the electronics industry, but capacitors constructed from aluminised dielectrics had the unusual property of self-healing. In effect, the self-healing property is achieved in the removal by evaporation of the metal film by arcing around the puncture in the insulator, preventing an electrical short circuit. Consequently, failure of equipment is avoided.

Although production of zinc coated paper was in vogue prior to the second world war and that during the war aluminised capacitors were used in this country, it was only in the post war era that American companies became interested. About this time and to a large extent, plastic films were replacing paper as the substrate for several reasons, although metallised paper capacitors are still in considerable use today. The advantages obtained are:—

1 Resistance to moisture is much superior. This is a serious problem

with paper based capacitors, necessitating vacuum sealing and plastic encapsulation.

2 Reduction in size and weight is possible because of the high dielectric strengths of the polymers used. For example 0·25 mil polyester film can replace 0·50 mil of multi-layer paper and yet obtain a better overall performance.

In general it may be claimed that their electrical, mechanical and chemical properties are superior to paper substrates. They are also comparable in price.

In the early years, the metal was deposited by metal spraying techniques but this proved to be unsuitable since the metal particles penetrated the substrate. Nowadays, all metallising of plastic film used in the manufacture of capacitors is carried out by vacuum deposition and this, because of the ease by which continuous metallising takes place, makes it a very economic proposition. The polymers used are generally polyesters, polystyrene and polycarbonates (for comparison of their properties see volume 2).

Since polyolefines and halogenated polyolefines possess such excellent properties it is surprising that they have not taken on. Admittedly the use of fluoroplastics would tend to increase the cost but, regardless of this, one would have envisaged outlets in military and space applications.

An early attempt to manufacture PTFE[23] capacitors resulted in the conclusion being drawn that silver was unsuitable (this being due to its poor adhesion to the polymer) but that evaporated copper was satisfactory. As a result, copper was used as a base on which to deposit a more suitable material, such as silver, either by further evaporation or by electroplating. As this took place prior to the publication of the "sodium" etchant treatments, the bond strengths must have been of a very low order indeed. That this was so is substantiated to some extent since the same company brought out a second patent[31] a few years later incorporating the sodium treatment of PTFE into the process of constructing capacitors. In the latter patent however, electroless deposition is favoured.

An interesting point which appears in the first patent is the reference to evaporated alkali metals on to PTFE which were observed to attack the polymer, however they were overlooked as surface preconditioners capable of improving adhesion.

Holland outlines the following requirements for metallised foil used in the manufacture of capacitors.

1 The metal deposited is a continuous film and of sufficient thickness to form a good electrical conductor. It must, however, be capable of being rendered discontinuous should electrical breakdown occur in a localised area.

2 The film should be of a uniform thickness throughout. Adhesion should be good, but penetration of the polymer should be avoided.

3 The metal deposited should be resistant to short term atmospheric exposure.
4 The production of capacitor foils should be such that the electrical and physical properties of the polymer should not be impaired by the process.

Printed Circuitry

Some years ago deposition techniques were investigated as possible competitors to those using copper clad laminates. Holland[16] confirms that the adhesion of copper to phenolic is greatly increased by initially depositing a film of nichrome. The resultant film is subsequently electroplated. No further progress seems to have been made in this direction.

There does not appear to be any outlet in the microcircuitry field, preferred substrates being glass or other nonconductors such as quartz. Perhaps this is partly due to the imposition of temperature limits and partly due to the fact that the surface of polymers cannot equal the smooth surface of glass.

Recording Media

Considerable use is made of vacuum deposited magnetic films on to tapes for use in recording media and for information storage in the computor industry.

Heating and Insulating

Cryogenic Insulation

A recent innovation in the field of metallised plastics affords considerable improvement in the technique of cryogenic insulation. Here is a space-age application where the necessity arises for storing cryogenic liquids, such as liquid hydrogen, in space for extended periods, using low density insulating materials.

In a vacuum, transfer of heat by convection is not possible and is therefore limited to radiation. Although aluminium foil is an effective lightweight radiation barrier, spacers must be provided to prevent conduction. If this is replaced by a metallised film of polyester, not only is a further reduction in weight obtained, which is all important, but it provides a higher reflectivity and far less lateral conductivity because of the overall amount of aluminium present (10^{-6} in). The low lateral conductivity is important for limiting localised heat leaks if the insulation is penetrated by supports or fill lines to the vessel.

Heating Mats

The relatively high electrical resistance offered by extremely thin vacuum metallised films can be utilised in certain applications. If a thin film is deposited on to an optical polymer, use is made of both the optical and conducting characteristics of the film to provide an efficient method of de-fogging and de-icing aircraft windshields by electrical heating. A gold film, 100 Å thick, will only reduce the light transmission by about 30% and yet have sufficient resistance (35 Ω per square) for heating.

Fabrics

Synthetic fibres (terylene, nylon) may be metallised and advantage taken of the heat reflection characteristics. For Arctic wear, a reduction in loss of body heat is achieved without adding to the bulk or weight of the garment and yet still allowing the material to breathe. On the other hand, in space applications the intense heat encountered is a problem. In this case it is reflected, allowing some degree of comfort and protection from radiation.

Due to the inflammability protection that the metal film imparts to the fibres, use is made of this property in protective clothing for fire fighting.

Optical

In optical applications, vacuum deposited coatings are normally preferred for the following reasons.

1 They are capable of being deposited on to smooth, highly polished surfaces and, although adhesion is not particularly high, in some cases it is superior to films deposited by other techniques under similar circumstances.

2 Higher purity metals can be deposited, resulting in superior reflecting properties. Vacuum deposited silver has greater reflecting power than chemically deposited silver and aluminium deposited by vacuum techniques has better reflecting properties when deposited from a high purity aluminium source (99·99%) as opposed to the commercial grade (99%).

3 Aluminium can be deposited by this technique but not by others. Although the reflectivity of aluminium is lower than that of silver in the visible and infra-red region, silver has the disadvantage of deteriorating rapidly, particularly in sulphur containing environments. Aluminium retains its reflectivity much longer, this being due to the natural oxide layer which forms on the surface, protecting it from corrosive atmospheres. A first or second surface coating may be applied. A first surface coating is one which is applied to the top surface, directly viewed, the other being a film deposited on the underside of a transparent polymer. Originally a second surface coating was used to protect the polymer from undue wear and abrasion. However, recent developments have found that the abrasion resistance can be improved considerably by the application of very durable top coats. Even so, second surface mirroring is still used on some applications such as medallions where a three-dimensional effect is required.

Reflectors

The manufacture of reflectors is a large commercial outlet for vacuum deposited coatings. A typical example is discussed.

In the manufacture of reflectors for use in flash photography, cellulose acetate butyrate is employed as the substrate and aluminium is the metal deposited. The following is a specification for the design and manufacture of such reflectors.

1 The base material must lend itself to accurate fabrication thus allowing itself to be formed into an optically designed contour

2 It should have a high reflectivity factor
3 Surface must not deteriorate even under severe exposure
4 Surface must not mar too easily
5 It must show good adhesion of the metal to the base
6 Must withstand reasonable impact
7 Must lend itself to large scale conveyor type production to minimise costs
8 Materials and production technique must be reproducible to ensure uniformity of product.

In addition to this, suitable applications of base and top coats are required, as mentioned earlier in the chapter.

Diffraction Gratings

Optical polymers have been used in producing diffraction gratings, aluminium being deposited for reflectivity purposes. Apparently polystyrene lends itself to producing a more accurate master replica than methyl methacrylate, both of them being superior to cellulosics.

Metallic films on optical polymers are also used for reflecting infra-red rays, reducing glare, absorbing ultra-violet and thereby protecting the polymer from possible degradation by affording an overall protection from eye damaging radiation and intense heat. Lightweight mirrors have also been produced (see polyesters, volume 2).

The variety of applications are innumerable. A fairly representative cross section would include dashboards, horn buttons and arm rests for the automobile industry. In the packaging field, metallised films are used for moisture proof packaging, since the metallic film reduces the permeability of the polymer to moisture vapour. The process is also used considerably for ornamental purposes in the manufacture of such articles as trophies, medallions, nameplates, radio and television dials and cheap costume jewellery.

Testing of Metallised Parts

When metallised plastics are used for decorative or semi-functional applications, in view of the particularly large number involved, it is obvious that some form of control must be exercised over the quality of the finished part. However, because of the exceptionally wide range of products, applications and industries covered, there is a large divergence in the type of quality tests used. For example, bottle caps may have to withstand the action of various chemicals, depending on the nature of the product enclosed. This may include alcohols and essential oils which are not likely to be encountered in applications involving automobile dashboards. Even within one industry, different manufacturers disagree over the content of specifications, so to quote standard tests would be quite pointless. Nevertheless, to give some idea of the types of test used, a few specific examples are cited below merely as a guide. In a few cases alternative tests are quoted to underline the aforementioned remarks.

Appearance

A uniformly reflective surface is required on all except attachment areas. No runs, sags, wrinkles or skips are permitted.

Adhesion

1 One test involves the application of a $\frac{3}{4}$ inch wide strip of adhesive Cellophane tape (M-6270) to the finished surface. Upon quick removal of the tape, none of the finish shall adhere to the tape. (Ford Motor Spec. P139)

2 Another "peel" test is described as follows. The finished surface is scratched through with a sharp point in a series of parallel lines about $\frac{1}{16}$ inch apart, and with a similar series at right angles, forming a cross hatched area. A piece of No. 600 Cellophane tape is firmly pressed into contact with the metallised surface in the area of the scratched lines. When the tape is pulled off quickly, there must be no peeling of the small squares in the surface. Removal of the finish at the edges of the scratches is permissible. (G. M. Fisher Body Division Spec. 9-26)

Wear

1 Parts must withstand 10,000 cycles of the following wear test without a "breakthrough" in the coating. A 3 inch strip of a 1·95 cotton drill is loaded with a 5 lb. weight and reciprocated across the surface of the part at the rate of 12 cycles per minute. The abrading strip must travel across the part surface for a distance of 8 inches. (G.M. Fisher Body Division Spec. 9-26)

2 A piece of $\frac{1}{2} \times \frac{1}{2}$ inch No. 10 cotton duck cloth is loaded to 10 lb/in^2 and is reciprocated across the surface of the part with a linear strike of 1 inch (minimum) at 90 to 100 cycles per minute. A failure constitutes any penetration through the top coat.

Temperature Resistance

Finished parts are exposed to a temperature of 79°C in a circulating oven for 24 hours, cooled to room temperature for 3 hours, then exposed to -29°C for 24 hours, followed by normal room temperature conditioning. During these exposures there must be no stickiness, blistering, loosening of the metallic film or visible effect, and the part must withstand the "cross hatch" peel test described above, after overnight room conditioning. (G. M. Fisher Body Division Spec. 9-26)

Weather Resistance

Finished parts will be exposed to Florida weather conditions for 220 sun hours. After exposure they must be free from visible deterioration and must withstand the "cross hatch" peel test described above. (G. M. Fisher Body Division Spec. 9-26)

Humidity Exposure

Finished parts must withstand three cycles of humidity and drying. Each cycle shall consist of 8 hours at 100% relative humidity at 38°C, followed by 16 hours of room temperature drying. During and after exposure, the parts must not show any blooming, white spots, blisters or any other surface defects affecting appearance and must also withstand the "cross hatch" peel test described above. (G. M. Fisher Body Division Spec. 9-26)

Exposure

The colour, adhesion and lustre of the finish on parts submitted to this specification, shall not be appreciably affected after five complete cycles of exposure as described below:—

8 hrs.—Salt spray, ASTM B117
6 hrs.—High humidity at 38°C
4 hrs.—Sunlight exposure at 66°C
6 hrs.—High humidity at 38°C

(Ford Motor Specification P139)

Perspiration Resistance

Synthetic perspirant solutions, as described in the Technical Manual of the American Association of Textile Chemists and Colorists, are used. (Fisher Test Method No. 15-52) The solutions, acid and alkali types, are each separately applied to the surface and remain in contact for 24 hours at 23°C (room temperature). The surface finish must not be visibly affected by these solutions. (G. M. Fisher Body Division Spec. 9-26)

A typical solution has the following composition:—

Sodium chloride	50 gm
Acetic acid, glacial	50 ml
Butyric acid	30 ml
Isovaleric acid	30 ml
Water	84 ml

Cleanability

Finished parts, as received, must withstand solvent cleaning to the same degree that is required on the base plastic. A piece of clean cloth moistened in F.S. 1062 (cleaners naphtha) or F.S. 1019, Fisher cleaner (85% cleaners naphtha-15% carbon tetrachloride) shall be rubbed lightly over the surface. There must be no evidence of coating removal on the cloth or softening of the surface of the part. (G. M. Fisher Body Division Spec. 9-26)

REFERENCES

1 Bauer E., Brunner R., *Helv. chim. acta*, **17**, 959 (1934).
2 Espe W., Knoll M., " Werkstoffkunde der Hochvakuum Technik," Springer, Berlin (1936).
3 Knoll M., Ollendorff F., Rompe E., " Gasentladungs-Tabellen," Springer, Berlin (1935).
4 Landolt-Börnstein," " *Phys. Chem. Tabellen*," 5th Edition, Springer, Berlin (1923-1936).
5 Leitgebel W., *Metallwirt.*, **14**, 267 (1935).
6 Pringsheim P., Pohl R., *Deutsch. Phys. Gesell. Verh.*, **14**, 546 (1912).

7 Faraday M., *Phil. Trans. R. Soc.*, **147**, 145 (1857).
8 Conn W. M., *Phys. Rev.*, **79**, 213 (1950).
9 Gaede W., *Annln Phys.*, **46**, 357 (1915).
10 Langmuir I., *Phys. Rev.*, **8**, 48 (1916).
11 Burch C. R., *Nature*, Lond., **122**, 3080, 729 (1928).
12 Ritschl R., *Z. Phys.*, **69**, 578 (1931).
13 Countryman M. A., *J. appl. Phys.*, **8**, 432 (1937).
14 Caldwell W. C., *J. appl. Phys.*, **12**, 779 (1941).
15 Olsen L. O., Smith C. S., Crittenden E. C., *J. appl. Phys.*, **16**, 425 (1945).
16 Holland L., " Vacuum Deposition of Thin Films," Chapman and Hall, London (1956).
17 Cartwright C. H., Strong J., *Rev. Scient. Instrum.*, **2**, 189 (1931).
18 Holland L., *Electronics Forum*, **12**, 5 (1948).
19 Shaw A., *Mod. Plast.*, **38**, 7, 114 (1961).
20 Schneider M., *Mod. Plast.*, **27**, 8, 135 (1950).
21 Clough P. J., Hansen J. V. E., *Metal Prog.*, **86**, 5, 93 (1964).
22 Bateson S., *Vacuum*, **3**, 1 (1953).
23 Burger F. J. P. S., West R., Shen T. E., Brit. Pat., 686, 031 (1950).
24 Murbach H. P., Wilman H., *Proc. phys. Soc.*, Lond., B, 66, 905 (1953).
25 Nixon G., *Metal Finish.*, **64**, 11, 70 (1966).
26 Hartman A. H., *Mod. Plast.*, **29**, 2, 115 (1952).
27 Navoy T. M., *Metal Finish.*, **48**, 11, 58 (1950).
28 Data supplied by National Plastics, London.
29 Benner F. C., *Elect. Mfg.*, **39**, 3, 107 (1947).
30 Mansbridge G. F., Brit. Pat., 19, 451 (1900).
31 Margolis D. S., Brit. Pat., 816, 641 (1958).
32 *Mod. Plast.*, **30**, 7. 110 (1953).

BIBLIOGRAPHY

1 " Ions, Electrons and Ionizing Radiations," J. A. Crowther, Arnold, London (1949).
2 " The Electrochemistry of Gases and Other Dielectrics," G. Glocker and S. C. Lind, Wiley, New York (1959).
3 " Structure and Properties of Thin Films," C. A. Neugebauer et al, Wiley, New York (1959).
4 " Thin Films and Surfaces," W. Lewis, Temple Press, London (1945).
5 " Physics of Thin Films," Vol. 1, G. Hass, Ed., Academic Press, New York (1963).
6 " Scientific Foundations of Vacuum Technique," S. A. Dushman, Wiley, New York (1949).
7 " High Vacuum Technique," J. Yarwood, Chapman and Hall, London (1943).
8 " Industrial High Vacuum," J. R. Davy, Pitman, London (1951).
9 " Modern Physical Laboratory Practice," J. Strong, Blackie, Glasgow (1944).
10 " Stress Annealing of Vacuum Deposited Copper Films," H. S. Story and R. W. Hoffman, *Proc. phys. Soc.*, **13**, 70, 950 (1957).
11 " The Growth and Structure of Thin Metallic Films," H. Levenstein, *J. appl. Phys.*, **20**, 306 (1049).
12 " Some Laboratory Techniques for Vacuum Coating of Plastic Films," J. Biram, *Vacuum*, **12**, 77 (1962).
13 " Thick Films: Promising Prospect for Vacuum Metallising," P. J. Clough and J. V. E. Hanson, *Metal Prog.*, **86**, 6, 78 (1964).
14 " The Design of Vacuum Evaporation Plant for Metallising Plastics," L. Holland, *Trans. Plast. Inst.*, Lond., **24**, 153 (1956).
15 " Bombardment of Plastics in a Glow Discharge," L. Holland, *Nature*, Lond., **181**, 4625, 1727 (1958).
16 " Preparation of Metal Film Resistors on Laminated Plastics," G. Siddal and G. Smith, *Brit. J. appl. Phys.*, **10**, 35 (1959).
17 " Studies on the Structure of Thin Metallic Films by Means of the Electron Microscope," R. G. Picard and O. S. Duffendack, *J. appl. Phys.*, **14**, 6, 291 (1943).
18 " Vacuum Metallising of Plastics Substrates," G. Pedrotti and G. Presti, *Riv. Mecc.*, **15**, 341, 51 (1964).

19 " Lacquering Techniques for Vacuum Metallising on Metals and Thermosetting Plastics," M. A. Self, *Metal Finish.*, **58**, 5, 40 (1960).
20 " Vacuum Metallising and Equipment," J. Th. Mall and J. Bennett, Plast. Inst. Conf., London (1966).
21 " The Decoration of Plastics by Vacuum Metallisation—Process, Methods, Uses, Performance, Requirements and Design," S. Kut, Plast. Inst. Conf., London (1966).
22 " Painting Plastics Manual," Bee Chemical Co. (1962).
23 " Vaccum Deposition of Thin Films," L. Holland, Chapman and Hall, London (1960).
24 " Vapour Deposition," C. F. Powell, S. H. Oxley and J. M. Blocher, Wiley, New York (1966)

CHAPTER 13

CATHODE SPUTTERING

This may be further subdivided into (a) physical sputtering and (b) electrochemical or reactive sputtering. In this chapter only the former category is discussed.

If an electrical discharge is produced between two electrodes in a partial vacuum, the cathode surface disintegrates because of bombardment by ionised gas molecules and this results in metal atoms leaving the cathode and condensing on nearby surfaces. The metal to be sputtered is made the cathode and is maintained at a high negative potential with respect to the anode which is made of some material like aluminium. The operation is performed in a vacuum chamber in the presence of a residual gas such as argon, krypton or air, which is the source of gas ions used for bombarding the cathode, at a pressure of between 10 and 50 microns.

When a potential is applied, ion bombardment of the cathode results in metal particles being emitted which travel along the electrostatic field created in the direction of the anode. The substrate to be coated is positioned between the electrodes and is subsequently coated with metal.

Since the removal of metal atoms from the cathode surface is accompanied by a stream of electrons leaving the surface at right angles and at high velocity, this results in a considerable amount of heat being generated on any surface with which they come into contact. Consequently the surface to be metallised becomes very hot and outside the temperature limits imposed on many thermoplastics. Water cooled electrodes may be used and are successful, even allowing for the poor thermal conductivity of plastics. As the process is extremely slow, it is not anticipated that this technique will find many applications in the field of metallised plastics.

Background

The phenomenon of cathode sputtering has been known for over a century since the observations of Grove[1] in 1852 and Plücker[2] in 1858, but it was not applied commercially until recent times. The initial discovery followed the observation by investigators working in the field of electrical discharges in gases, that at the negative electrode the wall of a glow discharge tube became coated with a metallic deposit. One of the earliest references to cathode sputtering for film deposition is that by Wright[3] in 1877. Today it is only used for special applications where vacuum evaporation is unsuitable and, in general, plays a secondary role to this technique.

Theory of Cathode Sputtering

The literature on this subject is voluminous and the number of papers published on the theory of cathode sputtering is not inconsiderable either. However, the investigators tend to be divided into two main groups, their explanations as to the mechanism of the phenomenon being as follows.
1 Because of the energy produced by the impact of the impinging positive ions, a high temperature is attained whereby the emission of cathode atoms takes place through thermal evaporation.
2 The gas ion transfers its energy to that of the metal atom which is analogous to the mechanism by which the energy of a light quantum is transferred to energy of an emitted electron.

Limitations

1 This technique may result in the degradation of some polymers. With optical polymers such as methyl methacrylate and polystyrene, the optical properties are likely to be impaired.
2 The very slow build up in thickness makes it impracticable except for work of a precise nature.
3 Heat transferred to the substrate by the thermal energy, released on impact by electrons emitted from the cathode, is rather high for many thermoplastics.

Metals Commonly Sputtered

Silver and copper are two of the easiest metals to sputter. In fact, the noble metals such as rhodium, palladium, ruthenium and gold may also be classified in this category. The iron and zinc groups offer no particular problems. Some difficulty is encountered with aluminium, chromium, beryllium and similar metals, this arising from the presence of the oxide layer with which they are associated. Nowadays, however, metals like aluminium are becoming much easier to sputter. This is perhaps attributable to a better understanding of the underlying fundamental principles of sputtering, such as the necessity for absolute contamination free atmospheres during deposition.

Sputtering in Inert Gases

Cathode disintegration increases when sputtering in the presence of an inert gas, the higher the atomic weight of the gas, the greater the sputtering rate. Some metals cannot be sputtered in oxygen (for example, aluminium) but will sputter in the lowest atomic weight gas, hydrogen. This is attributed to the prevention of oxidation on the cathode. Only noble metals can

197

be sputtered in an oxygen atmosphere, but even here palladium and platinum films are contaminated with oxides. Under such conditions only gold can be deposited to give an uncontaminated film.

Since the presence of oxygen is a distinct disadvantage, the speed of the pumping equipment should allow for fast entry of inert gas into the chamber to maintain the oxygen content at a very low level. It is also advisable to purge the system with the inert gas prior to sputtering, since a contamination free atmosphere lends itself to improving all aspects of the process.

Rate of Sputtering

The sputtering rate is dependent on a number of factors. Those which influence the rate of sputtering are as follows.

Residual Gas

The sputtering rate increases with the increase in atomic weight of the bombarding ions, but at a rate considerably less than proportional to its atomic weight. Therefore argon is greater than nitrogen which in turn is greater than hydrogen (fig. 13.1).[4, 5]

Temperature of Residual Gas

Sputtering rate increases with increasing temperature of discharge gas.

Pressure of Residual Gas

The sputtering rate(s) is dependent on the gas pressure (P) and distance (d) of the substrate from the cathode and may be expressed in the following manner:—

$$S \propto \frac{1}{dP}$$

provided that the sputtered atom is comparable in mass to the sputtering ion, that is copper in argon, but not for silver in hydrogen.

Cathode Geometry

Cathodes used are either in sheet or wire form. The rate of disintegration of wire is greater than that of sheet and has been found to increase with decreasing diameter (fig 13.2, 13.3).[6, 7, 8] This is partly due to the temperature of the cathode which, being of small thermal mass, is raised to a greater value by ionic bombardment. An increase in cathode temperature itself will result in an increase in the sputtering rate (fig. 13.4).[7]

Substrate Temperature

The rate of sputtering increases with increase in substrate temperature.

Current

The sputtering rate increases a little more than linearly with an increase of the sputtering current, depending somewhat on the conditions of temperature, pressure and geometry.

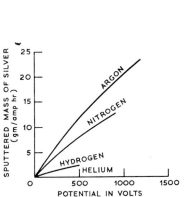

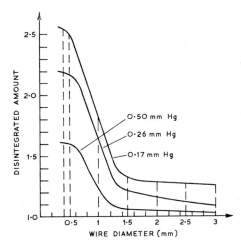

Fig. 13.1 Sputtering rates of silver in different gases. [Güntherschulze]

Fig. 13.2 Relative sputtering rates of copper wires of varying diameter and at different gas pressures. [Berghaus]

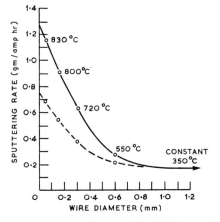

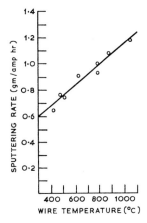

Fig. 13.3 Sputtering rate of molybdenum wires as a function of the wire diameter. [Fetz] Dotted line curve shows sputtering rate after temperature variation has been eliminated. [Holland]

Fig. 13.4 Increase in the sputtering rate of a molybdenum wire with temperature. [Fetz]

Applied Voltage

Sputtering will not occur under the critical voltage. In other words, it is virtually non-existent at applied voltages which are generally below about 400 volts. The sputtering rate however, increases proportionally to (V—Vc) where V is the applied voltage and Vc the critical voltage. If (I) is the current density, the rate of deposition may be expressed as:—

$$S \propto I (V-Vc)$$

Metal

The rate of deposition differs for each metal. According to Mayer and Günthershulze[4] the quantity of metal deposited cathodically is a function of the specific weight; the sputtering in this case was carried out in mercury vapour.

The parameters discussed above are somewhat more complex than the simplified version offered, since they are interrelated with each other. However, they serve as a useful guide.

Distribution of Sputtered Deposit

The uniformity of distribution is generally dependent on the ratio of cathode diameter (D) to the surface spacing (d), the greater the value of D/d the greater the uniformity, assuming uniform bombardment of the cathode.

Plant Required

The plant used for sputtering is very similar to that used for evaporation. For sputtering non-oxidisable metals like gold, a simple rotary pumping station will suffice, but for oxidisable metals like aluminium a complete booster plus diffusion pumping system is required. This is all the more necessary in order to cater for the outgassing of most plastic materials, by maintaining a high effective pumping rate which allows for high leakage rates of inert gases to be admitted during sputtering.

To prevent an undue rise in temperature of the heat sensitive polymers, a water-cooled cathode and substrate holder are used.

A direct current power supply which delivers a high tension voltage of 1,000 to 6,000 volts to the chamber at a maximum current of about 500 milliamperes is required. The door operates a safety switch which disconnects the high tension mains input when the work chamber is opened to the atmosphere. A typical layout is illustrated in fig. 13.5.[8]

Applications

Metallising of non-conductors by cathode sputtering is employed in a number of instances where accuracy, uniformity and precision are all important, one instance being that for the production of electronic components, for example microminiaturised circuitry. However, in the use of plastic substrates it is extremely doubtful whether any real commercial application of this process will be made. Only one application of significance has been uncovered; this concerns the manufacture of gramophone record masters, where palladium is deposited as the initial conducting film on to a cellulose base. It is claimed that unlike gold and silver, no diffusion takes place between palladium and the subsequent electroplated copper, the former being liable to produce roughness on the surface. Furthermore, it is reported that excellent reproduction is obtained with this process.

Cathode sputtering is sometimes preferred to vacuum evaporation for decorative finishes when using gold, since the slow deposition rate leads to careful control of thickness and hence economy in use.

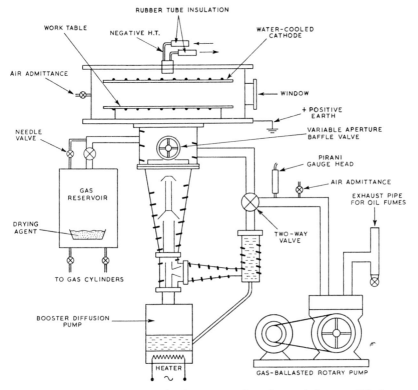

Fig. 13.5 Pumping layout of a large sputtering plant. A booster-diffusion pump is used to provide a high rate of gas flow during sputtering. The gas reservoir can be used for mixing gases when reactive sputtering. [Holland]

Comparison of Physical Vapour Deposition Processes

1 In cathode sputtering the temperature of the substrate increases somewhat whereas in metal evaporation it remains relatively cool.

2 Film formation in cathode sputtering is slow compared to that obtained by evaporation.

3 Throwing power of sputtering is excellent, that of evaporation is poor.
4 Sputtering requires only a partial vacuum, whereas evaporation is carried out in a high vacuum.
5 Thickness of films deposited by sputtering techniques can be controlled exceedingly well, but with evaporation the amount of control is relatively poor.
6 Cathode sputtering is normally used to deposit metals which exhibit low vapour pressures because of the difficulties encountered in providing a suitable source of high temperature. Examples in this class are palladium and platinum.
7 Adhesion of sputtered films is superior to evaporated films; this is due to the continual electron bombardment of the substrate.
8 Sputtered films are generally more granular than evaporated films, resulting in a rougher appearance. Consequently the reflectivity of evaporated films is higher than that of sputtered films.

REFERENCES

1 Grove W. R., *Phil. Trans. R. Soc., B*, 142, 87 (1852).
2 Plücker J., *Pogg. Ann.*, 103, 88 (1858).
3 Wright A. W., *Amer. J. Sci. and Arts*, 13, 49 (1877).
4 Güntherschulze A., *Z. Phys.*, 36, 563 (1926).
5 Güntherschulze A., *Z. Phys.*, 38, 575 (1926).
6 Berghaus B., Brit. Pat., 486, 629 (1936).
7 Fetz H., *Z. Phys.*, 119, 590 (1942).
8 Holland L., " Vacuum Deposition of Thin Films," Chapman and Hall, London (1960).

BIBLIOGRAPHY

1 " The Electrochemistry of Gases and Other Dielectrics," G. Glocker and S. C. Lind, Chapman and Hall, London (1939).
2 " Electronic and Ionic Impact Phenomena," H. S. Massey and E. H. S. Burhop, Clarendon Press, Oxford (1952).
3 " Thin Films and Surfaces," W. Lewis, Temple Press, London (1945).
4 V. Kohlschütter, *Jb. Radioakt. Electronik*, 9, 355 (1912).
5 J. Fischer, *Fortschr. Chem. Phys. phys. Chem.*, 19, 1 (1927).
6 " A New Apparatus for Cathode Sputtering," L. Holland, *Nature*, Lond., 177, 4522, 1229 (1956).
7 F. M. Penning, J. H. Moubis, *Proc. K. ned. Akad. Wet.*, 43, 41 (1940).
8 M. L. Oliphant, *Proc. Camb. phil. Soc. math. phys. Sci.*, 24, 451 (1928).
9 " Vacuum Deposition of Thin Films," L. Holland, Chapman and Hall, London (1960).

CHAPTER 14

CHEMICAL VAPOUR DEPOSITION

Chemical Vapour Deposition (CVD) has been in the past and still is, referred to synonymously as vapour plating, vapour pyrolysis, vapour metallurgy, vapour phase metallurgy, gas plating and thermal decomposition. However, the term chemical vapour deposition is now preferred as being the most precise description and prevents confusion with other techniques where a metal may be deposited from the vapour phase, such as vacuum evaporation (Physical Vapour Deposition).

The process is chemical. The metal passes through a vapour phase as a constituent of a volatile compound and, on arrival at a heated substrate, it decomposes to yield the metal as a deposit. The reaction is induced by maintaining a thermal gradient between the substrate and the plating vapour which disturbs the chemical equilibrium of the vapour when it impinges on the heated substrate and results in deposition taking place. Thick deposits may be built up quickly and although vacuum conditions are very often used they may be unnecessary in some cases.

Alternatively, vacuum evaporation may be regarded as a purely physical process where the transport of metal atoms takes place by a simple process of evaporation and condensation on a substrate which is normally at ambient temperatures. Thin deposits are obtained and unlike chemical vapour deposition, the utilisation of high vacuum techniques is essential.

Background

Metal carbonyls have interested scientists ever since the discovery of nickel carbonyl by Mond, Langer and Quinke[1] in 1890 and have long been recognised as a source from which a successful plating process might be developed. The first phenomenon which could really be associated with chemical vapour deposition can be traced back to 1852 when Bunsen[2] first observed the migration of Fe_2O_3 in a stream of gas containing HCl. The reaction is reversible and fundamentally involves a vapour generation step when it proceeds from left to right and a chemical vapour deposition step when the reaction is from right to left.

$$Fe_2O_3(s) + 6HCl(g) \rightleftharpoons 2FeCl_3(g) + 3H_2O(g)$$

A number of techniques and processes relevant to CVD were developed for the electric lamp industry just before the turn of the century. In an attempt to improve the physical properties of the fragile carbon filament, de Lodyguine[3] in 1893, deposited tungsten by heating the filaments in a mixture of hydrogen and tungsten hexachloride vapour. About this time, various other metals were also investigated, such as molybdenum, tantalum, titanium, chromium and vanadium.

In 1914, Weiss[4] first suggested the use of organo-metallic compounds such as acetylacetonates. Following this, various halide reduction and decomposition processes appeared. From 1935 until the outbreak of the war, attention was focussed on using the CVD process as a means of applying protective coatings.

In the early 1940's, the Commonwealth Engineering Company[5] of Dayton, Ohio, instigated an intensive research programme based on the original Mond process[1]. The major development to emerge from this programme was the use of an inert carrier gas which meant that far greater control could be exercised over the deposition.

Today, patent literature is replete with techniques for depositing various metals but there is noticeably a lack of information in many of these claims to substantiate their usefulness. The list of available compounds has increased and includes hydrides, nitrosyls and organic compounds. Until recently there was almost a complete dearth of theoretical knowledge and of a scientific approach to the problem. Industry, on the whole, has been slow to adapt this technique as a commercial outlet. According to Owen[6] the technique offers some limited potential for plating plastics, the carbonyl process for nickel offering the most promise of early application. This has been substantiated by the publication of a few isolated reports.

Advantages

1 Metals and alloys that cannot be deposited by other means may be deposited.

2 Ultra high purity metals may be deposited, which are extremely useful in electronics applications.

3 The throwing power in a system which is designed to provide the proper flow pattern is considered to be excellent since the vapour can flow around corners and penetrate cavities in the work.

4 Deposition rates may approach very high levels for certain processes (greater than 160 mil/hr), enabling the attainment of high production rates.

5 Porosity is as much a problem in chemical vapour deposition as in other processes where metals are deposited. However, thick deposits favour this process since a greater reduction in porosity is obtained with increased thickness under certain conditions.

Limitations

1 In general, the compounds used in this process tend to be reactive and easily decomposed by air or moisture, hence storage and handling problems exist which are less frequently encountered in other techniques. Some hydrides and metal alkyls for instance are susceptible to spontaneous combustion.

2 Some of the compounds used are not readily available which is reflected in their cost.

3 The temperature at which the majority of the processes operate severely restricts the number of polymers which can be plated and the choice of coating that can be applied.

4 Some compounds used are highly toxic. Nickel carbonyl, for example, is probably the most poisonous of the compounds used, being five times more poisonous than carbon monoxide. This hazard is intensified by its extreme volatility.

Nature of Chemical Reactions Involved in Chemical Vapour Deposition

There are three basic types of reaction involved in CVD, namely:—

    1 Thermal decomposition
    2 Hydrogen reduction
    3 Displacement

As the last named method involves a reaction with the surface to be plated which is normally a metallic substrate, this is not considered further.

Thermal Decomposition

Although volatile compounds such as hydrides, halides and organo-metallics may be used, carbonyls are perhaps the more commonly utilised. A typical reaction may be expressed by the following equation:—

$$Ni(CO)_4(g) \rightarrow Ni(s) + 4CO(g)$$

When using carbonyls for plating, this may be carried out at low, reduced, or atmospheric pressure and by using either static or dynamic systems.

Hydrogen Reduction

Hydrogen is saturated with the vapour of the metal to be deposited and the mixture passed over the heated substrate. If hydrogen reduces the compounds at the vaporising temperature, an inert gas is used to transport the vapour to the plating chamber where it then reacts with hydrogen in the vicinity of the substrate. Higher plating rates may be obtained with this technique. A typical reaction may be presented by the following equation:—

$$2MoCl_5 + 5H_2 \rightarrow 2Mo + 10\ HCl$$

Requirements for Chemical Vapour Deposition

The metal must form a volatile compound which can be dissociated or reduced at temperatures below the melting point of the substrate but sufficiently stable to prevent decomposition or reduction taking place before reaching the surface. The products of the reaction, excluding the deposit, must be gaseous.

In addition to this it should be mentioned that the compound, although volatile, should not be accompanied by excessive decomposition and it should preferably be reasonably insensitive to moisture and air. The by-product of the reaction should be both sufficiently stable and volatile to be pumped away.

Suitability

Although a number of metals can be deposited from the vapour phase, they do not always lend themselves as a source for obtaining ideal deposits. This may be due to a number of reasons such as brittle deposits, instability of the materials leading to excessive decomposition, poor deposition rates and so on. The restriction imposed by the operating temperatures used when depositing some metals also makes them prohibitive. Furthermore, there are only a few metals of this group which are suitable as initial deposits for subsequent electroplating. For example, there would be little interest in depositing molybdenum for plastics applications even if it could be satisfactorily deposited at low enough temperatures. It may be concluded that very few metals are suitable for plating on plastics except in specialised applications. In fact nickel, which is thermally decomposed from the carbonyl, is the only practicable metal at present. The following tables illustrate this point.

Table 14.1
Common Metals Deposited at Reasonably Low Temperatures
Carbonyls (Thermal Decomposition)

Metal	Compound	Vapg. Temp. °C	Plating Range °C	Optimum Temp. °C	Throwing Power	Nature of Deposit	Remarks
Cr	Cr(CO)$_6$	100	250-600	450-500	Good	Brittle	
Fe	Fe(CO)$_5$	100	180-400	370-400	Excellent	Brittle	Deposit requires heat treatment to become ductile
Ni	Ni(CO)$_4$	B.pt.40	150-250	180-210	Excellent	Ductile, Dense	May now be deposited at temperatures well below 100°C
Co	Co$_2$(CO)$_8$	M.pt.50	70	70	Poor		Excessive decomposition renders it unsuitable for plating

Table 14.2

Organo-Metallic Compounds (Thermal Decomposition)

Metal	Compound	Vapg. Temp. °C	Plating Range °C	Optimum Temp. °C	Throwing Power	Nature of Deposit	Remarks
Cu	Acety-lacetonate	250	350-400	350-400	Very Poor	Porous	Unable to build up thick deposits
Ni	Acety-lacetonate	165	230	230	Poor		Slow deposition rates due to decompo-sition
Co	Acety-lacetonate	140	200-450	318-352			
Al	Tri-isobutyl	160	265	265	Excellent	Heavy Deposits	Excellent for plating applications
Cr	Dicumene	165	300	300	Excellent	Brittle	

Hydrogen reduction processes are normally carried out at higher temperatures and are, therefore, further beyond the possibilities of depositing metals on to plastics. The best known processes for hydrogen reduction involve the refractory type metals which are unsuitable in any case.

Table 14.3

Metals Deposited by Hydrogen Reduction

Metal	Compound	Vapg. Temp. °C	Plating Range °C	Optimum Temp. °C	Throwing Power	Nature of Deposit	Remarks
Mo	MoCl₅	200	700-800	700-800	Fair	High Purity	Low rates of depo-sition
W	WF₆	Gas at R.T.	550-750	650	Excellent	High Purity	High rates obtainable

Table 14.4

Heat " Distortion " Points of Various Plastics
°C

Polymer	Pressure 66lb/in²	264lb/in²	Crystalline M.pt.	Vicat Softening pt.
Polyethylene, low density				85—87
high density				127
Polypropylene	105	60		150
4-Methyl Pentene -1			240	179
Polystyrene				73—103
Polymethyl methacrylate	74—113	71—102		100—112
ABS	98—113	89—109		
Polyphenylene oxide		191		
Polysulphone	181			
Polyacetal	158—170	110—124	163—175	

Equipment

In general, chemical vapour deposition is carried out at elevated temperatures, either at atmospheric or reduced pressures and by dynamic or static techniques, the conditions varying according to the properties of the compounds and materials used. When atmospheric pressure is used, it obviates the use of expensive vacuum equipment which is a definite advantage. Nevertheless, in many instances, the advantages of operating at reduced pressures are sufficient to warrant the somewhat more involved technique. For example, if toxic compounds are employed, reduced pressure prevents the premature reaction of the plating mixture and resultant formation of powdery, non-adherent deposits and the vapours escaping into the atmosphere.

The main components required for the deposition of metals from the vapour phase are:—

1. Vapour generator
2. Gas tight coating chamber
3. Carrier and diluent gas sources or pump
4. Heat source
5. Condenser

Ancillary equipment may be required including flow meters, pressure gauges, gas purification trains, control valves and thermocouples.

The reaction chamber should be gas tight and resistant to the chemicals used in the process. Generally the materials of construction are either pyrex or ceramic, although metals may be used provided they are not affected by the chemicals used or do not affect the vapour plating reaction. Owen[7] reports the use of polymethyl methacrylate for the deposition of nickel from the carbonyl.

Various methods of heating the substrate may be employed. These include the use of high frequency induction, resistance and radiation sources. Heating may also be accomplished using furnace techniques. This is the least desirable method, since the bulk of the plating action occurs on the hot walls of the plating chamber instead of on the object, resulting in a very low plating efficiency and non-uniform plating of the object.

Metal compounds which are not very volatile have to be heated so that they generate sufficient vapour to give an adequate plating rate, and there is the risk that the compound will condense out in the cooler parts of the system. To prevent this, all conduits and even parts of the chamber itself, have to be heated and maintained above ambient. With volatile compounds, such as nickel carbonyl, which have a vapour pressure of about 350 mm at room temperature, it is not necessary to employ heat; it is in fact advantageous to keep them cool so that there is no risk of condensation. If ice is used, a constant vapour pressure source is assured.

With processes operated at pressures above that of the source, a carrier gas must be used to transport vapour to the deposition chamber. The gas must be inert or favourable to the decomposition process. For example, H_2 in the hydrogen reduction process. Furthermore, before commencing plating operations the equipment must be purged of air with the carrier gas or an inert gas or it must be designed to withstand evacuation. With a process operated at pressures much lower than the vapour pressure of the source, the vapour will flow in the direction of the pressure gradient and no carrier gas is necessary. Whether or not a carrier gas is employed, it may be advantageous to use a diluent gas. This might merely be to achieve dilution of the vapour or might be another gas with some special favourable property, for example, hydrogen in the hydrogen reduction process (argon may be used for the carrier gas) or carbon monoxide in the carbonyl process.

Provision should be made for accepting the by-products of the reaction. As the plating compounds and by-products may be toxic, adequate extraction and safety measures should be taken. Since the compounds are also very expensive, they may be salvaged, allowing the repeated use of any unreacted compound.

The Controlling Variables of the Process

Of the several factors which influence the nature of the deposit, the temperature of the substrate to be plated is the most important. Processes operated at relatively low temperatures tend to give a finely crystalline deposit, whereas those operating at high temperatures tend to give coarsely crystalline deposits. The less stable plating compounds tend to be reduced or decomposed before they reach the heated surface, the tendency becoming more pronounced at higher deposition temperatures. Premature decomposition on reaction results in the formation of non-adherent powdery deposits or the formation of non-volatile decomposition products. Virtually amorphous deposits are obtained at the lowest deposition temperatures. Non-uniform substrate temperatures result in non-uniform deposits.

The flow rate of the metal compound vapour determines the rate of deposition. The faster the rate of flow of vapour, the faster the deposition rate; this is accompanied by a decrease in efficiency, slow rates of flow facilitating higher efficiencies. There is normally a range in which optimum plating characteristics and coating properties are obtained.

The advantages derived from plating at atmospheric pressure are that vacuum equipment is unnecessary and less restriction is placed on the size of the component to be metallised. However, using low pressure deposition techniques in a vacuum chamber allows greater control to be exercised over the process and the quality of the deposit. Lowering the pressure results in a decrease in the plating rate and favours large crystal formation. On the other hand, atmospheric pressure operations tend to favour fine crystal structures. With non-turbulent flow at near-atmospheric pressures, the material tends to deposit in pronounced streamlines and on the windward side of objects. The uniformity can be improved by rotating the specimen during plating. Operation at reduced pressures is sometimes helpful in improving uniformity.

Where diluent gases or hydrogen (halide reduction method) are employed, composition may be important since there is a range of dilutions outside of which inferior coatings are obtained or powdery decomposition occurs in the vapour phase. The linear velocity of the carrier gas and diluent gas is a factor which has also to be considered.

Efficiency

The efficiency of chemical vapour deposition processes is normally between 5% and 80% but under favourable conditions is generally greater than 50%. Efficiency varies with substrate temperature, rate of flow of the vapour, the composition of the plating vapour, but can be predetermined since it is a constant at fixed conditions of operation.

In many cases the efficiency can be improved by recovering and recycling unused plating compound.

Characteristics of Deposits

Structure

The structure of thin vapour deposited coatings may be nearly the same as that of the substrate (epitaxial growth). Massive deposits may consist of large equi-axed grains when deposition temperatures are high, which become columnar as deposition is continued. At lower temperatures and with correctly controlled deposition conditions very fine grained deposits (350Å) can be obtained.

Columnar structures are the most common in vapour deposition. By the use of (gaseous) addition agents the microstructure of the deposit can be altered to a laminated structure. Owen[8] has shown that the microstructure of nickel deposits obtained from the carybonyl process can be both columnar and laminar.

Chemical Properties

The use of highly purified source materials and gaseous reagents under optimum deposition conditions yields deposits of very high purity. Impurities such as oxygen, water vapour or oxyhalides in the plating atmosphere may exert a pronounced effect on the form of the deposit and affect its properties adversely. Oxygen or nitrogen form oxides or nitrides which lead to the formation of brittle deposits.

Mechanical Properties

With metals whose properties are sensitive to carbon and oxygen the coatings tend to be brittle and have a high hardness that is due to the uptake of these elements. If ductile deposits have to be achieved, oxygen, nitrogen and carbon impurities should be absent.

Very limited data is available at present on this subject.

Porosity

In some instances deposits can be obtained which are dense and essentially pore free in thicknesses of 1 mil or greater. Very thin films, however, are quite likely to have pin holes.

Similarities in Chemical Vapour Deposition and Electroplating

It is of interest to compare the properties of both processes. The purity of vapour deposited coatings is generally somewhat higher than those obtained by electrodeposition. Because of the purity of the deposits and the high temperatures employed they tend to be more crystalline in appearance and develop a matte texture at an earlier stage of growth than electrodeposited coatings. The problems of adhesion, stress and porosity are present as they are for all other metal deposition processes.

Non-uniform coatings are common to both processes. In chemical vapour deposition, deposition occurs faster at sharp corners and edges as observed in high current density areas in electroplating. In both cases one cure is to round edges and corners. Another is to use auxiliary anodes in electroplating and injectors in chemical vapour deposition. The injectors are small tubes which are placed in a suitable position close to the surface to allow one of the gases to flow on to the substrate at the appropriate point.

Striking similarities may be obtained in the structure of the metal deposited by both methods. Variation in plating conditions alters the structure of deposits obtained by chemical vapour deposition as it does in electroplating. The structure of deposits may undergo considerable change by the use of addition agents in both processes.

Brenner[9] points out that the reason for the close similarity between the structure of metals obtained by both processes is that they both involve crystallisation of the metal; that is, in each process atoms of the metals take up positions in a space lattice. The phenomena of crystallisation takes precedence over the type of process that produces the metal atoms in determining the structure. In both processes, the structure of the deposit is influenced by the factors that govern crystal nucleation and growth, such as concentration, diffusion, convection and impurities which operate in a similar fashion in both liquid and gas media.

Present Status of the Process With Respect to Metallising Plastics

Hoover[10] describes a method whereby deposition of nickel may take place at reduced temperatures, using H_2S as an addition agent. Only small additions are required to effectively reduce the plating temperature considerably. According to Owen[11] the H_2S acts as an accelerator being preferentially adsorbed at the nickel surface and displacing CO which retards the reaction:—

$$Ni\ (CO)_4 \xrightarrow[<60°C]{} Ni + 4CO$$

Published work by the last named investigator, employing a static system, has shown that nickel deposition up to a limited thickness may take place at room temperature. Beyond this thickness, deposition ceases because of carbon monoxide build-up, this being more readily adsorbed at the nickel surface than H_2S under these conditions.

At present, a useful deposition rate (several mil per hour) can be achieved at temperatures of about 50°C. Special apparatus has been designed that has commercial possibilities to operate the process without the need for continuous flows at atmospheric pressures which dispenses with flow meters and expensive equipment. Adhesion to plastics is reported to be fair although it is fully expected that preconditioning of the polymer will be essential in order to obtain the necessary bond strength for commercial usage.

Borinskii and Ivanov[12] disclose the use of tin dichloride evaporated at a temperature of 400 to 450° on to PTFE which has been heated to between 350 to 400°, the resultant tin oxide forming an adherent conducting film which is subsequently chemically silvered and electroplated.

There are a number of unexplained factors in this patent. First, the temperature scale is not specified. If it is in degrees Centigrade which is in the correct range for the chemical vapour deposition of tin from the chloride, the temperature is above the crystalline-to-amorphous transition stage of PTFE. On the other hand if degrees Fahrenheit is intended, this is well below the normal plating range of tin from the chloride. Secondly, if a conducting film is deposited, why chemically silver?

Homer and Whitacre[13] have successfully deposited nickel on cellulose acetate by decomposition of the carbonyl, the process being carried out as a continuous operation at atmospheric pressure. The material is fed into the plating chamber at a speed of about 15 ft per minute, following pre-heating to 138°C. The flow rate of nickel carbonyl is 1·8 ft^3 per minute.

The principal application is that of the production of a visor on vehicles to eliminate glare. The effect is achieved by the metallised film which has the capacity of filtering and dispersing strong rays and provides a valuable aid, particularly for night driving. When the metallised polymer is framed in metal, the development of static charge caused by the movement of the vehicle is inhibited.

Other polymers with light transmission characteristics have also been investigated. It is reported that polyethylene terephthalate has also been satisfactorily metallised by this technique.

Marvin[14] describes the manufacture of adhesive tape with a chemically vapour deposited film used for conducting purposes. The base may be cellulose acetate, the metal film being normally of copper or nickel. Applications mentioned include flexible conductors in printed circuitry and as windings around a plastic core to form coaxial cable.

REFERENCES

1 Mond L., Langer C., Quinke F., *J. chem. Soc.*, **57**, 749 (1890).
2 Bunsen R., *J. prakt. Chem.*, **56**, 53 (1852).
3 De Lodyguine A., U.S. Pat., 575, 002 (1897).
4 Van Liempt J. A. M., "The Deposition of Tungsten from Gaseous Compounds and its Applications," Muusses, Purmerend, Netherlands (1931).
5 Gurnham C. F., *Products Finish.*, **21**, 3, 68 (1956).
6 Owen L. W., "Chemical Vapour Deposition and Metal Coating Technique for Plastic Materials," Plast. Inst. Conf., London (1966).
7 Owen L. W., *Metal Ind.*, London., **92**, 12, 227 (1958).
8 Owen L. W., *Trans. Inst. Metal Finish*, **37**, 104 (1960).
9 Brenner A., *Trans. Inst. Metal Finish.*, **38**, 123 (1961).
10 Hoover T. B., U.S. Pat., 2, 881, 094 (1959).
11 Owen L. W., *Plating*, **50**, 10, 911 (1963).
12 Borinskii I. V., Ivanov A. G., U.S.S.R. Pat., 123,380 (1956).
13 Homer H. J., Whitacre J. R., U.S. Pat., 2, 884, 337 (1959).
14 Marvin P. R., U.S. Pat., 2, 916, 398 (1959).

BIBLIOGRAPHY

1 "Plating by Thermal Deposition," R. L. Hoyle, *Plating*, **59**, 11, 1173 (1962); **59**, 12, 1264 (1962); **60**, 1, 45 (1963); **60**, 2, 139 (1963).
2 "Vapour Plating," C. F. Powell, I. E. Campbell and B. W. Gonser, Wiley, New York (1955).
3 "Vapour Deposition," C. F. Powell, J. H. Oxley and J. M. Blocher, Wiley, New York (1966).
4 "Vapour Deposition: The First Hundred Years," E. M. Sherwood and J. M. Blocher, *J. metals*, N.Y., **17**, 594 (1965).

CHAPTER 15

METAL SPRAYING

One does not usually associate the spraying of molten metals on to plastics because of the temperature differential that immediately leaps to mind. This, of course, is rather deceiving, since the metal particles emerging from the pistol may have temperatures as low as 80°C, making it possible to metallise a number of polymeric materials.

Before the introduction of metal spraying, it had been known for some time that a jet of gas emanating from a nozzle at high velocity could cause fluids to break up into fine particles, that is, atomisation. Such a technique had been applied by Barnes (see chapter 11) in the field of aerosol deposition and the principle is also used in metal spraying. Consequently, the two methods have a number of points in common.

The source metal may be molten, wire, or in powder form. Heating methods may employ hot gases or electrical current.

Background

Some of the earliest attempts to spray metals date back to 1892.[1] In these early experiments the metal to be sprayed was either in the molten state or in powder form. The initial breakthrough was made by Schoop[2] in 1910 when he developed a process for spraying molten metal. Basically, the process consisted of pouring molten metal into a jet of gas issuing from a nozzle at high pressure. The apparatus used was extremely bulky and inefficient, but it can be considered as the forerunner of all subsequent metal spraying processes.

Schoop's attention then turned to utilising metal powder as the source and in the following year he produced a powder pistol which was the first commercially successful process for metal spraying.[3] In 1912[4] he and his co-workers developed a pistol which used wire, the method most widely used today.

Until this time, a variety of gases were used to heat the metal whether it was in powder or wire form. In 1914, however, Schoop[5] experimented with electricity as the means of heating which he did by arcing between the electrodes. The year 1923 heralded the appearance of the first "plasma"

214

torch (Gerdien)[6] although use was not made of this method until the late 1950's, since the high temperatures at which the process operated were unnecessary at the time of the invention. The molten metal technique up till that time had lain dormant due to over preoccupation with the wire pistol, but in 1924 the first commercialised version appeared designed by Jarg and Versteeg.[7,8]

Today, metal spraying is commonly referred to as the "Schoop" process,* since his wire and powder techniques are still in use today with minor modifications; so too is his method of electrical heating which is used in electric pistols.

Theory of Metallising

There is some controversy among the principal workers in this field about the theory behind metal spraying. Some factors remain unexplained. However, there is general agreement on some points.

Schoop[9] believes that the atomised metal particles solidify during flight and become molten again on impact and that this is due to the release of kinetic energy. Arnold[10] maintains, however, that the speed necessary to produce the required amount of heat is in excess of that obtained in the process. The theory favoured by Karg,[11] Kutscher[12] and Reininger[13] assumes that solid particles of metal are embedded into the pores of the substrate and that this is due to the magnitude of the driving force. Rollason[14] believes that the molten particles cool fairly slowly while being transported in the air stream and are still molten when they strike the surface (gun-substrate distance 1 in. to 3 in.). Splashes similar to fallen drops of solder are formed and interlock together. When examined under high magnifications, the microstructure exhibits columnar crystallisation and it is postulated that these crystals must have formed after the particles had come into contact with the substrate. Rollason continues to state that at greater distances the particles will be cooled below their freezing points and splashes will not form as above. Instead, with sufficient kinetic energy, deformation of the particles will occur resulting in a laminated packing enclosing fine pores. At still greater distances the particles form a "heaped" mass which is highly porous. This theory is more or less in agreement with that put forward by Turner and Budgen.[15]

When metal is used as the substrate, all workers agree that no alloying takes place. The most popular supposition is that the deposit interlocks with the interaction of the shot blasted substrate resulting in a dove-tailing effect which is, fundamentally, mechanical adhesion. Ballard[16] draws attention to the fact that if molten metal is allowed to solidify on a similar surface, the same degree of adhesion is not obtained. It is therefore concluded that some other contributing factor is involved.

---

*It is probably true to say that within the past decade this term has fallen into disuse to be replaced by "Flame Spraying."

Ballard bases his theory on the fact that since metals possess a high surface tension, each particle will assume a spherical shape. On arrival at the surface the particle may be (1) liquid, (2) solid, but not enough to be plastic, (3) solid, but cold and not easily deformed.

In the last case the velocity of the particles is high and one would expect a particle to bounce and be carried away in the gas stream, unless it was in collision with another particle and became entrapped.

Although unusual in wire processes, entrapments are common in powder techniques and entrapments of spherical bodies have been illustrated by Rollason[14] on examination of the microstructure.

Where the spherical drops are liquid on impact, they exhibit a definite splash formation. Ballard[16] suggests that the pattern of the splashes is similar in design to the formations observed towards the end of the cycle of incidents, before the drop becomes static, indicating that the freezing of the particles is not instantaneous.

The remaining case is that where the drops may be sufficiently hot to remain plastic at the time of impact. On impact their spherical form is flattened, likewise the top is also flattened by the impact of the next particle. The resulting shape is that of a plate. As the particle is subject to some cold work, an equi-axed structure is obtained, whereas the structure of the interior of the splashed drop is columnar.

Powder Process

This method is particularly suitable for brittle metals and alloys of high melting point which cannot be satisfactorily produced in wire form. Originally the powder was drawn into the pistol by suction, melted in the oxygen-fuel gas flame and propelled towards the surface by compressed air. Although good results were obtained by this method the desire to speed up the process made examination of pressure feeds a necessity.

The majority of pistols now operate on pressure feeds, the troubles initially encountered with this system being overcome by the introduction of high quality powder and of design modifications to the pistol.

Basically, a carrier gas, such as air or coal gas, is used to transport the powder to the flame at a sufficiently low pressure (about 10 p.s.i.) providing the powder with sufficient impetus to pass through the flame zone at a fairly low speed. The carrier gas should be moisture free since the introduction of moisture will result in clogging of the orifice. Around the orifice a number of grooves are arranged to allow the mixture of fuel gas (propane or acetylene) and oxygen to emerge, which is the source of the blow pipe flame which surrounds the powder. The flame must envelop the powder completely and must be of sufficient length for the transference of heat to take place. To propel the particles towards the substrate, compressed air is fed through a number of flutes in a nozzle surrounding the fuel gas nozzle. About 12 cubic feet of free air is used per minute at a pressure of 60 p.s.i. The powder should be as fine and uniform as possible to permit deposition, for the flame temperature is much lower than that used in wire spraying.

The amount of powder supported by the carrier gas is dependent on the gas used, its density, volume and velocity.

Wire Process

Irrespective of the design and manufacture of this pistol, the fundamental principles involved are the same, only the nozzles being subject to modifications. Nozzle design is a very important aspect of metal spraying, particularly in the wire process.

Compressed air, at a pressure of 60 to 70 p.s.i. and a flow rate of about 25 cubic feet per minute, is used not only for atomisation but 40% is utilised in driving a small air turbine. The turbine rotates at anything from 12,000 to 50,000 r.p.m. and drives, via reduction gears, two serrated rollers which grip the wire and feed it to the nozzle at a uniform rate; this is usually of the order of 6 to 30 feet per minute, the speed being regulated according to the melting point of the metal. The diameter of the wire used may vary from 1mm to 5mm depending on the pistol used, although they normally have a detachable and replaceable pinion which allows the use of different diameters of wire.

At the nozzle the wire is melted by an oxygen-fuel gas flame such as acetylene, propane or coal gas. Oxygen increases the temperature of the flame and stabilises it, whereas the fuel gas is the source of heat. The temperature obtained depends on the combination used, as does the respective volumes required for combustion. Very high temperatures are required to melt the wire satisfactorily.

A motor may replace the air turbine as the means of feeding wire to the nozzle. Electric pistols may also be used, instead of fuel gas, as the source of heating.

Molten Metal

The pistol is gravity fed from a container which holds the molten metal, the temperature being maintained by a burner operating on the Bunsen principle. Compressed oxygen and compressed fuel gas are therefore unnecessary, the coal gas obtained from the town mains supply being adequate. Consumption is about 50 cubic feet per hour. The pistol requires some 15 cubic feet per minute of free air at a pressure of 60 to 75 p.s.i. This passes in close proximity to the burner so that the air used for atomisation is preheated. A portion of the compressed air is diverted to the burner to produce a more intense flame.

Specially prepared metal is unnecessary, ingots being melted in an adjoining furnace and transferred to the container when molten. Because of the relatively low operating temperature of this process, only metals of low melting point can be used. Aluminium (melting point 659°C) is the highest used.

A disadvantage from which this form of metal spraying suffers is the corrosive effect that the molten metal has on the nozzle and other parts of the apparatus. As the nozzle wears, spraying becomes coarser and irregular and the speed has to be increased somewhat to maintain uniformity. Nozzles have to be replaced as frequently as every 1 to 2 hours and other parts at varying intervals. Consequently, the design and construction of the gun is extremely simple in order to facilitate changing and easy access to worn parts.

Electrical current may be used to heat both the crucible and the compressed air.

Advantages and Disadvantages of Metal Spraying Plastics

Advantages

1 Being essentially a dry method, no corrosive chemicals are absorbed by the materials to cause ill effects at a later date.
2 The process is exceedingly fast, very thick deposits being obtained in a short time.
3 Metals and alloys may be deposited which cannot be deposited by some other processes, e.g., aluminium, copper-manganese.

Disadvantages

1 Adhesion is poor.
2 Although it is not always essential to roughen the surface prior to metallising to obtain adhesion, in most cases it is certainly advisable.
3 Porosity is high.
4 Because of the oxide content, the conductivity is much lower than that obtained with other processes, a reduction of between 30% to 50% being obtained depending on the metal used for spraying. Consequently this invalidates its use for a number of electrical applications.
5 Thin walled substrates are generally unsuitable for metallising.

Rollason[17] has attempted to compare metal spraying with other techniques for depositing metallic films, but since the comparison was made some time ago, the progress which has taken place in each of the individual fields discussed may have altered the relative merits somewhat.

Temperature

A characteristic of the metal spraying process which is directly related to the metallising of plastics is that of the temperature of the particles at the time of impact. Regardless of the temperature of the molten metal at the nozzle of the pistol, the temperature on formation is relatively cool. In fig.15.1 it will be observed that as the nozzle-substrate distance increases, the temperature decreases.

The method adopted by Ballard[16] to estimate the temperature of the particles, involved exposing a very fine gauge nickel-nichrome thermocouple before the nozzle at varying distances and measuring the temperature of the gas stream. The thermocouples in these experiments were placed on the axis of the wire at the particular nozzles distances, fig. 15.1. These represent the maximum temperature obtained, the outer streams being much cooler. It may be observed that the temperature of the gas stream follows the order of the melting points of the metals examined.

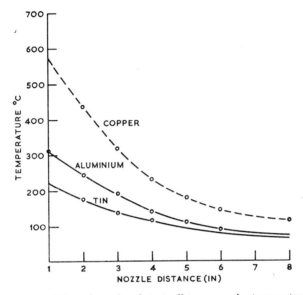

Fig. 15.1 Effect of nozzle-substrate distance on the temperature of the sprayed metal. [Ballard]

Porosity

The density of the sprayed metal is always less than that of the cast material (table 15.1). This is due partly to porosity and partly to oxide particles. Results show that the powder process produces deposits of the greatest porosity. On the other hand, deposits obtained from using the wire process exhibit the least porous structures (table 15.2). It may also be observed that porosity may be reduced by decreasing the nozzle-substrate distance. This is probably due to the fact that at great nozzle distances the particles are cooler and have less velocity, whereas at near distances the particles are sufficiently plastic to allow for interleaving.

Oxide Content

Many different opinions are available in the literature regarding the oxide content of sprayed metals. Bablic,[19] Schoop[20] and Arnold[10] maintain that oxidation of the particles in flight takes place when a highly oxidising flame is used. With the exception of copper, most metals offer experimental difficulties in the estimation of the oxygen content. Some typical figures for copper are given in table 15.3.

219

Table 15.1

Specific Gravity of Sprayed Metals (wire process)

Metal	A	B	C
Aluminium	2·4	2·3	2·54
Zinc	6·4	6·3	6·9
Tin	7·1	6·8	7·29
Copper	8·0	7·5	8·9

A—Turner & Ballard[18]
B—Arnold[19]
C—Cast Metal

Table 15.2

Effect of Parameters on Porosity

Distance (inches)	Porosity %		
	Wire (coal gas)	Molten Metal (acetylene)	Powder (acetylene)
1	1·1	10·6	
3	3·9	10·9	
5	4·5	11·7	
7	6·6	14·3	
8			13·8
9		14·4	
10	8·7		
11		16·5	
12			18·4
15			20·1

Condensed from Rollason.[14]

Table 15.3

Percentage of Oxygen in Copper Deposits[16]

Process	Nozzle-Substrate Distance (inches)	% Oxygen	% Cu₂O
Powder	8	2·84	25·6
	10	3·39	30·6
	12	3·17	28·4
Wire (coal gas)	3	1·02	9·2
Wire (acetylene)	3	0·59	5·3

It will be observed that the powder system contains the largest amount of oxide. This is partly due to the fact that granules of the powder have an oxide film already present and partly due to the mechanism of the process. In the molten metal process it is assumed that there is very little oxidation of the metal when in the molten state and oxidation can only occur in flight.

Ballard and Harris[21] have shown that the oxygen content of the coating is increased (table 15.4) as the oxygen pressure is increased. Reducing the nozzle-substrate distance tends to decrease the oxide content (table 15.3) since the particles are in a reducing part of the flame. To minimise oxidation it is advisable to use the wire process, slightly reducing flame, low oxygen pressure and reduce the nozzle distance as much as possible without over-heating the base.

Table 15.4

Effect of Varying the Oxygen Pressure[21]

Pressure lb/in^2	% Oxygen in deposit
11	0·30
16	0·32
20	0·34
24	0·36
34	0·52

Wire pistol, 3in. nozzle-substrate distance, acetylene used.

Substrates Used and Their Preparation

Metal spraying of thermosetting resins is, in general, more successful than that for thermoplastics, although this view is not shared by Cywinski and Baker.[22] This is not entirely due to the latter materials' lower softening points, but the hard surfaces of the thermosets do lend themselves better to accepting a deposit. Polymers, like polyethylene, with their smooth, waxlike, flexible surface are unsuitable for metal spraying unless an initial coat of zinc is used.

With thermosetting resins, fillers play an important role inasmuch that epoxy resins containing fillers such as $CaCO_3$ yield good bonds and the incorporation of slate powder results in poor bonding. As in the case of metals, the substrates are surface roughened prior to metallising. Alternatively, an adhesive may be used; when this is tacky, metal spraying is carried out sufficiently near to the surface for sufficient heat to be generated and polymerise the adhesive.

Aubry[23] suggests the use of a varnish comprising 10gm nylon in 50gm phenol, the material being sprayed or brushed; the coverage is 30gm/m². This mixture is heated in a water bath at a temperature of 50 to 100°C. It is claimed that zinc may be satisfactorily deposited although this has been questioned by Ballard.[24]

Cywinski and Baker[22] refer briefly to current development work on primers for thermosetting materials.

Applications

De-icing Systems[25]

The formation of ice on aircraft wings is a serious problem since the ice changes the contour of the aerofoil surface thereby reducing the lift coefficient. Using the electrical resistance properties of sprayed coatings, de-icing systems for aircraft are produced. A coating of aluminium or copper-manganese is deposited to a thickness of 3 to 10 mils on to an epoxy base which is about 30 mils thick, insulating the sprayed metal from the aerofoil surface. After spraying, another coating of resin approximately 10 mils thick is applied to provide further insulation and protection in service.

It is obvious that a heating mat, having a weight of only 0·27 to 0·37lb/ft^2 offers tremendous advantages in aircraft applications since it has little or no effect on the aerodynamic qualities of the wing section. As the electrical resistance is dependent on the thickness of the coating, it is important to maintain a uniform thickness during spraying. Resistance may be corrected by rubbing down or respraying where necessary.

In production, both manual and mechanical methods are used depending on the shape of the work and the quantity involved. The mechanical method is preferred because the spraying speed is more easily controlled and greater uniformity of the deposit is achieved. (plate 15.1)

Bannister[26] discloses in a recent paper a number of functional applications for the wire spraying process which he shows a distinct preference for, it being more amenable to the metallising of plastics. Among the applications cited are:—

Radio Frequency Aerials

Tubular polyester aerials are coated by metal spraying, the shrinkage effects of the sprayed metals on the plastic tubing serving to improve bonding characteristics to the sand blasted surface. However, the performance of the aerials is stated to be inferior to those which have been electroplated.

Waveguides

In view of the high strength/weight ratio of metal to plastic combinations, they are well suited for use in lightweight airborne radar equipment. It is maintained that complex wave guides can be produced to a tolerance of within ± 0·001in/in and with a surface finish of between 4 to 10 micro-inches. Epoxies have been used in this application. (plate 15.2)

Radar Reflectors

Large dishes have been fabricated from polyester resin to a tolerance on the curvature of ± 0·003in. The preferred metal is zinc which can be sprayed at maximum speeds without risk of stress blistering. It is stated that for typical radar aerial reflectors, it is more economical to manufacture them by metal spraying than by stretch-formed aluminium.

Plate 15.1 Production of a heating mat on aircraft wing section by metal spraying, using wire-fed pistol. [Courtesy of English Electric Aviation Ltd.]

Plate 15.2 Epoxy glass-fibre waveguide sprayed with high conductivity tin-silver alloy. [Courtesy of Plessey Radar Ltd.]

223

Screening

The interior of instrument cases and cabinets can be screened effectively and economically by metal spraying. An extension of this is the conductive metal coated plastics chassis to which soldered earth contacts are made. A further development is a glass fibre reinforced polyester computer cabinet for printed circuit boards, with metal sprayed edge contact strips.

Printed Wiring

Promising results have been obtained with high current carrying capacity circuits deposited on to epoxy glass laminate through rubber masks.

In the field of printed wiring, the plasma spray[27] technique which has been previously mentioned but omitted from the discussion, has been used to form conducting patterns on synthetic resins. Advantages claimed over the conventional metal spraying processes are:—

1 Adhesion can be obtained on smooth surfaces; this is due to the fine jet produced which results in a fine distribution of metal and

2 Very narrow wiring patterns may be produced directly without the use of masks. It may be necessary to form the circuit by intermittent spraying to avoid the possibility of overheating the base material.

Other Applications

Other applications include the manufacture of moulds, electrical screening purposes in general such as the screening of resin cored transformers, and in the manufacture of capacitors.

REFERENCES

1 Phipps A. E., *Metal Ind.*, Lond., **48**, 20, 553 (1936).
2 Schoop M. U., *Metall. chem. Engng*, **8**, 7, 404 (1910).
3 Schoop M. U., Brit. Pat., 21, 066 (1911).
4 Morf E., Brit. Pat., 28, 001 (1912).
5 Schoop M. U., Brit. Pat., 147, 901 (1921).
6 Gardien N., Lotz A., *Z. tech. Phys.*, **4**, 157 (1923).
7 Jarg C. J., Brit. Pat., 276, 955 (1928).
8 Jarg C. J., Brit. Pat., 276, 956 (1928).
9 Gunther H., Schoop M. U., " Das Schoopsche Metallspritzverfahren," Verlag Der Technischen Monatsschrifte, Stuttgart (1917).
10 Arnold H., *Z. angew. Chem.*, **30**, 209 (1917).
11 Karg H. R., *Korros. Metallschutz*, **3**, 110 (1927).
12 Kutscher G., *Apparatebau*, **36**, 261 (1924).
13 Reininger H., *Z. Metallk.*, **25**, 42 (1933).
14 Rollason E. C., *J. Inst. Metals*, **9**, 1, 35 (1937).
15 Turner T. H., Budgen N. F., " Metal Spraying," Griffin, London (1926).
16 Ballard W. E., *Proc. phys. Soc.*, Lond., **57** (Part 2), 320, 67 (1945).
17 Rollason E. C., " Metal Spraying," Griffin, London (1939).
18 Turner T. H., Ballard W. E., *J. Inst. Metals*, **32**, 291 (1924).
19 Bablik H., *Korros. Metallschutz*, **1**, 126 (1925).
20 Schoop M. U., Daeschle C. H., " Handbuch der Metallspritz—Technik," Rascher, Zurich (1935).
21 Ballard W. E., Harris D. E. W., 12th Int. Congr. Acet., Oxy-Acet., Welding and Allied Ind. (1936).
22 Cywinski J. W., Baker J. W., " Spraying of Metals and Plastics," Plast. Inst. Conf., London (1966).

23 Aubry N., Int. Inst. Welding Colloquium, Liege (1960).
24 Ballard W. E., " Metal Spraying and the Flame Depositions of Ceramics and Plastics,"
    Griffin, London (1963).
25 Information supplied by English Electric Aviation Ltd.
26 Bannister D. R., " Applications of Composites of Sprayed Metals and Plastics,"
    Plast. Inst. Conf., London (1966).
27 Brit. Pat. 987,785 to Standard Telephones and Cables Ltd. (1965).

BIBLIOGRAPHY

1 " Metallising Handbook," H. S. Ingham and A. P. Shepherd, Metco Ltd. (1949).
2 " Porodnik Metalizacji Natryskowej," J. Brennek, Z. Brodski, T. Drazkiewicz,
   S. Gebalski and Z. Kowalski, Panstwowe Wydawnick Techniczne, Warsaw (1959).
3 " Metal Spraying," T. H. Turner and N. F. Budgen, Griffin, London (1926).
4 " Metal Spraying," E. P. Rollason, Griffin, London (1939).
5 " Metal Spraying and the Flame Deposition of Ceramics and Plastics," W. E. Ballard,
   Griffin, London (1963).

CHAPTER 16

CONDUCTING PAINTS

The last few years have witnessed tremendous strides in this field, improved techniques becoming available on the market. In the original formulations the main fault was the high resistivity of the film, caused by its low metal content. This has been overcome somewhat and high metal contents are now available with a subsequent lowering of resistivity.

Metal content increases and resistivity decreases with increasing stoving temperature until pure metal is eventually obtained at a temperature of 400 to 500°C. Air drying films may have resistivities as low as 0·5 ohms per square and this may be reduced still further by stoving at temperatures below the distortion point of the plastic material being metallised. Where solvents are used as a vehicle for dispersions of the metal, they may also act as a solvent for the polymer being treated. In this case good adhesion is obtainable between the two.

Within their limitations, these films are quite good. The main drawback is that the adhesion of electrodeposited metals to these films is poor, making them ideal for electroforming but unsuitable for electroplated plastics.

An exception to this is when they are applied to ceramics or other materials which will withstand the high firing temperature. As metallic silver is obtained, adhesion is facilitated.

Thermosetting Preparations

These consist of a two component system which is an epoxy based preparation containing flake silver. The pot life of the mixture is limited to about 4 hours, the separate components themselves having a shelf life of approximately 6 months when kept in a commercial type of refrigerator.

The operation may be carried out by brushing or spraying. Air drying is recommended prior to stoving to prevent solvent being trapped in the film since this leads to blistering. Stoving conditions are 80°C for 60 to 90 minutes or 100°C for 30 to 60 minutes. The electrical resistance of a typical 0·006 inch thick film is about 0·55 ohms per square.

This type of film is suitable for electroplating from some acid baths provided that the surface has been lightly burnished prior to plating. It cannot be used as a base for soft soldering or as a conducting cement, although other preparations in this family can fulfil the latter role.

Metal Dispersions in Organic Vehicles

Silver is normally the metal used whether in flake or powder form, the organic vehicle being selected from the following (1) hydrocarbons (toluene), (2) alcohols (ethyl alcohol), (3) ketones (methyl isobutyl ketone) and (4) acetates (ethyl acetate).

These dispersions contain about 60 to 70% solids and can be air dried by solvent evaporation to give a highly conductive film. Stoving further increases the electrical conductivity of the film. Some of the films are solderable.

Table 16.1
Typical Electrical Characteristics of Films *

Organic Medium	Air Dried Films Resistance Ω per sq.	Stoved Films		
		Resistance Ω per sq.	Time min.	Temperature °C.
Toluene	1·0—2·0	0·5	60	140
Ethyl Alcohol	0·3—0·5	0·1 —0·2	20	165
MIBK	0·1—0·15	0·05—0·1	30	120
Acetates	0·2—2·0	0·1 —0·5	120	40

* Will depend on thickness of film.

Applications
Recording Tapes

May be used for brushing on to polyethylene terephthalate magnetic recording tapes. Small coated areas may be used to act as contacts to actuate stop switches. Because of the simplicity of application, this method is preferred to that of splicing in a piece of metal foil which was the original method. Another advantage is that it will give a signal for switching purposes without interrupting the information carried on the tape.

Screening

Can be used satisfactorily as an electrical screen on plastic and component cases.

Printed Wiring

Because of its low electrical resistance, it may be used for modifying prototype wiring boards.

Cine Film

Can be applied to cine film to operate relays for controlling curtains, lights and other scenic effects.

Other uses include potentiometer track terminations and capacitor terminations.

Graphite Dispersions

Although it may be argued against the inclusion of this " non metal," it is felt, since it does form a conductive film which can be electroplated and also functions in a similar capacity to metallised films, that this is sufficient reason to do so.

They are available as dispersions in water or organic solvents such as alcohols or aromatic hydrocarbons (naphtha). The resistances of these films vary considerably, but in general they are very high. They are resistant to electron bombardment, possess good black body characteristics and are chemically negative, although water dispersions are available which carry either a negative or a positive electrical charge.

Applications

Plastic Instrument Windows

The build-up of static charges on plastic instrument windows may affect the accuracy of instrument readings. A thin transparent coating of graphite will prevent this.

Electrodes

Graphite coatings make excellent electrodes in electronic equipment since they are electrically conducting but more or less immune to electromagnetic radiations. Applications are found in dose meters, ionisation chambers and Geiger counters.

Electrostatic Screening

Graphite films may be used as electrostatic screens. Examples include audio frequency amplifiers such as deaf aids and in television cabinets.

Plastic Cables

Certain materials, such as PVC which are used in the sheathing of electric cables, suffer from the disadvantage that static charges are built-up on the surfaces of the polymer not in direct contact with the conductor. In low voltage work, such as in microphone cables, this leads to the creation of noise. A thin film of graphite on the side of the polymer, so that it is tied to the conductor potential, will obviate such noise.

Although silver, in the form of flake or powder, and graphite are the two commonest materials to use, copper, bronze and zinc have also been employed but have never proved to be altogether satisfactory. Other systems are available besides those already mentioned using air drying resins or lacquers.

Platinum, palladium and gold have been used on materials such as ceramics which will withstand the firing temperatures demanded. Air drying or low bake temperature formulations are not available with these metals. In some of the applications mentioned, such as anti-static screening devices, the more popular method now is to incorporate anti-static agents into the polymer mix; these have proved very successful.

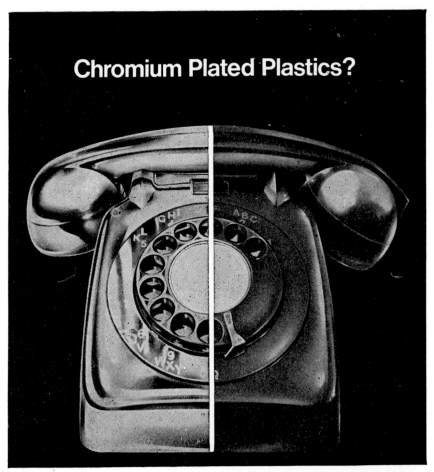